DANGER AND OPPORTUNITY

Dedication

To my parents and to Bruce, Gerald and Susanne

DANGER AND OPPORTUNITY

Explaining international crisis outcomes

ERIC HERRING

MANCHESTER UNIVERSITY PRESS
Manchester and New York
distributed exclusively in the USA and Canada by St Martin's Press

Published by Manchester University Press
Oxford Road, Manchester M13 9NR, UK
and Room 400, 175 Fifth Avenue, New York, NY 10010, USA

Distributed exclusively in the USA and Canada
by St Martin's Press, Inc., 175 Fifth Avenue, New York, NY 10010, USA

British Library Cataloguing-in-Publication Data
A catalogue record for this book is available from the British Library

Library of Congress Cataloging-in-Publication Data
Herring, Eric.
Danger and opportunity : explaining international crisis outcomes / Eric Herring.
p. cm.
Includes bibliographical references.
ISBN 0-7190-4292-5. — ISBN 0-7190-4293-3 (pbk.)
1. World politics—1945- 2. International relations. I. Title.
D843.H439 1995
327'.09'045—dc20 95-3507
CIP

ISBN 0 7190 4292 5 *hardback*
0 7190 4293 3 *paperback*

First published 1995

99 98 97 96 95 10 9 8 7 6 5 4 3 2 1

Typeset in Hong Kong
by Graphicraft Typesetters Ltd, Hong Kong

Printed in Great Britain
by Bell & Bain Ltd, Glasgow

CONTENTS

MAPS AND TABLES

Maps

Maps and tables

Tables

ACKNOWLEDGEMENTS

In the course of this research I accumulated many debts of gratitude and I am very happy to acknowledge them here. The generosity and supportiveness of the academic community was a regular reminder of how enjoyable it is to be part of it. Thanks to: the Social Science Research Council of the United Kingdom for funding and the Social Science Research Council of the United States for an SSRC MacArthur Foundation Fellowship in International Peace and Security; Maurice East, Dean of the School of Public and International Affairs of the George Washington University, Washington, DC, for being a friendly and helpful host while I was a Visiting Scholar; Robert Jervis for making the arrangements for me to be a Visiting Scholar at the Institute of War and Peace Studies, Columbia University, New York during the tenure of my SSRC MacArthur Fellowship; Mike MccGwire for very kindly providing me with accommodation for most of two summers in Washington, DC; Jack Snyder for being my thesis adviser while I was at Columbia, for teaching me important lessons in how to test ideas and for returning drafts very swiftly with exceedingly valuable comments; Pat Morgan for his extensive comments on Chapter One and for his very substantial support along the way; Ned Lebow and Celeste Wallander for their comments on particular draft chapters; Barry Buzan and Len Scott for their comments as examiners of the University of Wales PhD thesis on which this book is based; Nick Rengger for commenting on an earlier version of the entire manuscript; those who have responded to my presentations of drafts to conferences and seminars; those who have been kind enough to send me their draft manuscripts; those whose research I have discussed and upon whose shoulders this work stands; those students in my classes in the Department of Politics at the University of Bristol with whom I have had the pleasure of discussing crisis behaviour; my family for their support over the years, and to whom this book is dedicated; my thesis adviser, Ken Booth, for his phone call to Lancaster, for his unflagging support ever since and for his inspirational teaching; Richard Purslow, editorial director at Manchester University Press, for his receptiveness and enthusiasm and his comments on the draft manuscript; and Julian Ellis for his hard work in compiling the index. Finally, I would like to thank my partner Susanna Reid for putting up with a long summer and autumn of rewriting and for sustaining my sense of perspective. I bear sole responsibility for the contents and especially the limitations of this book.

ABBREVIATIONS

CDSP	Current Digest of the Soviet Press
CIA	Central Intelligence Agency
CINCPAC	Commander-in-Chief Pacific
COMECON	Council for Mutual Economic Assistance
DefCon	Defence Condition
EMP	Electromagnetic pulse
Ex Comm	Executive Committee of the NSC
FRG	Federal Republic of Germany
FRUS	*Foreign Relations of the United States*
GDR	German Democratic Republic
ICBM	Intercontinental Ballistic Missile
IISS	International Institute for Strategic Studies
IPPNW	International Physicians for the Prevention of Nuclear War
IRBM	Intermediate Range Ballistic Missile
JCS	Joint Chiefs of Staff
JSTPS	Joint Strategic Target Planning Staff
KGB	Committee for State Security
MAD	Mutual Assured Destruction
MIRV	Multiple Independently-targetable Re-entry Vehicle
MND	Minimum Nuclear Deterrence
MRBM	Medium Range Ballistic Missile
NATO	North Atlantic Treaty Organisation
NBC	Nuclear, Biological and Chemical
NIE	National Intelligence Estimate
NLF	National Liberation Front
NPT	Non-Proliferation Treaty
NSC	National Security Council

OPEC	Organisation of Petroleum Exporting Countries
PLA	People's Liberation Army
PLO	Palestine Liberation Organisation
PoW	Prisoner of War
PPS	Policy Planning Staff
PRC	People's Republic of China
RCC	Revolutionary Command Council
ROC	Republic of China [Taiwan]
SAC	Strategic Air Command
SALT	Strategic Arms Limitation Talks
SAM	Surface-to-Air Missile
SE	Special Estimate
SIOP	Single Integrated Operational Plan
SIPRI	Stockholm International Peace Research Institute
SLBM	Submarine Launched Ballistic Missile
SNIE	Special National Intelligence Estimate
SSBN	Strategic Nuclear Ballistic Missile Submarine
START	Strategic Arms Reduction Talks
TASM	Tactical Air-to-Surface Missile
UAE	United Arab Emirates
UN	United Nations
USAF	United States Air Force
WSAG	Washington Special Action Group
WTO	Warsaw Treaty Organisation [Warsaw Pact]

INTRODUCTION

What explains international crisis outcomes? This is the main question which I seek to answer. To do so, I develop an approach which takes into account the deterrence-compellence distinction, the military balance, the interests at stake, and psychological and strategic cultural factors. Much has been written on each of these separate factors but much remains to be done to integrate those insights.[1] I draw on primary historical sources and the case-study literature and I focus very specifically on crisis outcomes: the aim of the case-study chapters is not to retell or rewrite the full story of each crisis. For example, in this study I do not want to know simply whether psychological biases influenced decision-makers: I want to know whether psychological biases influenced the crisis outcome. Overall, my approach is based on integration of theory and a focus on outcomes.

DANGER, OPPORTUNITY AND THE CHARACTERISTICS OF CRISES

In politics, a crisis involves unusually intense conflict. Often it is a point at which conflict is likely to increase or be resolved. Definitions of crisis often focus on danger and do not acknowledge that crises may also be about opportunity, even when opportunity is a factor in the rest of the analysis.[2] Awareness of both dimensions is encapsulated neatly in the Chinese ideograph for crisis (*weiji*), which is a combination of the characters for danger (*wei*) and opportunity (*ji*).[3] Opportunity for one side may represent danger for another: more commonly, both sides in a crisis experience a mix of danger and opportunity. This will be a persistent theme throughout this study. In some cases, only one side may perceive the existence of a crisis. For example, in 1983 a crisis in the Soviet Union was produced by a combination of a large-scale North Atlantic Treaty Organisation (NATO) exercise, President Reagan's aggressive anti-Soviet rhetoric, and his administration's unusual frankness about seeking to be able to fight and win (and if necessary initiate) a nuclear war. The existence of this war scare was not picked up by the West immediately.[4] Danger may exist in terms of the risk of war or in terms of threat to interests. For the purposes of this study, a crisis exists when key decision-makers perceive a significant probability of war, time pressure, and a threat to their interests or opportunity to advance their interests.[5] Crises are characterised by conflicting pressures. Deterrence must be combined with reassurance, otherwise threats may provoke the very attack they were designed to deter (Jervis 1976: 58–113; 1978; Lebow, Stein 1987a: 41–63; Stein 1991a,b). Crises involve pressures to avoid war and yet defend one's interests, and pressures to give diplomacy and other non-military options more time and yet to use force before the opponent takes steps to neutralise the military option. These conflicting pressures are familiar in theoretical terms, but discussing all of these conflicting pressures together helps to stress the essential duality of crises. For example, Glenn H. Snyder and Paul Diesing point out that decision-makers tend to be torn between making commitments and preserving their options, winning and avoiding risks, making explicit threats and making ambiguous ones, maximising pressure and minimising provocation, reaching a settlement and avoiding losses, and going public and maintaining secrecy (1977: 207–81). To this could be added the desire to acquire and keep allies and the desire not to be dragged into conflicts by them. Sometimes decision-makers and theorists fail to recognise the need to balance these conflicting pressures, and thus their policies and theories can be one-sided and as a result dangerously flawed. The duality of crises also flows from the similarities and differences between Cold War, non-Cold War crises and post-Cold War crises.

Time pressure

A sense of time pressure is relative and subjective. A crisis may last months, but initiatives by the adversary will often require decisions to be made under short-term time pressure. Alternatively, the overall structure of the crisis may impose time pressure. The Western allies had to respond quickly to the Soviet blockade of Berlin in 1948 in order to supply the city. The most obvious kind of time pressure involves a deadline. Decision-makers tend to avoid being clear about deadlines in order to give themselves room for manoeuvre. In the Berlin crisis of 1958–62, Khrushchev set a deadline but did not say when the clock started ticking and eventually extended and suspended the vague deadline. Alternatively, decision-makers may try to increase the credibility of their threats through the self-imposed time pressure of a clear deadline. In the Gulf crisis of 1990–91, the coalition led by the United States against Iraq secured a UN Security Council resolution with a clear deadline of 15 January 1991 for the complete and unconditional withdrawal of Iraq from Kuwait, which had been invaded in August 1990. If Iraq did not comply, the use of force to retake Kuwait would then have UN backing. However, this deadline was not as clear as it looked because it did not say when the punishment for non-compliance would be meted out. Hence the satirical magazine *Private Eye* had on the cover of its 4 January 1991 issue a picture of President George Bush at a press conference with a speech bubble saying 'If Saddam doesn't withdraw from Kuwait . . . I'll issue another ultimatum'. There was much speculation about whether it would take days or even weeks before force was used, and there was uncertainty about whether signs of apparent withdrawal would be sufficient to constitute compliance. As it turned out, force was used immediately on the expiry of the deadline, apparently because the deadline was derived from expectations about the optimum date to begin military operations.

Interests: threats and opportunities

The idea of interests is analysed in depth in Chapter Two, but a few points should be made here. Leaders are usually motivated by a mixture of threat to their interests and opportunity to advance them, and a debate has arisen about which motivation tends to be dominant. For example, the Iraqi invasion of Kuwait in 1990 was motivated both by concern about the damage being caused to Iraq's economy by Kuwait's over-production of oil, and by the desire to possess Kuwait. This debate is taken up in Chapters Two and Three, but it is logical to build both approaches into the definition of crisis at this stage. Actions taken to exploit an opportunity often involve risks of loss. The reverse also applies: actions taken to protect threatened interests may create opportunities for gain. The United States intervened in the Korean War in order to prevent South Korea from losing the war, and soon found itself presented with what it saw as an opportunity to reunite Korea.

METHODOLOGICAL ISSUES

I use a structured, focused comparison approach (George 1979) and place it within a framework of crisis behaviour theory. This methodology provides structure through explicit definitions of key terms, provides focus by selecting a set of hypotheses to consider and provides comparison through a set of case studies, with the intention of discovering causal patterns. An approach which seeks to examine the relative weight of different factors must consider the extent to which those factors are discrete and rankable. It is likely that there will be connections between factors: for example, a favourable military balance may create more opportunities for promoting interests that otherwise would not be defined as interests, or may create fears in the minds of opponents, who then take counter-action which puts interests in danger. The links between factors will be explored at length. Once these links are understood, it becomes easier to rank the importance of the factors which have been analysed. The methodology used in this study is strongly influenced by Jack Snyder's efforts to encourage a balance between the parsimony of social science methods and the eclectic insights of holism (1984–85, 1988. See also Russett [1970] 1974; Achen, Snidal 1989; Hollis, Smith 1990; Huth, Russett 1990; King, Keohane, Verba 1994). The holistic approach stresses details of historical, political and cultural context, and examines questions from the various subjective viewpoints of the individual actors. In contrast, the social science approach adopts more scientific methods of theory testing, tries to separate causes from effects, has more (but by no means complete) faith that theory and evidence can be distinguished from each other, and seeks to develop cumulative knowledge.[6] In reading the case studies, some historians will be uncomfortable at the way in which the factors are separated out and then compared against each other. This may be seen as a somewhat artificial exercise. However, even historians cannot escape the fact that they are engaged in an artificial exercise of selecting and organising the infinite complexity of events into a linear narrative. Furthermore, historians routinely rank causal factors without dealing with the associated conceptual and theoretical problems and without making explicit their criteria beyond strength of empirical evidence, even though facts and theories blend into each other to some extent. Where historical debates exist on aspects of the case studies, these will be discussed. However, unrealistic expectations that these can be resolved – that someone can have the last word – should be discarded. Not only are specific events disputed by historians: there are also differences about whether to focus on, or how to weigh against each other, the immediate versus underlying causes of events. New information on the cases selected continues to emerge, especially on Soviet decision-making in the wake of the collapse of the Soviet Union, but also due to the continuing declassification of US and even some Chinese documents. These documents have also allowed interviewers to prise further insights from former crisis participants.[7] Although it will be many years before key historical documents on the Kuwait crisis of 1990–91 are available (and, especially on the Iraqi side, they may either never surface or may never have existed), the sprint into print which accompanies – never mind follows – modern crises has helped to shed some light. Furthermore, it is an important case because it was the first big political-military crisis after the end of the Cold War and because, regardless of the truth, lessons are already being drawn from it. There is a more general point here: lessons based on limited information, including information regarding decision-making in closed societies, are going to be drawn from past crises. Scholars ought not to sit back and refuse to engage until large amounts of high-quality information is available. Instead, they ought to do the best they can with the limited information available while emphasising that further information may require a reassessment of their conclusions.

Although studies of crisis behaviour often appear to be talking about the same case, such as 'Berlin', 'Korea' and so on, each supposedly single case actually involves multiple stages. For example, the Korean War had numerous stages, such as the North

Korean decision to attack South Korea, the decision of the United States to intervene, its decision to try to reunite the whole of Korea once it was winning, its failure to take seriously the Chinese attempts to deter its approach to the Yalu River, the Chinese decision to intervene and the Chinese decision in 1953 to make the concessions necessary to break the stalemate at the Panmunjom talks to end the war. In the Gulf there were at least two crises, with Iraq at the centre of both. During the first in 1990, Iraq decided to invade Kuwait. The second revolved around whether or not Iraq would bow to the US ultimatum for it to withdraw from Kuwait in January 1991. In addition, at any one of the many stages, each actor will be pursuing multiple objectives. For example, in wanting to complete the installation process of nuclear-armed missiles during the Cuban missile crisis, Khrushchev was seeking to find a quick fix to the Soviet Union's nuclear inferiority relative to the United States, to provide a force which would deter future attacks by the United States on its ally, to avoid being seen to be deserting an ally in the face of pressure from the United States and to secure a foreign policy victory which would bolster his own position domestically and that of the Soviet Union in its rivalry with China. The clarity of the objectives of the protagonists also varies from case to case. Sometimes the main objective is fairly clear, such as the Chinese aim in 1950 of discouraging the mainly US forces under the United Nations (UN) flag from crossing the 38th parallel into North Korea. On other occasions, such as during the Taiwan Straits crisis of 1954–55, it was more difficult to identify the main Chinese objective. In focusing on the primary objective involved in a particular crisis decision, history is effectively freeze-framed. A long hard look can be taken to assess the role of the various factors at work. This is not ahistorical and certainly does not assume that political calculations are constant; indeed, because the balance of political factors changes so frequently, it is important to focus on a particular decision point. From this decision point, history can be rewound in order to see how far back the causal chain needs to be pursued and to get a sense of the relative weight of underlying versus proximate factors. However, fundamentally, this debate cannot be resolved because it is rooted in different assumptions about epistemology and the causes of human action. On this issue, my inclination is to focus primarily on proximate factors on the grounds that an emphasis on underlying factors is liable to provide under-determined explanations of crisis outcomes, that is, a particular set of underlying factors can be compatible with a wide range of crisis outcomes.[8] That said, underlying factors are still important in setting the context for crisis behaviour.

Case selection

Eight crises have been selected for study in detail. The number of cases selected is intended to be large enough to provide a reasonable range of cases from which to generate generalisations, and small enough to enable a fair amount of historical detail to be used so that the cases are not caricatured. As no pretensions are made about being scientific or about being able to generate statistical probabilities, no attempt has been made to draw a random sample from the universe of cases which fall within the definition of crisis given above. The cases selected are the Berlin blockade of 1948–49, the US invasion of North Korea in 1950, the Taiwan Straits crisis of 1954–55, the lengthy Berlin crisis of 1958–62, the Cuban missile crisis in 1962, the Sino-Soviet border crisis in 1969, the Argentine invasion of the Falkland Islands in 1982 and the Iraqi refusal to withdraw from Kuwait in 1990–91. As the decisions and calculations of actors are interdependent, the perceptions and positions of all the main actors are explored in each case.

The non-random selection of the cases raises the possibility that the conclusions drawn will be skewed by some unintentional bias. The most obvious possible unintentional bias is that most of the cases are from the Cold War. There are three responses to this point. First, the cases span Cold War, non-Cold War and post-Cold War contexts and actors. Korea, Taiwan, Berlin and Cuba were all East-West Cold War cases: they will be compared with the Sino-Soviet border clashes as an intra-Communist Cold War case, the Falklands as non-Cold War and the Gulf as post-Cold War. Second, there is a substantial diversity among the Cold War cases which is unlikely to have been overridden by the fact that they took place during the Cold War. There are some cases of deterrence and some of compellence; some cases where one side had a nuclear monopoly and others where both sides had nuclear weapons; some which ended peacefully and others which ended in war; some where it seems that psychological or strategic cultural factors loomed large and some where they did not. Third, the importance of the Cold War aspect to some cases will be assessed explicitly in the Conclusion. Overall, the variety of cases helps ensure that, once a hypothesis is formulated, there is the possibility of falsifying it or indicating the limits of its applicability by examining cases in which it does not seem to apply. Comparison will also be made with the conclusions of some large-scale statistical analyses of crisis behaviour, which span many contexts and actors.

STRUCTURE OF THE BOOK

The book is divided into three parts. Part I explains the theoretical dimensions of the study's model of international crisis outcomes. Within Part I, the meaning of the concepts of deterrence and compellence is explored in Chapter One, the nature of the military balance and the balance of interests is considered in Chapter Two, and the role of psychological and strategic cultural factors is considered in Chapter Three. In Part II, the theoretical model developed in Part I is applied systematically to eight case-study chapters in turn in order to shed light on the outcome of each case. In Part III, the objective is to identify patterns and general conclusions which have emerged from the application of the theoretical material to the cases. Near the beginning of each chapter I have provided a section which summarises the main issues discussed and conclusions offered. In the mean time, it is worth summarising my main conclusions very briefly here. Some analysts view crises from a perspective in which the opponent is an aggressor seeking to exploit opportunities. Others see decision-makers as driven by fear of loss, which results in psychological biases and disastrous policy choices. In my case studies I find that both factors are present, but I find the latter is more important. The conventional wisdom that deterrence is easier than 'compellence' (making someone do something) actually remains to be proven. While the differences between the two influenced crisis tactics, they were not central to explaining outcomes. Nuclear superiority also had little effect in securing favourable outcomes. Conventional military superiority – especially locally – can be important but decision-makers who think they have military superiority tend to be surprised when opponents stand up to them, and tend to misperceive them as irrational. Having more at stake than the opponent is often a crucial advantage as long as both sides do not want war. Strategic culture affects outcomes indirectly by shaping perceptions of interests, options and opponents.

NOTES

[1] Studies which address the question of the relative importance of the military balance and the balance of interests include McConnell 1979; Maoz 1983; Betts 1987; Huth, Russett 1984; Huth 1988b; George, Simons 1994 and Paul 1994. Although Huth and Russett have written a number of influential pieces (Russett 1963, 1967; Huth, Russett 1984, 1988; Huth 1988a, 1988b), their 1984 article and the book by Huth (1988b) are selected for discussion in this study as the most advanced representations of their work (see Levy 1988, 1989). Studies which also consider psychological factors are Adomeit 1982, Stein 1985a and b, Lieberman 1992 and Lebow, Stein 1994: 111, 227, 228, 301, 309–17, 320, 321, 501n. I will address their perspectives and conclusions at appropriate points throughout the book.

[2] For examples of influential definitions of crisis which focus only on danger and not also on opportunity, see Hermann 1969: 414; Snyder, Diesing 1977: 6; Lebow 1981: 10–12 and Brecher, Wilkenfeld 1989b: 5.

[3] *Wei* is 危, *ji* is 机, and *weiji* is 危机. See page 74.

[4] This incident was reported by KGB Colonel Oleg Gordievsky who spied for the West (Brook-Shepherd 1988: 269–70; Andrew, Gordievsky 1990: 599–600). I am grateful to Len Scott for emphasising to me the importance of this case. Ib Damgaard Petersen and Paul Smoker (1993: 193–200) claim that the United States knew about the war scare at the time and made vigorous efforts to reassure the Soviet Union, whereas Martin Walker (1994: 275–7) and Bruce Blair (1993: 180–1) maintain that the United States only found out some time later. According to Blair, US government intelligence analysts disagree over whether there was a Soviet alert or even whether a war scare occurred at all (1993: 340n).

[5] I exclude from my definition the concept of surprise because decision-makers are often not surprised when a crisis occurs, and often choose or feel the need to start them. When Saddam Hussein invaded Kuwait, he was not surprised that a crisis followed, although he miscalculated what

the outcome would be. Stalin deliberately induced a crisis over West Berlin to achieve his political objectives. On the Western side, tension in relations with the Soviet Union plus the vulnerability of West Berlin, isolated deep in what was to become East Germany, meant that decision-makers were hardly surprised that the Soviet Union exerted pressure.

[6] On the distinction between social science explanation and holistic understanding, see Hollis, Smith 1990. I address its implications for this study on pages 22–5, 64, 71 and 249. My use of the term 'explaining' for the subtitle of this book is meant in its less specific conventional sense. Throughout this book I try to combine where possible the social science and holistic modes of analysis.

[7] On the need to handle with care information derived from oral history, see Kramer 1990. For valuable discussions of how to use this kind of source properly, see Garthoff 1990b and Lebow, Stein 1994: 9–14.

[8] For more arguments in support of this preference, see Lebow 1981: 1–4.

Part I

THEORY

Chapter One

DETERRENCE AND COMPELLENCE

> 'That's a great deal to make one word mean,' Alice said in a thoughtful tone.
> 'When I make a word do a lot of work like that,' said Humpty Dumpty, 'I always pay it extra.'
>
> Lewis Carroll ([1872] 1988: 275)

Is it easier to secure a favourable crisis outcome if one is engaged in deterrence rather than compellence? In this chapter I argue that, despite arguments to the contrary, the distinction between deterrence and compellence is semantically viable. I offer definitions of the various kinds of deterrence and compellence – immediate, general, direct and extended. I consider the debate between Paul Huth and Bruce Russett on one side and Ned Lebow and Janice Stein on the other in relation to the task of coding (that is classifying or categorising) cases as examples of successful or failed deterrence or compellence. I then suggest what would constitute an adequate test of the relative difficulty of deterrence versus compellence. I point out that the method of structured, focused comparison is designed only to identify causal patterns (if they exist) and not statistical success rates. The alternative I propose is that the case studies ought to consider whether the two types of situation – deterrent and compellent – are associated with different causal patterns; whether decision-makers hold the belief that deterrence is easier than compellence; and whether decision-makers try to ensure that their task is one of deterrence rather than compellence. I emphasise that the achievement of the main deterrent or compellent objective in a crisis does not necessarily mean that the crisis outcome is favourable overall: for example, compromise may be necessary on related issues so that the overall outcome is roughly equal.

THE DISTINCTION BETWEEN DETERRENCE AND COMPELLENCE

The words with which students of strategy are normally comfortable upon closer attention prove to be uncertain and flimsy, and their meanings need to be thought through carefully. As David Baldwin writes: 'Conceptual analysis is neither impossible nor merely a matter of taste; it is a necessary first step towards clear thinking' (1985: 30). Baldwin proposes two criteria in choosing a definition of an established concept: it should help in the development and assessment of policy options and it should not depart unnecessarily from common usage (1985: 30). In any conceptual analysis, one comes across limitations in current concepts which raise the question of whether to create new terms. For conceptual innovations, a third condition should be applied: the new term should have some reasonable chance of catching on. Stickiness matters: if a label keeps falling off, then it is of little value. This chapter keeps conceptual innovations to a minimum and concentrates on clarifying existing concepts and the relationships between them.

Military and non-military deterrence and compellence

Deterrence is the use of threats to prevent someone from doing something whereas compellence is the use of threats to make someone do something (cf. Schelling [1960] 1980: 195). One can deter a military action with military means, a military action with non-military means, a non-military action with military means, and a non-military action with non-military means, as Huth and Russett note (1990: 473). They restrict their analysis to threats of military force to prevent the use of military force on the grounds that conclusions cannot easily be drawn across classes of cases due to the differences in the actions considered and the instruments used. It would follow from this that much of crisis behaviour is not about deterrence or compellence.[1] This is perfectly reasonable, but it is not self-evident that the differences between deterrence of attack and deterrence of other undesired actions are so great that it is always inappropriate to analyse them together. For example, trying to deter crime through threat of imprisonment shares important characteristics with trying to deter attack through threat of a military response (a poor success rate, the sceptic might say). Deterrence of action in general seems to be a reasonable 'class of case'.[2] I will make it clear in the theoretical and case-study chapters when I am referring to military deterrence of military action or when I have in mind something broader.

The semantic viability of the distinction

The semantic viability of the deterrence-compellence distinction is questioned by Baldwin.[3] He argues that 'From a purely semantic standpoint, any deterrent threat can be stated in compellent terms, and any compellent threat can be stated in deterrent terms' (1979: 188). He suggests that one can speak in terms of 'deterring South Africans from doing X (when X is continued white dominance)' (1979: 188). However, there is a distinction: Thomas Schelling defines deterrence in terms of preventing another actor from 'starting something', and the whites started dominating South Africa many years ago. Thus, to demand that they cease doing it is a form of compellence. Just as in the example below from Schelling's own writings, the phrase to 'deter continuance' of something is a contradiction in terms when looked at in the light of Schelling's own definitions. Baldwin says 'we could talk about compelling the Russians to do X (when X is anything except launching a nuclear attack)' (1979: 188). That is not the case: no demands were made of the Russians that they do anything, coupled with threats of punishment for non-compliance. In his example, the Russians could basically do what they liked as long as they did not launch that nuclear attack, for which punishment is promised. Thus overall, the deterrence-compellence distinction is semantically viable.

The practical differences between deterrence and compellence are discussed by Schelling at some length (1966: 66–91). His arguments relate to who has to make the first move, the necessity of inflicting harm to establish credibility, the mode and style of creating the context, the role of deadlines, the relative clarity of demands and the consequent problems of complying and identifying compliance, and the closeness of the link between the demand and the threatened punishment for non-compliance. In the case studies to follow, the practical significance of these points will be considered. Baldwin claims that these differences are probably unimportant (1979: 189–91): this is a matter for empirical analysis. No comment is made by Baldwin on Schelling's view that in the conduct of a crisis 'the difference between deterrence and compellence, like the difference between defense and offense, may disappear' (1966: 80). He discusses the case of the Cuban missile crisis in which the United States failed to deter the Soviets from deploying their forces, sought to compel the Soviets to remove them, and 'by good fortune' found a threat (a naval blockade) to help achieve this objective 'that had some of the static qualities of a deterrent threat' (1966: 80–2). This does not offer support for Baldwin's position because the overlap is situational rather than one of semantics. The fact that a threat can have multiple objectives suggests a reason why Baldwin is led to argue that any deterrence threat can be restated in terms of compellence.

'Cease doing' and 'continue doing'

As stated earlier, compellence is defined here as the use of threats to make someone do something. In 1960 in *The Strategy of Conflict*, Schelling describes compellence as involving 'a threat intended to make an adversary *do* something (or cease doing something)' ([1960] 1980: 195), while in 1966 in *Arms and Influence*, he drops the phrase 'or cease doing something' from his definition without explanation (1966: 69). The objectives of making an opponent 'cease doing' something – or 'continue doing' something – fall in a hazy overlap of deterrence and compellence. A number of pages after offering his revised definition of compellence he writes the following: 'Note that to deter *continuance* of something the opponent is already doing – harassment, overflight, blockade, occupation of some island or territory, electronic disturbance, subversive activity, holding prisoners or whatever it may be – has some of the characteristics of a compellent threat' (1966: 77). The similarity of 'cease doing' and deterrence lies in the fact that the objective in both cases is inaction on the part of the target. The similarity of the two increases if the prohibited action is actually a series of actions, so that what is being deterred is the next action in the series. However, the usage of 'deterrence' in the example just given still seems to contradict Schelling's own definition. If deterrence is about preventing someone from 'starting something', then attempting to prevent the continuation of something which has already started cannot be considered an attempt at deterrence. In his own terms, making someone stop doing something is a case of compellence. 'Cease doing' appears to be more a part of compellence in that what is required is a change in the current behaviour of the target. Trying to make someone cease doing something or continue doing something (an objective which could also be restated as trying to prevent someone from ceasing doing something!) cannot be categorised clearly as either deterrence or compellence. In other words, Schelling's 1966 quiet modification of his definition of compellence makes sense.

TYPES OF DETERRENCE

General and immediate deterrence

Morgan suggests that we distinguish between general and immediate deterrence. This idea has justifiably become part of the basic lexicon of deterrence theorists, although there has been very little analysis of general deterrence.[4] According to Morgan, general deterrence exists when:

> 1. Relations between opponents are such that leaders in at least one [state] would consider resorting to force if the opportunity arose . . . 2. The other side, precisely because it believes that the opponent would be willing to consider resort to force, maintains forces of its own and offers warnings to respond in kind to attempts to use force contrary to its interests . . . 3. The decisionmakers at whom the general deterrent threat is aimed do not go beyond preliminary consideration of resorting to force because of the expectation that such a policy would result in a corresponding resort to force of some sort by leaders of the opposing state.
>
> (1980: 42–4)

On the other hand, immediate deterrence has the following characteristics:

> 1. In a relationship between two hostile states the officials in at least one of them are considering attacking the other or attacking some area of the world the other deems important. 2. Key officials of the other state realize this. 3. Realizing that an attack is a distinct possibility, the latter set of officials threaten the use of force in retaliation in an attempt to prevent the attack. 4. Leaders of the state planning to attack decide to desist primarily because of the retaliatory threat(s). (1980: 38)

Morgan's summary definitions are that immediate deterrence 'concerns the relationship between opposing states where at least one side is seriously considering an attack while the other is mounting a threat of retaliation in order to prevent it', while general deterrence 'relates to opponents who maintain armed forces to regulate their relationship even though neither is anywhere near mounting an attack' (1980: 30). Deterrence of attack is treated as a special case of deterrence in this study, as has been explained earlier. For the purposes of this study, general deterrence is the use of a standing threat in order to prevent someone from seriously considering doing something, while immediate deterrence is the use of specific threats to prevent someone from doing something which is being seriously considered. Immediate deterrence may rely on a single specific threat, but in practice more than one kind of threat or more than one of the same kind of threat tends to be issued. One has to be careful not to mistake general deterrence for immediate deterrence. The mere existence of a military establishment represents a standing threat, and occasional declarations of willingness to use force if necessary are made to draw attention to this. Often threats are issued in order to prevent serious consideration of attack. This still falls under the heading of general deterrence because an attack is not yet being seriously considered. But it starts to look rather like immediate deterrence because the opponent seems to be close to considering an attack. Indeed, in these situations the deterrer is unlikely to be sure either way, and in effect plays 'safe' (in a way which might turn out to be provocative) by assuming that its task is immediate deterrence.

Direct and extended deterrence

Direct deterrence is the use of threats to prevent someone from doing something to the deterrer, and extended deterrence is the use of threats to prevent someone from doing something to someone else. Although discussions of extended deterrence usually revolve around the use of threats of force to prevent an attack on another state, they are also often concerned with deterring attempts at political intimidation. From this point on, for the sake of brevity, references simply to 'deterrence' and 'compellence' are usually to immediate and direct (rather than general or extended) deterrence and compellence, unless the context makes it clear otherwise (as in the use of the heading 'Types of Compellence').

TYPES OF COMPELLENCE

General and immediate compellence

General compellence is the use of a standing threat to make someone do something. This is very like the phenomenon that has become known as 'Finlandization'.[5] Although tremendously difficult to demonstrate, it is widely believed that a backdrop of military superiority can be used to make leaders in other countries anxious to initiate acts they believe to be desired by the stronger state, or stop doing what they fear might antagonise it (Garnett 1975a: 55). In contrast, immediate compellence is the use of specific threats to make someone do something. This is what analysts normally have in mind when they refer to compellence.

Direct and extended compellence

In order to make the conceptual analysis complete, the applicability of the direct-extended distinction to compellence needs to be considered. The only use of the phrase 'extended compellence' in the literature is by Lebow and Stein. Although they do not provide a definition, one can try to deduce a definition from the cases they cite. They seem to have examined cases which Huth and Russett have classified as immediate extended deterrence, decided that they are actually cases of compellence and then apparently assumed that the idea of (immediate) extended compellence makes sense (1990a: 352). In 1964–65, according to Lebow and Stein, the United States failed to compel North Vietnam to cease supporting the National Liberation Front (NLF) in South Vietnam.[6] They categorise the role of the United States in Laos in 1961 as extended compellence success (whereas Huth and Russett see it as an immediate extended deterrence success). Essentially, the United States committed itself to sending troops to defend the Laotian capital Vientiane, held by pro-US General Phoumi Nosavan, and demanded a cease-fire and negotiations leading to the formation of a neutral coalition government, to which the alliance of neutralist and Communist forces agreed. President Kennedy was motivated by the fear that the Communist Pathet Lao would take over if the civil war continued. Lebow and Stein are not clear on why this is extended compellence. Perhaps it is because the US objective involved getting the opposition to do something they did not want to do, that is, participate in the (re)establishment of a neutral government, and the US pressure was brought to bear through third parties, namely the Soviet Union and North Vietnam. It was also compellence in that the United States was trying to get the opposition forces to cease doing something, that is, cease fighting.

On the basis of the Laotian case, extended compellence might be defined as the use of threats in order to make someone get a third party to do something (including cease doing something). However, this is not compatible with the use of the phrase by Lebow and Stein elsewhere in the same article (the numbers in brackets followed by dates refer to the case number and year of the Huth and Russett studies):

> Extended compellence succeeded in 1913, when Austria-Hungary compelled Serbia to end its occupation of northern Albania (case 16: 1984); in 1970, when the United States and Israel compelled Syria to halt its attack against Jordan (case 49: 1984) . . . Extended compellence failed in 1964–65, when the United States failed to compel North Vietnam to cease its support of the Viet Cong (case 45: 1984); in 1979, when Libya failed to compel Tanzania to withdraw its forces from Uganda (case 54: 1984); and in 1922, when Britain failed to compel Turkey to withdraw its forces from Chanak (case 4: 1988).
> (1990a: 352)

From this list, they appear also to define extended compellence as the use of threats to make a state do something or cease doing something with regard to a third party. However, this is contradicted by their following examples of direct compellence: 'direct rather than extended compellence succeeded in 1906, when Britain compelled a Turkish withdrawal from Taba (case 2: 1988) and in 1921, when the United States compelled Panama to surrender territory to Costa Rica (case 3: 1988)' (1990a: 352). It is not clear why Austria compelling Serbia to withdraw from northern Albania is extended compellence whereas Britain compelling Turkey to withdraw from Taba is direct compellence. The definitions of these concepts as used in this study are that direct compellence is the use of threats to make someone do something, and extended compellence is the use of threats to make someone get a third party to do something. This approach is consistent with the general usage of the terms 'direct' and 'extended'.[7]

PROBLEMS OF TESTING DETERRENCE AND COMPELLENCE THEORY: LEBOW AND STEIN VERSUS HUTH AND RUSSETT

The potential for drastic disagreement on how to test deterrence and compellence theory is demonstrated by the debate between Huth and Russett on the one hand and Lebow and Stein on the other.[8] The debate receives a substantial amount of attention in this chapter because their work is at the cutting edge. If one accepts the analysis of Lebow and Stein, then all of the conclusions of the very influential and widely-cited Huth and Russett studies must be discounted.[9] In their assessment of the 1984 Huth and Russett study, Lebow and Stein eliminate forty-one of the fifty-four cases of immediate extended deterrence. They argue that in ten cases there was no serious intention to attack, in eight there was no attempt to deter, and in a further nineteen cases neither condition was present. They reclassify four cases as compellence, two as direct deterrence and four as ambiguous. In his 1988 study, Huth – without explanation – drops sixteen cases, adds thirteen and recodes five. Of the thirteen new cases, Lebow and Stein accept only one as a case of immediate extended deterrence. They reclassify four cases as compellence, two as ambiguous and eliminate the remaining six. In the six cases they eliminate, they argue that there was no serious intention to attack in one, there was no attempt to deter in one, and neither condition was present in a further five.

Competing measures of consideration of attack and attempts to deter or compel

The disagreement between the two sides flows in part from the fact that Lebow and Stein have stricter criteria for deciding what constitutes serious consideration of attack or an attempt to deter. Lebow and Stein argue that Huth and Russett rely primarily on surrogate measures of the intention to attack and of the attempt to deter – namely threats and military movements – in spite of the fact that such words and actions are often bluffs, reassurances to allies, temporising activities until the situation becomes clearer, signals of concern or resolve, or desire to negotiate and many things other than serious consideration of attack. While Huth and Russett measure possible intent to use force by implicit or explicit verbal threats to use force or the 'movement, buildup, and/or positioning of military forces near or along the border or coastline' of the target state, they also argue that they take steps to winnow out spurious cases by looking for 'contextual evidence' that might indicate a threat 'intended *only* to: (1) deflect attention from the attacker's own domestic political unrest and instability; (2) draw into the dispute an outside party who would then exert pressure on the protégé [the country to which deterrence is being extended] to make concessions; or (3) force the protégé to enter into negotiations' (1990: 483). The fact that Huth and Russett have this procedure shows that there can be no objective criteria for case selection. They criticise Lebow and Stein for not operationalising 'serious consideration of attack' by the use of clearly observable indicators. Yet Huth and Russett do not provide such operationalisation for measuring the deflection of attention, drawing in outside parties or forcing negotiations. They refer to contextual evidence: to the extent that this means direct historical evidence, they then run into the same problems of using historical evidence as Lebow and Stein (or anyone else). If they are not referring to direct historical evidence, then it is not clear to what they are referring. It should be emphasised that the procedure of excluding competing explanations is not simply a minor safeguard but is central to the case selection process. In the end, there is no escape from in-depth historical analysis and subjective judgements on coding.

Huth and Russett claim that Lebow and Stein believe that analysis of the historical record provides a 'high confidence' measure of serious consideration of attack (1990: 481). However, Lebow and Stein seem instead to be arguing that (if used properly, of course) it is the highest confidence method. Huth and Russett note that Lebow and Stein do not address directly in their article the difficulties of using documentary evidence, such as the limitations of decision-makers' own self-awareness as to their own intentions; the fact that they may not articulate their intentions when they do know them; their intentions may change but they might not express this change; they may express conflicting intentions; and they may try to mislead as to their real intentions (1990: 481). In part this is simply a matter of good historical judgement and understanding of psychology, rather than an effective criticism of Lebow and Stein, who pay a great deal more attention to the issue of psychology than Huth and Russett. However, it also involves the more important point that historical evidence, however well researched it may be, has inherent limitations. Aside from this, it is not clear what Lebow and Stein mean by a serious intention to attack. Huth and Russett infer that Lebow and Stein require that the potential attacker has decided to use force from the start. In contrast, Morgan's original definition only requires serious *consideration* of attack. However, it is possible that what Lebow and Stein want is clearer historical evidence that such consideration took place. Focusing on historical debates helps to reduce the temptation of casual coding. In order to avoid forcing cases into categories, it makes sense to follow Lebow and Stein in having a category of 'ambiguous cases'. However, where the circumstantial evidence is very strong in terms of the criteria used by Huth and Russett, it also makes sense to include the case. Thus, in this study, serious consideration of an action exists when there is direct historical evidence of that consideration, or where there are verbal statements of intent and/or actions consonant with preparation for that action and where there is no strong circumstantial evidence to suggest that the statements were made or actions performed primarily for other purposes. Deterrence has been attempted, according to Huth and Russett 'as long as the defender issued at least one verbal warning or initiated a show of force near the border or off the coast of the potential attacker' (1990: 489). For Lebow and Stein this is crucial, on the grounds that it is much easier to identify the practice of deterrence than to identify seriousness of intention to attack. They argue that any serious attempt to deter was absent from nearly all of the cases they eliminate from the Huth and Russett studies. Exactly the same points made above with regard to serious consideration of attack apply to the seriousness of an attempt to deter or compel: there is no escape from detailed historical study, and one must be careful to exclude, or at least classify as ambiguous, cases where alternative interpretations are plausible.

False positives versus false negatives

One of the aims of Lebow and Stein is to screen out many spurious cases (false positives) which they believe Huth and Russett let slip through. Huth and Russett accept that some spurious cases may be included, but argue that it is preferable to admit the occasional spurious case than to restrict the definition of serious intention to attack or of an attempt to deter to such a degree that many genuine cases are excluded (false negatives). They claim that, if very strong historical evidence of serious consideration of attack is required, then the analysis will be biased towards finding cases of deterrence failure, and that this will therefore under-represent the degree to which immediate deterrence succeeds (1990: 483, 489. Cf. Huth, Russett 1993: 62). It is difficult to choose between the two sides on this point, because knowing which trade-off is preferable depends on a comparison of the number of spurious cases included with the number of successes excluded, and a comparison of the sensitivity of the conclusions of the study to these inclusions and exclusions.

Cold War bias versus revisionist bias

Unconscious Cold War bias is perceived by Lebow and Stein to permeate the work of Huth and Russett. This is supposed to have led them to see (and to rely on sources which also perceived) Soviet and Chinese intention to attack where none existed or where the evidence of such intention is actually weak or ambiguous (1990a: 345–8, 353–5; 1990b: 42–3). The retort of Huth and Russett is that Lebow and Stein are too quick to accept revisionist interpretations of the case studies and are not aware of (or do not attach sufficient weight to) evidence of Soviet and Chinese consideration of the use of force (1990: 487). In the case-study chapters, positions will be taken on their competing interpretations; clearly, it is important to avoid revisionist bias as well as Cold War bias. As with the issue of false positives versus false negatives, the two perspectives need to be compared to judge the sensitivity of conclusions regarding causal patterns to their differing assessments of individual cases. Although there is no escape from subjectivity, and different generations and cultures will reinterpret history from their own perspective, not all historical accounts are equally accurate: one can still achieve 'qualified objectivity' (Appleby, Hunt, Jacob 1994).

Single cases, multiple dimensions

Much of the recoding by Lebow and Stein is based, according to Huth and Russett, on a failure to apply the point that a single case can have multiple deterrent and compellent dimensions. Certainly, Huth and Russett show that Lebow and Stein misunderstood their classification of a number of cases (e.g. 1990: 484–7; forthcoming). The practical, immediate task in hand can often be identified clearly, regardless of how actors perceive their own motivations. The concentration of this study on operational objectives is designed to avoid the question of broader offensive or defensive motivations, although it is addressed in Chapters Two and Three. One can designate particular aspects of a crisis as involving deterrence or compellence. For example, after Iraq invaded Kuwait, Iraq's objective was to deter the use of force by the allies to drive it out of Kuwait. The allies hoped to deter chemical weapon attacks by Iraq, but this was very much subordinate to their main goal of compelling Iraq to withdraw. An actor may pursue a deterrent, compellent or mixed strategy.

The links with offence and defence

Deterrence theory is seen by Lebow and Stein as involving the assumption that the opponent is offensively or aggressively motivated. According to Lebow 'deterrence is unabashedly a theory of opportunity. It assumes that adversaries are risk-prone maximisers who seek opportunities to make military gains and pounce when they find them' (quoted in Huth, Russett 1990: 487; see also Lebow, Stein 1990b: 64). However, Huth and Russett argue correctly that, while such assumptions tend to be associated with deterrence theory, they are auxiliary and not a necessary part of rational deterrence theory, which could have a completely different set of auxiliary assumptions about motivations (1990: 472, 487). Deterrence may be used for offensive motives and compellence for defensive motives, and either may be used for a mixture of motives.[10] Furthermore, defensive and offensive motivations may not be clearly distinguishable. These are themes which are threaded throughout this book and reflect the way in which decision-makers are motivated by varying mixtures of danger and opportunity.

Competing measures of success and failure

If fewer than around 250 casualties result from deliberate use of force from an attacker with the capability to escalate the use of force further, and the deterrer does not capitulate, then this is still a military deterrence success, according to Huth and Russett (1990: 490–1). Of course, any use of force represents a failure of general deterrence. Lebow and Stein reject the casualty-figure approach as arbitrary and not derived from deterrence theory (which normally refers only to the prevention of the proscribed action) (1990a: 344–5). In contrast, Huth and Russett argue that, as Alexander George and Richard Smoke (1974) have shown, limited force can be used to probe a deterrence commitment. Furthermore, Huth and Russett indicate that there is a strong tendency towards conflicts either involving fewer than 300 casualties or over 1,000, with few cases in between (1990: 490–1). Hence, to phrase the definition in the broad fashion used in this study, immediate deterrence is successful if (a) a contemplated action does not occur mainly because of the threats of the deterrer or if a deterree, capable of doing more, marginally oversteps the bounds of permitted action to probe the commitment of the deterrer and (b) the deterrer does not capitulate to the demands of the potential attacker. At most, the probe should be seen as a partial failure of immediate deterrence. Potential attackers would generally rather not use force to attain their objectives, so demands are almost always implicit in any communicated consideration of attack. Immediate deterrence has failed if the deterree does the proscribed action, or tries to do so in the face of resistance.

Similarly, immediate compellence is successful if the target performs the required action mainly because of the threats of the deterrer and has failed if the target does not perform the required action to a significant extent. A possible objection to the definition of successful compellence offered here is that compellence is often associated with the imposition of sanctions which are lifted only when the required action is performed, whereas deterrence tends to be associated with a sanction which is only imposed when a proscribed action is performed (Huth, Russett 1990: 475). However, these associations are not definitional necessities. Force can be used to shore up deterrence, and when force is used to encourage compliance with a compellent demand, that use of force is intended to increase the credibility of the threat to use additional force.

DETERRENCE, COMPELLENCE AND CRISIS OUTCOMES

Long-run versus initial outcomes

Positive outcomes are often partial and reversible (Blechman, Kaplan 1978: 87; Huth, Russett 1988; Lebow, Stein 1990a: 13–14; 1991: 11–13; 1994). I concentrate on operational objectives and short-term outcomes because of the relative directness of the causal links (cf. Blechman, Kaplan 1978: 65). This does not mean that the short-term outcome is necessarily more important than the longer-term outcome, either in terms of the specific issue in dispute or in terms of broader implications for relations between the states involved. It is possible that partial success is more successful in the long run than total success, on the grounds that the loser will be more strongly motivated to exact revenge at a later date. Then again, if the winner succeeds sufficiently well, the capability of the loser to challenge can be crippled for a long time. Studies of the longer-term impact of international crisis outcomes on relations between states are important, but it is also important to understand what brings about initial outcomes.

Deterrence and compellence outcomes versus crisis outcomes

The outcome of a crisis as a whole must also be distinguished from the outcome or any particular deterrent or compellent dimension of a crisis.[11] For example, although the United States successfully compelled the withdrawal of Soviet missiles from Cuba, one possible interpretation of the crisis outcome as a whole is that the United States conceded as much as the Soviet Union. The dependent variable – the thing to be explained – in this study is not deterrence or compellence outcomes but crisis outcomes, in which deterrence or compellence may be independent variables (i.e. form part of the explanation). It is perfectly reasonable to construct more narrowly based studies in which the universe of case studies is defined solely in terms of, say, immediate extended deterrence. In that study, immediate extended deterrence would be the dependent variable. However, the preference here is to develop a broader explanation of crisis outcomes.

In order to code the outcome of a crisis, the extent to which the actors achieved their objectives must be assessed. Success may be outright or it may involve compromise. In zero-sum contexts (where one side's gain is the loss of the other) it requires the achievement of objectives to a greater extent than the opponent. In a power struggle, decision-makers may be concerned primarily with maximising their gains relative to their opponent. Thus one state may be worse off in absolute terms (due to, say, the costs of a military build-up) but better off relative to a rival state (due to, say, political concessions by the opponent in order to avoid escalation to war).[12] The subjectivity of this exercise lies in the fact that like is rarely being compared with like and in the ways decision-makers (and analysts) intentionally and unintentionally interpret outcomes or argue about what were the objectives.

An important aspect of the links between deterrence, compellence and crisis outcomes is the claim that deterrence is easier than compellence. It is to this argument that I now turn.

IS DETERRENCE EASIER THAN COMPELLENCE?

The reason why one threat fails and another succeeds might simply be because, as Thomas Schelling claims, 'It is easier to *deter* than to *compel*'.[13] This point is familiar to all deterrence theorists, but familiarity has bred neglect in that the validity of Schelling's distinction has rarely been explored in any detail.[14] Walter Petersen's study (1986) is the only substantial assessment on the practical importance of the difference between deterrence and compellence.[15] Unfortunately, his article on 135 interstate disputes between 1823 and 1973 contains serious flaws. He defines compellence and deterrence as follows: 'an explicit and specific threat to use military force in an effort either to change the status quo (compellence) or to deter the opponent from attempting to change the existing situation (deterrence)' (1986: 270). The definitions which Petersen uses unwittingly shift the focus away from what Schelling had in mind. In another context Robert Jervis observes that 'Deterrence usually seeks to uphold the status quo and compellence to change it, but Schelling's distinction refers to the adversary's behaviour whereas the status quo refers to a situation.'[16] There can be cases where threats are issued to make an opponent do something in order to maintain the status quo. One country can try to compel another to sign a border treaty which involves acceptance of the status quo. There can also be cases where threats are issued to prevent an opponent from doing something (such as clamp down on demonstrators) in order to bring about a change in the status quo (such as bring down the regime against which the people are demonstrating).

Even if we accept Petersen's redefinition of the basic concepts, his coding does not adhere to the new definitions, as can be demonstrated by a few examples. There is not space in this study to go through all or many of his 135 cases, but the difficulties with the cases examined are unsettling. For example, in 1939, the Soviet Union demanded that Finland cede territory to it, and backed up its demands with threats of force. When Finland refused, the Soviet Union took the territory by force. In 1956, Hungary declared and then maintained its neutrality in spite of Soviet threats. As a result, the Soviet Union and other Warsaw Treaty Organisation (WTO or Warsaw Pact) allies invaded Hungary and installed a pliant government. The Finnish example was an example of failed compellence and the Hungarian case could possibly be failed deterrence followed by failed compellence (although it is unclear that either strategy was attempted seriously), yet Petersen codes them both as examples of successful compellence by the Soviet Union.

In the case of the Cuban missile crisis, Petersen codes the Soviet Union as the initiator who changed the status quo and then conceded to the United States. It is true that the Soviet Union changed the status quo by emplacing missiles on Cuba, but it is strange to code the crisis as an example of a failed Soviet attempt at compellence. The Soviet Union was not trying to get the United States to do anything other than accept what it (the Soviet Union) was doing. In reality, it was the United States which deterred the Soviet Union from completing its deployment and compelled it to withdraw its missiles. Compellence is about A convincing B that B should do something, not about A using force to bring it about: that is the offensive application of force, not compellence. On the same logic, deterrence is about A convincing B that B should not do the proscribed action, not about A resisting B while B tries to do the proscribed action: that is the defensive use of force, not deterrence.

Even if threats are made and the required outcome results, other factors could have brought about the outcome, as was pointed out earlier. In 1956, Britain, France and Israel colluded in an invasion of Egypt, but Britain and France were forced to withdraw. Petersen codes this as two cases of successful Soviet deterrence (where the 'initiator defends [the] status quo') in spite of the fact that the drastic economic sanctions imposed by the United States are generally seen as the key reason for the collapse of the British military effort, and, without Britain, France would not go it alone. The Soviet Union did issue military threats after the invasion took place, but much less weight is attached to them by analysts in comparison with the economic sanctions of the United States. Although the British Prime Minister, Anthony Eden, was concerned about the Soviet military threat, the immediate and crippling damage being inflicted by the sanctions was decisive in his calculations.[17] Furthermore, it might be seen as successful US non-military compellence because the United States required that Britain do something – that is, withdraw.

The weaknesses of Petersen's article are a product of his underestimation of the problems of coding, which seems to be due to his desire to get on with testing theory. It is not as if coding is an uncontroversial business: coding is the social science term for categorising aspects of history, and historians make their living by coding and re-coding cases, as it were. If Petersen had provided detailed evidence for his coding decisions, the problems would have been immediately obvious to readers of his article. Indeed, more direct familiarity with the historical evidence might have made the problems obvious to him. As it was he relied wholly on the codings in only three other studies (Petersen 1986: 273).

The apparent relative ease of deterrence may turn out to be illusory. Baldwin argues that this is so simply because 'deterrent threats are used for easy tasks while compellent threats are used for hard tasks'. Thus 'The person who tries to prevent unlikely things from happening will probably succeed; while the person who tries to cause unlikely things to happen will probably fail' (1979: 189). Baldwin cannot have it both ways: if he claims that any deterrent threat can be restated in terms of compellence and vice versa, as was discussed earlier, then his claim that deterrence is used for harder tasks than compellence is meaningless. This study argues that Baldwin is wrong about the supposed semantic unviability of the deterrence-compellence distinction, but is right to argue that the relative inherent difficulty of the two has not been tested. It follows from Baldwin's argument that, in order to find out whether deterrence is easier than compellence, one must look at their success rates with regard to tasks with the same degree of difficulty. One might be tempted simply to compare similar tasks, but there are two problems with this. First, the exact opposite of 'don't do X' is 'do X'; 'cease doing X' or 'undo X' do not quite suffice. However, for 'don't do X' one can rarely think of an example of 'do X' that one might ask of an opponent which keeps X constant. For example, one might demand of an opponent 'don't deploy missiles' or 'don't attack', but one would rarely demand of an opponent 'deploy missiles' or 'attack'. Ironically, these polar opposites apply more easily to allies, although allies are usually threatened with non-military sanctions for non-compliance with demands. In contrast, the demands 'cease deploying missiles' or 'undo your deployment of missiles' can plausibly apply to both opponents and allies. The second problem is crucial: just because tasks are similar does not mean that they are of a similar degree of difficulty – they may be, but one cannot assume that they are.

For deterrence to be easier than compellence, two conditions must obtain. First, the action to be deterred must be equally as likely to occur (in the absence of the deterrent threat) as the action to be compelled was to not occur (in the absence of the compellent threat). This incorporates the idea of 'autonomous probability', which Baldwin borrows from Karl Deutsch (Baldwin 1979: 189). Second, in these circumstances, the success rate of deterrence in preventing the action must be higher than the success rate of compellence in making the same or any other action occur. This would be a fair test of the proposition that deterrence is easier than compellence. It is by no means clear how to calculate autonomous probability, and until this is done Schelling's proposition cannot be tested. Apparently fair comparisons, such as those suggested above between deploying missiles and removing them, may not be fair because one does not know that the autonomous probability that the hypothetical missiles would not have been deployed anyway was equal to the autonomous probability that the missiles would have been removed anyway. Dissimilar situations – such as the deterrence of limited use of force and the compellence of a signature on a peace treaty – may have the same autonomous probability and thus be a good test of whether or not deterrence is easier than compellence. But the identical nature of the autonomous probability will be difficult to discover and inevitably will be subjective.

Although the comparative case-study approach lends itself to the discovery of causal patterns rather than success rates (which require statistical analysis), causal patterns can be suggestive. Lebow and Stein claim to have identified successful compellence in five out of eight attempts (six extended and two direct) and thus argue that it is plausible that deterrence may not be easier than compellence (1990a: 351–2). However, their application of compellence might be questioned as being too broad: for example, they suggest that 'it can even be argued that the airlift constituted successful compellence by the western powers as it convinced the Soviet Union to discontinue the blockade' (1990a: 369; cf. Huth, Russett 1990: 477). Furthermore, deterrence may be easier than compellence, all other things being equal, but all other things may rarely be sufficiently equal for the relative ease of deterrence to have an effect on the outcome.[18] One should also be careful to compare like with like. It is generally believed that extended deterrence is more difficult than direct deterrence. If this belief is true, then a comparison of immediate extended deterrence with immediate direct compellence will under-represent the relative difficulty of deterrence and compellence.

CONCLUSION: OBJECTIVES, THREATS AND CRISIS OUTCOMES

Deterrence is about preventing someone from doing something, whereas compellence is about making someone do something. As defined in this study, both rely on threats of military action which may come about through deliberate escalation or the potential for loss of control, although broader and narrower definitions of both in other studies are reasonable and useful in allowing for comparison. In actual crisis behaviour the differences between deterrence and compellence may be eroded, and this erosion may be the deliberate result of crisis tactics. Virtually all aspects of how to test deterrence and compellence theory are disputed. In this study, the identification of consideration of attack and attempted deterrence (and the identification of a desire not to undertake a particular action and attempted compellence) requires substantial historical evidence of words and actions which cannot be persuasively construed otherwise. The avoidance of false positives and Cold War bias on the one hand must be balanced with the avoidance of false negatives and revisionist bias on the other. In assessing the cases, one needs to separate their various deterrent and compellent dimensions from the issue of defensive or offensive motivations. I focus primarily on initial crisis outcomes (without denying the importance of the long run) so that the cause-effect connection is not too distant. The outcome of an attempt to deter or compel is not the same thing as the crisis outcome as a whole: it is only part of the broader outcome.

Now that I have proposed an approach to the role of deterrence and compellence, I turn to the development of the next stage of my approach to explaining international crisis outcomes, that is, a consideration of how to assess the military balance and the balance of interests.

NOTES

1 See, for example, note 10 below, which discusses 'coercive diplomacy'.

2 Lebow and Stein (1990a) have analysed military threats to deter attack and non-military threats to deter attack in order to compare their

relative effectiveness. They conclude that non-military threats are more effective. For a critical response, see Huth, Russett 1990: 473–5.

[3] I am grateful to David Baldwin for his comments on this section of the chapter.

[4] The exceptions are Freedman 1989b, Huth, Russett 1993 and Lebow, Stein 1994, especially pp. 49, 50, 92, 93 and 351–5.

[5] Whether Finland was Finlandized (and whether Western Europe had anything to worry about even if it was) during the Cold War was debated vigorously. See Singleton 1978, Laqueur 1979, Maude 1981, Matson 1983 and Allison 1985. There are parallels between Finlandization and the idea of bandwagoning to avoid loss (on the latter point see pp. 47–8).

[6] 1990a: 366–8. Huth and Russett in their 1988 study define it as failed immediate extended deterrence. The intention here is not to choose the most appropriate categorisation of this particular case, but to develop a definition of extended compellence.

[7] Upon reading a draft of this chapter, Lebow accepted that he and Stein 'mixed together' extended and direct compellence (correspondence, Lebow to Herring, 31 July 1991).

[8] See Huth, Russett 1990, and forthcoming and Lebow, Stein 1990a and b, forthcoming. Russett has been through this before in more general terms in his debate with Oran Young. See Young 1969 and Russett 1969. For further discussion of the Huth-Russett and Lebow-Stein debate, see pp. 64 and 249.

[9] Huth and Russett argue that their findings would still stand if the recodings by Lebow and Stein of *individual* aspects of their analysis were incorporated into their analysis (1990: 468, 492–6).

[10] Alexander L. George and William E. Simons do not use the term 'compellance' (sic) because they say, correctly, that it does not distinguish between offence and defence. They prefer to distinguish between 'coercive diplomacy' which they see as defensive because it involves 'efforts to persuade an opponent to stop or reverse an action' and 'blackmail strategy', which is the offensive use of coercive threats 'employed aggressively to persuade an opponent to give up something of value without putting up resistance'. They maintain that 'Defensive uses are quite distinct from offensive ones' (George 1994: 7). The value of this approach is that it suggests that there can be more to objectives in a crisis than deterrence or compellence. However, the emotive, pejorative term 'blackmail' is unhelpful, and the offence-defence distinction is much more problematic than they suggest. On the offence-defence distinction in military terms, see Quester 1977, Levy 1984, Snyder 1984 and Hopf 1991. Furthermore,

their approach confuses motivations (offence/aggression and defence) and objectives (stop, reverse and give something up). An actor can have offensive (or mixed) political motivations behind persuading an opponent to stop doing something, and so on. Some have attributed such motivations to the Soviet attempts to stop the airlift to West Berlin in 1948–49 (although alternative interpretations have also been offered).

[11] This is yet another issue on which Lebow and Stein take Huth and Russett to task and another reason for their different assessment of the cases they examine (1990a: 345).

[12] On the issue of relative versus absolute gains, see Snidal 1991, Baldwin 1993, Jervis 1993, Huntington 1993 and Stein, Pauly 1993.

[13] 1966: 100. If, as Schelling claims, deterrence is easier than compellence, and 'cease doing' shares some of the characteristics of both, then it follows that we will have, on a scale of ascending difficulty, 'don't do', 'cease doing', and 'do'. The relative degree of difficulty in making someone cease doing something in comparison to ensuring that they continue doing something is less clear. I am grateful to Celeste Wallander for her observations on this point. A similar position to that of Schelling is taken by George and Simons, who choose to have four categories on what they believe to be a scale of increasing difficulty: deterrence ('Persuade opponent not to initiate an action'), type A coercive diplomacy ('Persuade opponent to stop short of the goal'), type B coercive diplomacy ('Persuade opponent to undo the action') and type C coercive diplomacy ('Persuade opponent to make changes in government') (1994: 9). This is a revised version of the taxonomy in an earlier edition of this work (George, Hall, Simons 1971: 24. See also Blechman, Kaplan 1978: 98–101, 105–7).

[14] On a related point, see Barry Buzan on the implications of nuclear deterrence being easy or difficult (1987: 167–72). Colin S. Gray argues that Buzan's view that nuclear deterrence is easy runs the risk of 'confusing ease of deterrence success with an absence of need for deterrence' (1993: 665).

[15] But see the brief exchange in Lebow, Stein 1990a: 351–4, and Huth, Russett 1990: 477. See also Hayes 1991 on US nuclear deterrence, compellence and reassurance in Korea since 1945.

[16] Jervis 1989b: 29–30. See also Jervis 1984: 134, 153–4. Like Petersen, Betts (1987: 138) confuses the two ideas.

[17] Ovendale 1985: 160–1, Betts 1987: 62–5, Carlton 1988: 73–80, Kunz 1989: 226–7, Golan 1990: 278–82 and Kyle 1991: 500–14.

[18] Lebow and Stein have stated that: 'In contrast to deterrence, which requires the target merely to refrain from some action – often an invisible

concession – compellence requires the target to act in ways that are highly visible' (1994: 377n). One would have thought that, all other things being equal, this difference would tend to make deterrence easier than compellence.

Chapter Two

THE MILITARY BALANCE AND THE BALANCE OF INTERESTS

> [There] has been an unreasonable fear concerning what Albert Wohlstetter, in the late 1950s, called the 'delicate balance of terror' . . . Deterrence addicts have an unbalanced terror of delicacy.
>
> Ken Booth (1987a: 260)

> It is Kissinger's idea . . . that it is a good thing to make a false threat that the enemy believes is a true threat. It is a bad thing if we are threatening an enemy with a true threat and the enemy believes it is a false threat. I told Kissinger that 'False or true, we Vietnamese don't mind. There must be a third category – for those who don't care whether the threat is true or false.'
>
> Nguyen Co Thach, North Vietnamese Foreign Minister (quoted in Hersh 1983: 134)

From the military balance perspective, the side which is militarily inferior will back down first or most in a crisis. From the balance of interests perspective, the side with less at stake will back down first or concede most. When the military balance is roughly equal, a crisis outcome which favours one side over another might be explained in terms of the balance of interests. The balance of interests is linked to the willingness of actors to suffer or risk suffering for what they value. For this reason, the North Vietnamese, for example, sought to portray themselves as indifferent to threats of punishment. Backing down first or most also requires that the costs of doing so are not expected to exceed the benefits of non-compliance. In this chapter I propose to measure the conventional balance in terms of perceptions of the local, short-term and general war forces. I outline the two main attitudes to nuclear weapons –

nuclear war-fighting strategy (which aims to reinforce deterrence and make nuclear use rational by developing nuclear military strategies), and the mutual vulnerability perspective (which argues that the political effects of nuclear weapons rest on the possibility of uncontrolled escalation, not rational nuclear use). I suggest that the nuclear balance should be measured in terms of perceptions of the tactical, theatre and strategic nuclear balances and how they relate to ability to fight a nuclear war or to escalate, to take the two competing perspectives into account. In the next part of the chapter I explain the importance of the balance of interests between compliance and non-compliance, discuss the nature of interests, and suggest that interests be categorised as personal, intrinsic and strategic. I assess the logical and theoretical promise and limitations of a number of arguments which might explain when the balance of interests favours one side over another. First, seeking to avoid losses might be a more powerful motivating factor than seeking to make gains. Second, strength of motivation needs to be considered alongside extent of opportunity. Third, it may be easier to defend the status quo than overturn it. I conclude by pointing out that psychological and strategic cultural factors sometimes influence these rational calculations and perceptions; these are assessed in Chapter Three.

THE MILITARY BALANCE

The role of the military balance is influenced by trends and expectations of trends by reducing or increasing perceptions of time pressure, threats and opportunities (Johnson 1983; Maoz 1983; Lebow 1984; Levy 1987). Military threats may rely on the possibility of cool, rational and deliberate use of force. This is what Betts terms the 'chess model' (1987: 10–16). They may also rely on the risk of irrationality or loss of control. Schelling calls this 'the threat which leaves something to chance' (1966: 92–125) while Betts terms this the 'Russian roulette model' (1987: 10–16). It is plausible that a stress on the latter – on competitive risk-taking – is more marked in the nuclear than the conventional context because it is more difficult to see nuclear use as rational. However, it may also play an important role in the operation of conventional military threats.

Military balance and balance of interests

The balance of conventional forces

The balance of conventional forces can be broken down into three measures: the local balance (those forces immediately available for combat over the main operational objective in the crisis); the short-term balance (the local military balance plus those forces which can be sent at short notice to supplement them); and the general war balance (all forces actually and potentially available for combat).[1] These measures are not entirely independent of each other, as the general war balance incorporates the forces in the short-term and local balance, and the short-term balance incorporates those in the local balance.

Nuclear war-fighting strategy

The categorisation of nuclear weapons which is normally used in the West has its origins in the US geopolitical position. Strategic weapons are defined as being of intercontinental range because of the distance between the United States and what was the Soviet Union; theatre weapons are those which could strike Soviet or East European territory from the Eurasian landmass or from the territory, airspace or waters of US allies; and tactical weapons are short-range devices which the United States expected to use mostly on the territory of its allies. In contrast, the Soviet Union perceived US theatre nuclear weapons as strategic because they could hit Soviet territory and Soviet strategic nuclear forces, while France refers to its tactical nuclear weapons as 'pre-strategic' to emphasise their role in beginning the process of nuclear escalation to the highest levels (Schubert 1991: 181). On some levels the perspectives converge: for example, both the United States and Soviet Union perceived each other's intercontinental forces as strategic. In this study, tactical nuclear weapons refers to those intended to be used in battles or smaller scale engagements and of such short range that they must be launched in the vicinity of those battles or engagements. Theatre nuclear weapons refers to those intended to be used in battles from hundreds of miles away or to strike non-strategic targets well to the rear of potential or actual battles. Strategic nuclear weapons refers to those intended to be used to strike the opponent's main homeland population, industrial or command centres, or nuclear forces intended for use against the same assets of the attacker. These definitions treat nuclear weapons as essentially the same as conventional weapons – they are to be used to deter attack by demonstrating an ability to win nuclear war if it occurs and deny opponents the ability to achieve their objectives, or even to start a nuclear war if it is perceived as necessary. War-fighting strategy is intended to provide the most credible form of deterrence and to provide decision-makers with usable nuclear options if they come under nuclear attack or feel the need to launch a nuclear attack.[2]

War-fighting has been the primary (but not sole) criterion in the planning, acquisition, force structuring, operational and to a lesser extent declaratory policies of all of the states which have openly deployed nuclear weapons – the United States, Soviet Union, Britain, France and China.[3] Blair has shown that Schelling's concern that the reciprocal fear of surprise attack could generate a nuclear war was closer to reality than has ever been believed in the past.[4] The United States and Soviet Union both felt vulnerable to a decapitating nuclear attack, that is, an attack against the political leadership and command structures which would lead to paralysis of their retaliatory capabilities and to surrender (once a leader and a communication system could be located). Although it is generally believed that they intended to absorb an initial nuclear strike before responding, Blair shows that, from the early 1980s, they quietly adopted policies of Launch on Warning (LoW): they would launch before the opponent's warheads began to strike their targets. The danger was that, in a crisis, decision-makers might mistakenly interpret ambiguous warning information as unambiguous evidence that an attack was imminent or under way and launch large numbers of nuclear weapons. Their fear that the balance of terror was, as Albert Wohlstetter (1959) put it, 'delicate' resulted in actions which helped to make it so. Fortunately, in the wake of the end of the Cold War and the collapse of the Soviet Union, numbers of US and Russian nuclear weapons and, more importantly, alert levels are being reduced drastically; Kazakhstan and Belarus are handing over their nuclear weapons to Russia; and Ukraine is also on a very low nuclear alert level and claims that it will also become non-nuclear. Of course, these positive trends may be reversed; in particular, it is possible that Ukraine may retain nuclear weapons.

Mutual vulnerability and the risk of escalation

The other mainstream perspective on nuclear weapons is that they are fundamentally different from conventional weapons. This view emphasises the importance of mutual nuclear vulnerability, which Steven Kull has summarised as:

> 1. The existence of large and redundant nuclear arsenals capable of inflicting unacceptable damage even after absorbing an all-out first strike (generally known as secure second strike or MAD [Mutually Assured Destruction] capabilities
> 2. The secure option, in a military conflict . . . to escalate to unacceptable levels
> 3. The option to launch missiles that are (either directly or via the command and control center that controls them) threatened by incoming warheads
> 4. The extraordinary difficulty in meaningfully defending populations when such a small percentage of deliverable warheads would destroy such a large percentage of the population.
>
> (1988: 30)

This perspective argues that the political value of nuclear weapons stems from the potential for escalation. It also argues that excessive concern for deterrence credibility – part of the deterrence 'addiction' perceived by Booth (1987: 260) – is dangerous because it risks creating inadvertent nuclear war through mutual fear of surprise attack. Deterrence of nuclear attack or even total defeat in a homeland conventional war does not require rationally usable options (Jervis 1989b: especially 15, 81). The result of mutual vulnerability, according to McGeorge Bundy, is 'existential deterrence', which hinges upon the existence of mutual vulnerability rather than the existence of any particular options or categories of weapon (1984; 1988: 593–4). This is similar to, but slightly broader than, Morgan's notion of general deterrence discussed in the previous chapter. Nuclear security is not seen as guaranteed: it may all go terribly wrong. Indeed, the credibility of the threat to escalate rests on the possibility that either side or both sides will lose control or act irrationally. This risk may be created deliberately or it may be an unintended consequence of refusing to back down in a crisis. Even if options are developed to make the use of limited force apparently more safe, decision-makers may simply compensate by taking more risks (Bradley 1993). In this context, nuclear weapons are not military weapons but, as Morton H. Halperin puts it, '"explosive devices" that may, under certain extreme circumstances, be used to demonstrate national resolve but never as weapons to fight wars' (1987: 49). As will be explained in my concluding chapter, there is some evidence that a nuclear taboo and a tradition of the non-use of nuclear weapons have developed in response to their potential destructiveness. Political victory is still possible in that, for example, an opponent may be intimidated by fear of escalation into not capitalising to the full on conventional military success. However, the mechanism for this political victory is not the threat to wage nuclear war successfully but the threat to escalate even to mutual and utter destruction. Distinctions between tactical, theatre and strategic nuclear weapons are not very meaningful in this perspective: all nuclear weapons serve the same purpose of influencing the risk of escalation. For this reason, I will examine perceptions not only of the tactical, theatre and strategic nuclear balances but of the potential for nuclear escalation. The war-fighting approach may have dominated nuclear weapons policy, but whether chess-like emphasis on rational, usable options was as important as fear of uncontrolled escalation in influencing crisis outcomes is a different question, which will be considered in the case studies.

THE BALANCE OF INTERESTS BETWEEN PEACE AND WAR

It has been argued so far that the side which is militarily inferior or with less at stake in a crisis should be the side which backs down. However, this will be the case only if the side which backs down believes that its interests are best served by peace rather than war. The importance of this can be illustrated by contrasting the cases of the Cuban missile crisis and Kuwait. In the former case, neither side was prepared to go to war and the crisis was about who would be the first to comply with the wishes of the other. In the latter, both sides were prepared to go to war and neither was willing to comply with the wishes of the other. Similar processes operate during intra-war crises, when decision-makers compare the balance of interests between compliance and non-compliance; for example, in the 1960s and early 1970s North

Vietnam continued to supply forces in the South in spite of threatened and actual US escalation. As Nguyen Co Thach, North Vietnamese Foreign Minister, said in response to US threats: 'There must be a . . . category . . . for those who don't care whether the threat is true or false' (quoted in Hersh 1983: 134). This balance of interests is not built into approaches to crisis behaviour as often as it might be.[5]

THE NATURE OF INTERESTS

Interests are not static or eternal and this study does not assume them to be so. What one values is contingent. What is valued one day (such as an ally) can become a liability on another; indeed, allies can be assets and liabilities simultaneously – they create dangers and opportunities. The fact that perceptions of interests are contingent and tend to alter underlines the value of analysing perceptions at the time of the crisis outcome. This freeze-frame approach ensures that the weighting given to any particular interest is historically contingent, not ahistorical. From this point, the historical events can be rewound as far as is necessary to understand perceptions and behaviour at the time of the outcome. How interests are formed is a disputed and unresolved question in international relations theory (Klotz 1992: 4). National interests are not defined arbitrarily and are not simply the wants or desires of decision-makers. Instead, they are social constructions which are rooted in particular conceptions of the nature of politics and which decision-makers have to justify in terms of their normative basis and the expected consequences for the political community (Kratochwil 1982; see also Kratochwil 1989; Klotz 1992; Wendt 1992). These constructions may vary from decision-maker to decision-maker or they may be shared by decision-makers but vary from era to era.[6] Within those social constructions there is plenty of scope for varied perceptions and assessments of issues, both in terms of norms and consequences, and for manipulation of those assessments.[7]

Personal, intrinsic and strategic interests

The question remains as to how to categorise interests – that is, those things valued by actors. Interests may be abstract and concrete, and they may be relevant to later crises as well as the one under way at the time. In this study, intrinsic interests are those concrete and abstract things valued for their own sake, while strategic interests are those concrete and abstract things valued for their relevance to subsequent bargaining. In addition, this study also considers personal interests, that is, those abstract and concrete things valued by leaders for the protection and promotion of their position as individuals (cf. Snyder, Diesing 1977: 183–4; Jervis 1979; Stein 1985a: 39).

Personal, intrinsic and strategic interests are not fully independent of each other; for example, the intrinsic interests lost in one crisis are not available for subsequent crises, and what serves the state often serves the individual leader. Sometimes, perhaps often, the interests of the leader and the interests of the state or many of the population diverge strongly. Most Iraqis and the Iraqi state would have been better off if Saddam Hussein had withdrawn from Kuwait before the allies forced him out. However, from Saddam Hussein's perspective, a humiliating withdrawal was likely to be more of a threat to his power (and his life) than a military defeat in which he could have claimed to have taken on the world and thus have satisfied honour. Similarly, in August 1969, US National Security Adviser Henry Kissinger tried to manipulate this perception of a leader willing to let his country suffer to preserve his personal prestige. According to Nixon, Kissinger said to the North Vietnamese that they had stressed that it was 'Mr. Nixon's war' and that '"We do not believe it is in your interest . . . because if it is Mr. Nixon's war, then he cannot afford not to win it"' (quoted in Nixon 1978: 396). The belief that domestic political calculations – including electoral, elite and coalition politics – affect crisis decision-making is well established and will be examined in the case studies. The idea of the national interest has fallen out of favour in academic analysis as an explicit concept because, in policy terms, the national interest is seen to be simply whatever the key decision-makers prioritise. However, as was discussed above, there are substantial constraints on their choices, and it is still valuable to distinguish between the personal interests of leaders and national interests (whether intrinsic or strategic). While intrinsic interests may matter, their role in explaining crisis outcomes may be undermined if decision-makers believe that broader, strategic interests are at stake as well. Concerns about strategic interests are usually couched in terms of beliefs about the impact of the outcome of the crisis under way on the outcomes of other conflicts of interest. Great powers, and even more so superpowers, are likely to inflate the assessment of the interests at stake beyond the intrinsic interests. They believe they have a world to win or lose, and that successes and failures in any part of the world will have implications for them in the other parts.

Some interests are described as 'vital' by decision-makers and analysts. Vital interests may be personal, intrinsic or strategic. The most basic value is survival in tolerable conditions. For great powers and superpowers, the existence of an acceptable regional or international order is also often seen as a basic value: satisfied actors seek to maintain the order while revisionist ones seek to overturn it. Bernard Brodie pointed out that 'According to customary usage, those of our interests are "vital" that we are ready to fight to preserve' (1973: 342). From this perspective, it is not possible by definition to go to war for less than vital interests. In order to avoid tautology, threat to vital interests must be defined independently of the probability of war. Decision-makers may go to war or risk being attacked over issues that they regard as trivial, and the possibility should not be ruled out in advance. Furthermore, on occasion, interests may simply not be defensible through war and may require the avoidance of war. This is likely to be true in the nuclear context, or when the basic value under threat is that of the promotion of a world order in which disputes, including clashes of basic values, are resolved non-violently. In bargaining terms, to the extent that values or commitments are seen to be interdependent – that is, failure to stand firm in one place or at one time will lead to challenges in other places or at other times – then apparently small threats loom much larger (Schelling 1966: 55–9; Jervis, Snyder 1991).

IS SEEKING TO AVOID LOSSES A MORE POWERFUL MOTIVE THAN SEEKING TO MAKE GAINS?

Categorising interests does not explain why the balance of interests may favour one side in a crisis. I now turn to a possible explanation, namely that seeking to avoid losses is a more powerful motivator than seeking to make gains (Stein, Pauly 1992). One of the arguments for this rests on the neo-realist premise that states are concerned primarily with security and are therefore averse to the risks associated with trying to make gains; I deal with the psychological aspects of this issue in Chapter Three.

Bandwagoning, dominoes and balancing

The belief that an unfavourable outcome will make further unfavourable outcomes more likely (an element of domino theory) will increase a decision-maker's incentive to avoid losing. The other side of the coin is the belief that favourable outcomes will make further favourable outcomes more likely (an element of bandwagon theory). This will increase a decision-maker's incentive to win (Jervis, Snyder 1991; see also Snyder 1991c). For example, at a meeting between Truman, Attlee and their advisers in the White House on 4 December 1950 after the Chinese intervention in the Korean War, Acheson said that 'if we now give up in the Far East, we are through. The Russians and the Chinese are coming in and other Far Eastern peoples would make their best terms'. In response, looking at it from the Soviet and Chinese perspective, Attlee remarked that 'this was the bandwagon psychology' (*FRUS 1950* 7: 1369). Domino and bandwagon theories both assume that trends, either positive or negative, tend to continue and accelerate, if not counteracted (Snyder 1991a: 10). However, if an actor with allies under threat believes in the domino theory, then it is more likely to take action to prevent dominoes from falling and thus to disprove the theory (Jervis 1989b: 194, 232–3; 1991: 36–8).

The expectation of a general tendency towards counteraction rather than bandwagoning or falling dominoes is built into the neo-realist conception of balance of power theory, which claims that balances of power tend to form (Waltz 1979); in more general terms, trends tend to be reversed. In a refinement of neo-realist theory, Stephen Walt (1985, 1987, 1988, 1989, 1991, 1992) argues that balance of threat is a more accurate phrase, in that states tend to balance not against the most powerful state (which may be perceived as benign) but against the most threatening one. Hence, for example, Canada balanced militarily against the Soviet Union (the most threatening state) rather than the United States (the most powerful state). The basic argument, however, remains the same – that potential or actual loss generally produces balancing behaviour. In balancing behaviour one can, of course, be worried about intrinsic or personal as well as strategic interests.

Status quo and revisionist states see the balance of interests differently

The insight that expectations about trends in crisis outcomes will influence perceptions about the extent and nature of interests at stake in a crisis is an important one. However, Randall Schweller has shown that the now substantial literature on balancing and bandwagoning which has developed in the wake of Walt's research all shares the false assumption that 'bandwagoning and balancing are opposite behaviors motivated by the same goal: to achieve greater security'.[8] Bandwagoning is generally presented as appeasement, giving in to threats and capitulation. Instead, he shows that balancing is motivated by loss avoidance, whereas bandwagoning is frequently motivated by opportunity for gain (although it can be the result of giving in to threats). Defined in this way, bandwagoning is much more common than neo-realists have suggested, so that the claim that balancing is the norm and bandwagoning the exception has to be questioned.[9]

The neo-realist failure to perceive the importance of opportunistic bandwagoning flows from neo-realism's status quo bias; in particular, it assumes that 'states are willing to pay high costs and take great risks to protect the values they possess, but will only pay a small price and take low risks to improve their position in the system' (Schweller 1994: 85; see also Glaser 1992: 507). This assumption ignores revisionist states, which are more concerned with making gains than avoiding losses and which are prepared to take great risks to make those gains. The leading revisionist state is the bandwagon upon which lesser revisionist states jump. Status quo powers do seek to maximise security, but revisionist states seek to maximise power. The revival of the traditional realist distinction between revisionist and status quo (or satisfied) states[10] provides a superior explanation of alliance formation and international system stability:

> the most important determinant of alignment decisions is the compatibility of political goals, not imbalances of power or threat. Satisfied powers will join the status-quo coalition, even when it is the stronger side; dissatisfied powers, motivated more by profit than security, will bandwagon with an ascending revisionist state.
>
> (Schweller 1994: 88)

He develops this into what he calls a 'balance of interests' theory of alliance formation (1994: 99–106). At the unit level of analysis, if a state's balance of interests is such that it is willing to incur more costs to extend than to defend its values, it is a revisionist state; if the reverse applies, it is a status quo state. At the systemic level of analysis, the balance of interests 'refers to the relative strengths of status quo and revisionist states' (1994: 99). An international system is stable if the former are stronger and unstable if the latter are stronger. In a crisis between a revisionist state and a status quo state, the original proposition – that seeking to avoid losses is a more powerful motive than seeking to make gains – still holds only if the revisionist state does not value making gains over avoiding losses to the same extent that the status quo state values avoiding losses over making gains. This might be the case in circumstances where keeping what you have is a necessary prerequisite for acquiring what you covet. The original proposition would also hold in a crisis between status quo actors: if one side is seeking to avoid a loss and the other is seeking to make a gain, the former will be at an advantage. In a crisis between revisionist states, one possible inference based on Schweller's analysis is the curious argument that the one seeking to make a gain is at an advantage over the one seeking to avoid a loss.

This approach underlines the value of defining crisis in terms of danger and opportunity. To define crisis only in terms of danger is to see crisis from a status quo perspective. However, Schweller's view of status quo and revisionist is based on an overall assessment of a state's view of the international order as a whole: it is not clear that this will apply directly to explaining crisis outcomes. For example, even if a state is dissatisfied with the international order as a whole, in a particular crisis it may be concerned more with avoiding losses than making gains. Similarly, a status quo power in a particular crisis may be aiming primarily to make gains. Hence I will not undertake the task of classifying the various actors in my case studies according to Schweller's approach, although a separate study to see if it yields any results would be worth undertaking. I concentrate on analysing the status quo primarily as the existing situation rather than as the orientation (or not) of particular states.

Perceptions about the potential for gain or loss and the actions that result need to be assessed in the context of motivation and opportunity. These factors will now be considered.

WHERE THERE'S A WILL? STRENGTH OF MOTIVATION AND EXTENT OF OPPORTUNITY

In pursuing their interests, decision-makers will act according to the strength of their motivation and the extent of opportunity. Lebow and Stein claim that deterrence theory assumes that challengers are motivated by the existence of an opportunity to challenge, that no challenge will take place if there is no opportunity, and that the attacker's cost-benefit calculation can be influenced by the deterrer (Lebow 1989: 28, Table 2.1; Lebow, Stein 1990b: 66, Table IV). The first of the three assumptions attributed by Lebow and Stein to deterrence theory is not a necessary part of deterrence theory: a very different auxiliary assumption could be associated with it.[11] However, the 'deterrence model' does tend to be associated with that and similar assumptions (Jervis 1976: 58–113; Huth, Russett 1990: 471–2; Glaser 1992: 503n). The deterring state is often presumed to be trying to maintain the status quo, and the target of the deterrent threat is often presumed to be a revisionist state. Lebow and Stein argue that decision-makers are more often motivated by need – strategic vulnerability or domestic political weakness – than opportunity, so that a challenge will not be made if there is low need for it even if an opportunity exists. Although they claim that low need in the context of an opportunity will result in no challenge (Lebow 1989: 29; Lebow, Stein 1990b: 66), 'unlikely' would be more accurate.[12] Indeed, Lebow refers to India's attack on Pakistan in 1971, Iraq's attack on Iran in 1980 and Israel's intervention in the Lebanon in 1982 as 'opportunity-based challenges' (1989: 29; but on Iran-Iraq, see also 30). From this perspective, challenges are very likely when need is combined with opportunity, and fairly likely, even in the absence

Table 2.1 *Motivation, opportunity and probability of challenge*

	Dubious opportunity	*Good opportunity*
	Box 1	*Box 2*
Weak motivation	No challenge	Challenge unlikely
	Box 3	*Box 4*
Strong motivation	Challenge fairly likely	Challenge very likely

of a reasonable opportunity, where there is high need (Lebow 1989: 28, Table 2.1; Lebow, Stein 1990b: 66, Table IV). Although such pressures can produce irrational behaviour (discussed in Chapter Three), it is important to note that it can be rational to challenge if a very high level of need makes even a very small prospect of success worth the risk.

The dichotomy of need versus opportunity proposed by Lebow and Stein conflates opportunity as a motivation and opportunity as a situation. Decision-makers may be motivated by potential loss or potential gain, and how they act may also be influenced by the extent of opportunity available to avert losses or make gains. Furthermore, Lebow and Stein equate need with potential loss, yet a decision-maker may feel strongly the need to act in order to satisfy ambition, and their categorisation omits completely the possibility that a decision-maker may be strongly motivated to try to make a gain even when there exists no good opportunity to do so. The categories of strength of motivation (strong or weak) and extent of opportunity (dubious or good) ought to be used. Table 2.1, which is an adaptation of the Lebow-Stein table, illustrates this modified approach. Just as the traditional focus of the deterrence model on the ambitions of and opportunities for the challenger is insufficient, so the traditional focus of crisis behaviour literature on threats to interests is inadequate. As both sides may be motivated simultaneously by a mix of potential gain and potential loss, this should be encompassed by the definition of crisis. For this reason, in the introduction I defined a crisis as existing when key decision-makers perceive a significant probability of war, time pressure and a threat to their interests or an opportunity to advance their interests. It is not easy to judge the relative weight of extent of opportunity against strength of motivation, just as it is difficult to weigh various opportunities against each other or various motivations against each other. In the end, the process is an impressionistic one of historical judgement. In assessing motivations and opportunities, the domestic and international dimensions of both should be taken into account (Knorr, Morgan 1983; Morgan 1991). It is possible that potential losses or gains in foreign policy are more manipulable (through reassurance and deterrence respectively) by other states than potential losses or gains in domestic policy, but this need not be the case and domestic and international policy issues may be blurred.

Deterrence: attempting to reduce opportunity

If a decision-maker is heavily influenced by the existence of an opportunity, then increasing the deterrent component in signalling may help. However, stronger deterrence efforts may be provocative if a decision-maker is strongly motivated to challenge, if that motivation is based on perceived necessity rather than choice (Jervis 1976: 58–113; Lebow, Stein 1987a: 6, 14–15) and if the deterrent means are not unambiguously defensive. If the target is motivated by a sense of threat, then increasing that sense of threat is likely to be counter-productive. Increased deterrence may not be provocative if the perception of any opportunity can be eliminated, but this may be impractical due to the inherent uncertainties in human behaviour reinforced by wishful thinking, which almost always leave some scope for hope of a favourable outcome.

Reassurance: attempting to reduce strength of motivation

When deterrence will not work, what will? The other way of preventing a challenge is to reduce the strength of motivation of the potential challenger. The most recent version of the idea of reassurance focuses on the reduction of the opponent's fear of loss.[13] However, reassurance can also be about satisfying the opponent's desire for gain. This reassurance strategy is known pejoratively as appeasement, but it can be the right option if it will reduce the opponent's strength of motivation to pursue further gains. How practical reassurance of the opponent is will vary from case to case.[14] Even if reducing an actor's potential gain is possible, it may not be acceptable if its objectives are not seen as legitimate, or if the fulfilment of its desires threaten important interests. The unacceptability of satisfying the desires or allaying the fears of an actor is increased by the fact that decision-makers usually believe that their broader strategic interests as well as – or rather than – intrinsic interests are involved in crises.

Implications for compellence

Although the discussion of motivation and opportunity has been couched mainly in terms of deterrence, it can be restated more generally to take into account compellence, as is the case in Table 2.2. Compellence is based on threats and, like deterrence, it may fail or even be provocative if the target of the threats is strongly motivated to refuse to co-operate. In such cases, the prospects for success could be increased by reassurance in the form of reducing the extent of the compellent demands. However, the perception that this would be appeasement plays a role in eliminating this as an option. On other occasions, the target may be motivated by the belief that it has an opportunity to get away with non-compliance with the compellent demand due to the weak credibility or extent of the threats it faces. In these circumstances, amelioration of the compellent demands might be less important for success than increasing the credibility of the threats.

Threats, reassurance and crisis outcomes

To summarise, if an actor is mainly motivated by potential loss, then threats may fail because they may be provocative, and reassurance may succeed because it may help allay the opponent's fears (see Table 2.2). If the actor is mainly motivated by potential gain then threats may succeed in averting a challenge by reducing the perception of opportunity, and reassurance may fail by increasing that sense of opportunity. Sometimes the politically acceptable range of threats, reassurances or combination thereof will not work if the potential challenger's balance of interests still favours

Table 2.2 *Threats, reassurance and crisis outcomes*

		Appropriate response
Actor's dominant motivation	Danger (potential loss)	Reassurance better than threats (but reassurance may still fail)
	Opportunity (potential gain)	Threats better than reassurance (but threats may still fail)

non-compliance over compliance. It is difficult to know at the time which motivation is dominant in the opponent's mind and therefore which strategy will be the most successful. The extent to which deterrence and reassurance are incompatible or complementary strategies also needs to be established. For example, the reassurances in a mixed signal may be drowned out by the accompanying threats: this was the case in US diplomacy towards China as its forces approached China's border during its invasion of North Korea. Alternatively, in preparing to carry out threats decision-makers might claim, for moral or prudential reasons, that the target should only be reassured minimally: this was central to US policy in the Gulf crisis and to British policy after the Argentine invasion of the Falkland Islands.

IS IT EASIER TO DEFEND THE STATUS QUO THAN OVERTURN IT?

A possible surrogate measure of the balance of interests is to argue that the balance of interests favours the side which is defending the status quo. This approach has been adopted in a number of studies (Payne 1970; Snyder, Diesing 1977; McConnell 1979; Maoz 1983; Jervis 1984, 1991; Betts 1987). Just as it is widely accepted that deterrence is easier than compellence, so it is often assumed to be easier to defend the status quo than overturn it (for example Jervis 1989b: 30–1, 35, 41, 227). However, defending the status quo is easier only under certain circumstances, as will be explained.

The status quo is defined here simply as the existing situation, and as any situation has many dimensions, then each side may be trying to maintain certain aspects of the status quo while trying to change others (Wolfers 1962: 84–6, 125; Payne 1970: 71; McConnell 1979; Betts 1987: 139; Glaser 1992: 501n). For this reason, it will be difficult to operationalise the concept and then say which side it favours overall. The fact that the status quo is multidimensional is not the only problem: in each dimension, although the status quo can be static (such as US nuclear superiority), it might also be seen as a trend (such as that which existed towards US-Soviet nuclear parity). If the United States had tried to reverse the trend, then it could have been perceived as trying to defend the static status quo but trying to overturn the dynamic status quo.[15] A trend may be thought of as either undermining the status quo or as being the status quo (cf. Snyder, Diesing 1977: 25–6; Jervis 1989b: 32–3). Although the latter seems to be something of an oxymoron, it can still acquire political significance. Furthermore, in a fluid crisis, the 'existing situation' may not exist for long, so that the defender of the status quo will become the one pressing for a change in the status quo in order to secure a return to the status quo ante (McConnell 1979: 246; Betts 1987: 139; Jervis 1989b: 33, 168–71).

Potential losses versus potential gains: the argument revisited

An important underpinning of the claim that there is a systematic advantage to being the defender of the status quo is the belief that decision-makers worry more about potential losses than potential gains. The discussion earlier in this chapter indicated some of the limitations of this line of argument, but did not find it to be groundless. The defender of the status quo will also be more strongly motivated if losses are perceived to involve extra damage to strategic interests while the challenger does not envisage further strategic gains. This is reinforced when concessions on the status quo are seen as permanent losses, but when backing down from a challenge to the status quo is seen as only temporary (Snyder, Diesing 1977: 25). It would have been harder for the West to retrieve concessions on the status of West Berlin than it would for the Soviet Union to renew its pressure at a later date if concessions were not made. Once again, this requires that there be a clear difference between the two: if a challenger backs down from its attempt to change the status quo, is this a loss for the challenger or simply a failure to make a gain? If it is the former, then the threat has become part of the status quo (the existing situation) (Levy 1989: 126–7). Furthermore, an apparent compromise can be one-sided: the defender of the status quo may be at a disadvantage if the challenger offers to compromise on its demands, because failure to compromise on defence of the status quo may be perceived to be unreasonable inflexibility (Snyder, Diesing 1977: 24–5). This was the case in the weeks preceding the Argentine invasion of the Falkland Islands. In other words, meeting the challenger's demands half-way would result in a net loss for the defender but a net gain for the challenger. However, the other side of the coin is that this inability to compromise represents bargaining strength, as the defender of the status quo has little incentive to compromise.

The territorial status quo

One possible simple way of defining the status quo is to concentrate on possession of territory (Payne 1970: 69–71; McConnell 1979: 245). James L. Payne argues that states are more likely to go to war over even a small change in the territorial status quo than over issues such as the development of an anti-ballistic missile (ABM) system by an opponent. This is partly because 'territory is so vitally important, being the *sine qua non* for the exercise of many other rights', but mainly because it is such a blatant and mutually perceptible challenge to the rights of the other side (Payne 1970: 71). Payne does not provide the necessary empirical support for his assertion that states are more likely to go to war over territory than over other issues. The argument which adds to the plausibility of his position is that military power is more directly relevant to territorial disputes than to some other issues, such as international financial matters: territory can be taken and held by force. When the territorial status quo is violated, the wronged state and its allies must react to the violation immediately, otherwise their right to a return to the status quo ante will wither, and an attempt to do so much later will be seen by many as aggression (Payne 1970: 77–8). That reaction should involve an effort to reverse the violation of the status quo, should be proportional to the original violation and should take place only in the same place as the original violation (Payne 1970: 78–81). As time passes, if the violation has not been reversed, a new status quo comes into existence, even if its legitimacy is disputed (Payne 1970: 77–8, 82; McConnell 1979: 246–7). However, many continuing territorial claims, such as the Spanish one regarding Gibraltar or the Argentine one regarding the Falkland Islands, show that time does not heal all breaches of the status quo. Overall, it is not clear that this particular dimension of the status quo should be elevated above all the others.

Legitimacy

The legitimacy of a territorial status quo is strengthened by renunciation of right to that territory by other states (Payne 1970: 68–71). Yet it is often the case that existing treaties and promises do not involve a clear and mutually perceptible renunciation of territorial claims, and failure to renounce is usually based on the disputable grounds of morality and justice. Snyder and Diesing believe that 'Legitimacy often derives from defense of a long-term [not necessarily territorial] status quo against the attempt to change it by force' (1977: 498; see also 25, 184). Indeed, their primary concern is with the concept of legitimacy, which they see as the most important part of the balance of interests in determining crisis outcomes, rather than the status quo itself (see also Stern *et al.* 1989: 298–304; Welch 1993b). They argue that when the status quo is seen as illegitimate, then the advantage lies with the actor trying to change it (1977: 498–9; see also Betts 1987: 139). On the fourteen occasions among their cases when they believe that one side had legitimacy on its side, it achieved a favourable outcome. In the two cases in which they believed legitimacy to have been equal, the outcome was a compromise. This contradicts Betts' proposition that, when the balance of legitimacy is equal, the defender of the status quo has an advantage (1987: 138). The fact that in all sixteen of the cases examined by Snyder and Diesing, the outcome corresponds with the balance of legitimacy (1977: 498–500) leads one to suspect tautology, although insufficient detail is provided on the case studies to make this judgement with any confidence. One also ought to quarrel with their implicit view that the status quo is generally mutually perceptible, and with their claim that the decision-makers who lost in crises accepted that their actions were illegitimate (1977: 498–9). Decision-makers do not have to see their own actions as illegitimate for the balance of interests thesis to be valid (cf. Betts 1987: 136). However, a decision-maker could be lent an advantage if the opponent knows that the international community in general, and possibly domestic factions, may oppose the challenge due to the issue of legitimacy.

The burden of the first use of force

Another way in which defence of the status quo might be advantageous is when the defender can relinquish the initiative in a way which requires the opponent to make the first move (Schelling [1960] 1980: 37–8, 137–9; 1966: 43–9; Jervis 1989: 31–2). The burden of the first use of force is likely to be relatively clear and also a relatively heavy burden. Decision-makers relying on the balance of interests will concentrate on trying to pass the last clear chance for avoiding war to the adversary, on giving up the initiative, on achieving *faits accomplis* (George, Smoke 1974: 536–40), and on manoeuvring so that the opponent has to move first if it wants to achieve its objective. These tactics are all different, so one can be used to try to undermine others. For example, putting the burden of the first use of force on the opponent is one way of undermining the opponent's advantage of being the defender of the territorial status quo. For this reason the Soviet Union blockaded ground access to West Berlin in the hope that resupply by air would not work, and that the allies would be faced with the choice of making concessions or using force to reopen land access. The idea is to make defence of the territorial status quo unsustainable by peaceful means in a context in which the use of force might be excessively dangerous. The use of a *fait accompli* to overturn a status quo may be a dangerous tactic, according to Jervis, because the side which has been taken by surprise will see itself as the defender of the 'real', original status quo and will therefore feel strongly motivated to act against the *fait accompli.* At the same time, the state which had carried out the *fait accompli* will see itself as the defender of the status quo. These were the respective positions of Britain and Argentina over the Falklands and the United States and Soviet Union during the Cuban missile crisis. Hence both sides will see themselves as acting to avoid incurring a loss, and possibly perceive the opponent as acting to make a gain (Jervis 1989b: 171). There is no reason why the tactics discussed here cannot supplement reliance on military superiority. However, the state which is relying on the balance of interests must work to indicate that, although it is inferior or equal in terms of military capability, it is more willing to go to war or keep fighting because it has too much to lose by giving in.

The conditional advantage of defending the status quo

The defender of the status quo will be at an advantage only if the status quo is being defended mainly by one side; if the status quo is mutually perceptible, territorial, legitimate, and tolerable to the potential challenger; and if the defender is motivated by loss avoidance and the challenger motivated by a desire for gain. One could also add that it helps if the defender conservatively attaches great importance to order, if revisionist claims are unrealistic (such as Chinese demands for the return from the Soviet Union of vast tracts of territory) and if the status quo seems natural (unlike attempts by the colonial powers to hang on to their overseas empires after the Second World War).[16] To claim that there is an advantage in being the defender of the status quo is to argue that there is a strong tendency for these conditions to exist. Otherwise the claim is meaningless and what one is actually saying is that, for example, a state has an advantage when its position is perceived to be legitimate.

CONCLUSION

As a crisis may result in war, the balance of military capabilities available to fight that war or conduct that escalation may influence the outcome of the crisis. All other things being equal, the side that is more likely to lose the war should back down first or concede most. Alternatively or additionally, the outcome of the crisis may be influenced by the relative importance of the interests at stake for each side and by each side's calculation of its balance of interests between war and peace. Interests are socially constructed and changing, so it makes sense to identify perceptions of interests at the point of the crisis outcome. Interests can be categorised comprehensively in terms of personal, intrinsic and strategic interests, which may be abstract and/or concrete. They may also be seen as vital interests. In considering motivations for crisis behaviour the problematic need and opportunity dichotomy ought to be replaced with a dichotomy of strength of motivation and extent of opportunity. Amongst other things, this allows for a clearer understanding of the role of threats in closing off opportunities for an adversary and the role of reassurance in reducing the opponent's strength of motivation. The proposition that defending the status quo is easier than overturning it may reflect the status quo bias of neo-realism, which posits security as the primary goal of states, although revisionist states may value making gains (power maximisation) over avoiding losses (security). In addition, the view that defending the status quo is easier than overturning it often rests on other propositions regarding avoiding losses versus making gains, the territorial status quo, legitimacy and the burden of the first use of force.

Up to this point I have presumed rationality in order to assist with the development of my explanation of crisis outcomes. In the next chapter I consider what it means to be rational and I assess the relevance of the interaction of psychological and strategic cultural factors with deterrence, compellence, the military balance and the balance of interests for explanations of crisis outcomes.

NOTES

[1] This breakdown has been influenced by the work of Huth and Russett (Huth, Russett 1984; Huth 1988b). Huth states mistakenly in *Extended Deterrence and the Prevention of War* that the short-term balance in that book corresponds to the existing local balance in the 1984 Huth and Russett study (1988b: 60). As they state elsewhere, the short-term balance actually corresponds to the existing overall balance (1988: 6n. See also Levy 1988: 503; 1989: 25).

[2] For advocacies of war-fighting strategy, see Kahn 1960, 1962, 1965; Pipes 1977, 1982; Gray 1979, 1982a, 1982b, 1986; and Gray, Payne 1980. For mainstream critiques see Arnett 1979; Keeny, Panofsky 1981–82; MccGwire 1984, 1985–86; Halperin 1987; Kull 1988; Jervis 1984, 1989b; Ball 1981, 1990; and Howard 1981. For the anti-nuclear perspective, see Green 1966; Lifton, Falk 1982; Schell 1982, 1984; Booth 1987a; and Lifton, Markusen 1990.

[3] On the dominance of war-fighting in US nuclear strategy see Friedberg 1980; Rosenberg 1982, 1983, 1987; Pringle, Arkin 1983; Scheer 1983; Kaplan 1984; Herken 1987; Trachtenberg 1988a and b; Nolan 1989; Sagan 1989; and Ball 1990. On Soviet nuclear strategy see Garthoff 1958, 1966, 1978, 1982; Dinerstein 1959; Arnett 1979; Gray 1979, 1986; and MccGwire 1987, 1991. On the reduced emphasis on nuclear war-fighting in the Gorbachev era see MccGwire 1987, 1991; Shenfield 1987, 1989; and Garthoff 1990a. On British, French and Chinese nuclear strategy see Freedman 1989a; and Karp 1991. On Chinese nuclear strategy see Liu 1972; Gelber 1973; Lewis, Litai 1988; and Lin 1988.

[4] Blair 1993. Schelling [1960] 1980: 207–29. On nuclear command and control in general see also Ball 1981; Bracken 1983; Pringle, Arkin 1983; Blair 1985; Carter, Steinbruner, Zraket 1987; Feaver 1992; and Sagan 1993.

[5] For example, Huth and Russett note that, in their studies of immediate extended deterrence, they do not include a calculation of 'the expected utility of peace to the attacker; that is, the attacker's utility for not actually pressing ahead with attack on the protégé' (1984: 514). They justify this on the grounds that such a calculation is more subjective than their other variables and because, they say, the potential attacker's calculation of this factor can change dramatically and do so quickly (1984: 514). Yet they felt able to identify two important cases in which actors attached so little value to peace that they were prepared to run great risks and suffer great damage. These cases were the Japanese decision to attack the United States in 1941 (Russett 1963) and North Vietnamese willingness to fight to reunify the country (Huth, Russett 1984: 519–20). If the balance of interests between challenge and compliance can be identified in those cases, it can be identified in others, although not necessarily in all (cf. Stein 1985a: 49–51).

[6] On related points regarding strategic culture see p. 81.

[7] On the manipulation of perceptions of interests, see Maoz 1990.

[8] Schweller 1993: 74. The literature includes David 1991a and b, 1992–93; Jervis, Snyder 1991; Levy, Barnett 1991, 1992; Kaufman 1992; and Labs 1992. For Walt's reply to Kaufman and Labs see Walt 1992. On the problems of distinguishing between balancing and bandwagoning and between *détente* and bandwagoning, and on the importance of distinguishing between alliances and alignments (which Walt does not), see Wohlforth 1993, especially pp. 26–8.

[9] Schweller elaborates upon a number of differing types of opportunistic bandwagoning, including 'jackal' bandwagoning, which seeks to cash

in on successful revisionism (such as that of Mussolini's alliance with Hitler); 'piling on' bandwagoning, which seeks to benefit from a war which is about to be won (such as Stalin's declaration of war against Japan in the last days of the Second World War); and 'wave of the future' bandwagoning, which is motivated by the desire to be part of a successful historical or ideological movement (such as the rejection of Communism in favour of market democracy in Eastern Europe) (1994: 92–8).

[10] The examples Schweller (1994: 85n) cites include Carr 1946, Morgenthau 1948, Kissinger 1957 and Wolfers 1962: 125–6.

[11] This was discussed briefly on p. 26.

[12] I am indebted to Piers Hillier for this point.

[13] Lebow, Stein 1987a,b; Lebow 1989; Stein 1991a,b. See also George, Smoke 1974: 604–10; Howard 1983; MccGwire 1984: 78; Huth, Russett 1990: 471n. Schelling argued in favour of 'reassuring' behaviour to reduce the opponent's fear of surprise attack ([1960] 1980: 240–1). In addition, he stressed the 'critical role of "assurances" in completing the structure of a threat, in making the threatened consequences persuasively *conditional* on behavior so that the victim is offered a choice' (1966: 74).

[14] Stein (1991a and b) explores acting with restraint, developing shared norms of competition and shared principles and procedures, making an irrevocable and substantial concession to show benign intentions, and encouraging co-operation through reciprocal actions. Charles Glaser explains the value of options such as a defensive military posture, arms control, unilateral restraint, and what he calls reactive offence (1992: 526–33). Glaser's work is particularly interesting for its development of nuanced options calibrated to whether or not the opponent is a secure expansionist state (considered in Jervis's deterrence model); an insecure status quo state (considered in Jervis's spiral model); or an insecure expansionist state (a category not considered by Jervis) – obviously, secure status quo states do not pose much of a problem other than making sure that they remain that type of state.

[15] I am indebted to Patrick Morgan for corresponding with me on this matter.

[16] Thanks again to Patrick Morgan for his comments.

Chapter Three

PSYCHOLOGY AND STRATEGIC CULTURE

> So it is said that if you know others and know yourself, you will not be imperiled in a hundred battles; if you do not know others but know yourself, you win one and lose one; if you do not know others and do not know yourself, you will be imperiled in every single battle.
>
> Sun Tzu ([*c.*400 BC] 1988: 82)

> Understanding a people's culture exposes their normalness without reducing their particularity.
>
> Clifford Geertz (1973: 14)

Up to this point, I have assumed that decision-makers will be rational and I have treated what it means to be rational as unproblematic. However, the rationality of decision-makers can be flawed due to psychological or strategic cultural biases.[1] In this chapter I explain what I mean by rationality. I argue that psychological and strategic cultural factors are short cuts to rationality in the sense that they serve the necessary function of simplifying an infinitely complex world. I also argue that the process of simplification may contain serious flaws and thus short-circuit rationality. In my explanation of international crisis outcomes I do not assume rationality; nor do I adopt a psychological or strategic cultural model of crisis behaviour. Instead, I explain the premises of each approach and I assess the possible impact of psychological and strategic cultural factors on the approaches to deterrence and compellence, the military balance and the balance of interests developed in the preceding chapters. This is necessary preparation for the case-study chapters, in which I consider the role of the two approaches in explaining the crisis outcomes, and for the conclusion, in which I consider whether any overall patterns have emerged. I stress the importance of distinguishing between those occasions on which psychological and strategic cultural factors alter outcomes and those occasions on which they merely warp the processes leading to the same outcome.

SHORT CUTS TO RATIONALITY AND SHORT-CIRCUITS OF RATIONALITY

Being rational – more or less

I make three assumptions about rationality. First, what is being assessed is the rationality of the means used to achieve given ends rather than the rationality of the ends themselves. This is not to deny that decision-makers' ends are often means to achieve other ends. For example, the secret shipment of missiles to Cuba was a means to achieve the end of establishing missile bases on Cuba; the missile bases were a means to achieve the end of reducing US nuclear superiority; the reduction of US nuclear superiority was a means to achieve the end of improving the Soviet crisis bargaining position, and so on. While objectives are not just arbitrary wants and so their rationality can be judged (Kratochwil 1992; Rescher 1988: 92–106), my concern is to judge whether or not behaviour leading to a particular crisis outcome is rational or not. In addition to the rationality of the means used – 'substantive' rationality – I am also interested in 'procedural' rationality, that is, the rationality of the decision-making process used (Simon [1976] 1982). Second, rationality will be judged from the perspective of the individual decision-maker operating in an environment of uncertainty, rather than from the perspective of an omniscient observer. Third, decision-makers can only be more or less rational rather than perfectly so. This is what Herbert Simon called 'bounded' rationality ([1972] 1982). Time limits, changing circumstances and uncertainty ensure that they cannot compare all the costs and benefits of all options or compare all the trade-offs. Instead, it is enough that they consider the costs, benefits, probabilities and trade-offs of a reasonable range of options. The implication of this position is that the difference between rationality and irrationality is a continuum rather than a sharp dichotomy. Different decision-makers (or the same decision-makers at different times) may be rational in different ways. They may seek to maximise their subjective expected utility: the calculation is based on their values and viewpoint and their calculations about the future. Alternatively, with MINIMAX rationality decision-makers place greatest weight on minimising the maximum possibility of loss and are prepared to forego otherwise more attractive options if they lack this characteristic. Hence more than one rational response to the same situation is possible.[2]

Many ideas about crisis behaviour have been derived deductively and have assumed rationality. Case studies show that decision-makers often discuss policy options in a way which does not seem fully rational, which might be taken to mean that theories based on the rationality assumption are not valid. This perspective implies that the key criterion for a good theory is that it must provide a good match with what decision-makers said or wrote regarding their thought processes. There are two defences against this argument. First, the social science criterion for good theory is not that the theory matches the historical record, but that, as Jervis puts it, the theory must produce propositions that are 'significant, testable, and valid' (1985: 5; see also Wagner 1988). This takes us back to what constitutes an adequate test: the former criterion is preferred by the holistic tradition and the latter by the social science tradition (Hollis, Smith 1990). This split is at the unresolvable heart of the Lebow and Stein versus Huth and Russett debate.[3] In the social science approach, propositions based on deductive logic – for example, that the possession of a capability to punish reduces the likelihood that a state will be attacked – may be borne out by the examination of a large number of cases using more 'objective' measures, such as those employed by Huth and Russett. The second defence is that history cannot record the thoughts of decision-makers directly. Human thought processes are still fairly mysterious in important ways. Even if documents provide a great deal of information on the calculations of individuals, those individuals may have been influenced by factors about which they were unaware. The thought processes involved in a particular decision may be much more crude or much more sophisticated than historical documents would lead us to believe. A commonplace illustration of this point is that sometimes the best way to analyse something is to stop thinking about it consciously but instead set it aside, in order to come back to it later after allowing your brain to sort it out all by itself, as it were. In addition to unconscious influences, decision-makers may try to mislead as to the factors involved in a decision. Thus, in the testing of theories regarding human behaviour, there is no final court of appeal – certainly, the historians do not have the final say.

Those employing the rationality assumption are playing a percentage game. That is, they are talking in terms of tendencies, such as a supposed tendency of decision-makers to balance rather than bandwagon, or for deterrence to be easier than compellence, or for defending the status quo to be easier than overturning it. The theory will not always be right, but the aim is only to reduce the rate of error and come out ahead of a naive approach. In contrast, analysts worried about those occasions when decision-makers are irrational tend to focus on how things can go wrong rather than how often they go right. The avoidance of conventional war is a percentage game in that wars continue to occur, and the reduction of their frequency (and intensity) is a reasonable objective. The avoidance of nuclear war is generally perceived more as one requiring indefinite success. However, even in this context percentages have a part to play: because there is a significant amount of uncertainty about exactly what is needed to prevent a nuclear war, decision-makers must gamble, and it is rational to gamble on the option with the best percentage. The art lies in trying to judge the percentages. The alternative to assuming rationality for the purposes of theory is to assume irrationality (sometimes called nonrationality). That sounds rather strange, but simply means the development of an alternative model of thought processes. Psychological bias-based models could compete in the percentage game against ones based on the rationality assumption. We do not yet have an alternative deductive theory of crisis behaviour which does not rely on the rationality postulate.[4] However, a great deal of progress has been made on how to integrate ideas about cognitive and motivated biases, how to consider how various biases interact and how to incorporate more of the political and strategic factors which induce bias (for example, Stein 1988).

Seeing what you expect or want to see

Decision-makers may be rational but still choose the wrong option if they do not have the information they need. Psychological bias exists when decision-makers have (to a reasonable degree) the information they need but still choose the wrong option. Psychological biases are normally divided into cognitive biases and motivated biases.[5] Cognitive (also known as unmotivated) biases are distortions in the 'cold' (i.e., unemotional) processes of reasoning, decision-making and judgement. They may be produced by information overload or scarcity, and can involve seeing what you expect to see. The value of cognitive biases is to reduce the complexity of the environment to manageable levels: they are short cuts to rationality as well as short-circuits of rationality. Motivated biases (also known as affective biases) are 'hot' processes in which biases are produced because of some need to misperceive (such as a desire to resolve painful value trade-offs); in other words, the person engages in wishful thinking. Decision-makers see what they want to see, or, in the case of denial, fail to see what they do not want to see. In practice, cognitive and motivated biases can be very difficult to distinguish. For example, the faulty application of a heuristic such as a historical analogy may be produced by either.[6]

IMPLICATIONS FOR THE ANALYSIS OF CRISIS OUTCOMES

Warped processes or altered outcomes?

Even when evidence which suggests the workings of psychological biases is found, it must still be put in overall context. The basic question is whether they were vital to the outcome of a crisis. Warped processes may reinforce rather than work against the direction in which a rational decision-maker would take a crisis. Psychological biases can make a decision-maker more effective by increasing confidence, reducing the pain of value conflicts and dealing with informational uncertainties, although rational behaviour is generally the better bet for a favourable outcome.[7] A decision may be taken rationally and then all sorts of irrational, illogical or inaccurate arguments used to maximise support for the decision. In one sense this is a rational strategy in that it may maximise support for the decision. On the other hand it may alienate those who see the spuriousness of the bolstering arguments. There is the further problem of the 'echo effect': that decision-makers may adjust their objectives to match their rhetoric, either because they come to believe their own rhetoric or because their domestic or allied audience believe it and expect action accordingly (Jervis 1989b: 191–2).

Deterrence, compellence and the military balance

The assumptions made by decision-makers when assessing the military balance may be reasonable ones which may turn out to be wrong, or they may be psychologically biased. This can have a profound effect on deterrence and compellence. If decision-makers do not believe their own negative threat assessments but are manipulating them in order to gain support for military expenditure, then this is rational (if possibly short-sighted) behaviour. Decision-makers may believe that they are unlikely to win a war but engage in a desperate gamble and put a brave face on it. They may be motivated to use force in spite of an unfavourable military balance because they expect it to deteriorate even further in the future. This 'better war now than war later' view is rational only if there was a sufficiently likely probability of a war with sufficient net costs in future. A rational decision-maker must also consider the possibility that, as Brodie puts it, 'Wars avoided are sometimes totally avoided' (1973: 148).

Deterrence, compellence and the balance of interests

Assessments of interests when warped by psychological biases might be flawed in a number of ways. Decision-makers might focus only on their own interests and not attempt to estimate what the opponent has at stake. When they focus on their own interests, they might exaggerate them, and just assume that they have more at stake than the opponent. Often it may be the case that it is so obvious that an opponent will respond to the use of force that there may seem to be no need to examine its interests in any detail. However, judgement of the scale, nature and timing of the opponent's forcible response would seem to require close examination of its interests. The expectation that an opponent will not respond to the use of force – the view of the Argentine junta regarding the anticipated British reaction to its invasion of the Falkland Islands – goes against much of the grain of experience and thus requires even more careful justification. An assessment of the military balance is not enough: the interests at stake must also be considered.

When the interests of the opponent are considered, decision-makers might miscalculate due to motivated bias by focusing on the aspect of the balance of interests which favours them. Alternatively, they may not compare like with like: for example, they may tend to compare their own strategic and/or personal interests with the intrinsic interests of the opponent. This does not necessarily mean that they will consistently see the balance of interests as favourable. However, decision-makers may tend to value strategic interests over intrinsic interests and may tend to assess their own strategic interests but only the opponent's intrinsic interests. If they consistently value their own interests over those of their opponents (Stein 1985a: 41), then the balance of interests alone cannot explain variations in outcomes. Decision-makers may also employ a distorted form of MINIMAX thinking by choosing the option with the least anticipated cost, regardless of probabilities and benefits. Alternatively, they may avoid facing up to trade-offs by claiming that their preferred policy option is in all respects better than the others (Stein 1985b: 61).

The hypothesis that decision-makers are more likely to take risks in order to avoid losses than to make gains was discussed in the previous chapter. It was argued that this is characteristic of status quo-orientated actors rather than being universal. The work of Amos Tversky and Daniel Kahneman (1981, 1986) in experimental psychology found a general tendency for people to take risks to avoid losses and avoid risks in pursuit of gains. They might have achieved different results with subjects from a less satisfied section of the population. Another of their findings is that risk acceptance can be turned into risk aversion, and vice versa, towards the *same* situation merely by a change of emphasis in presentation – in other words, a change in how the situation is framed (see also Stein, Pauly 1993). Potentially high losses combined with lack of opportunity (see Table 2.1, box 3) tend to promote irrationality as actors engage in wishful thinking to relieve the psychological pressure. In addition, decision-makers who are powerfully motivated by desire for gain might, through motivated bias, mistakenly perceive the existence of an opportunity. This was the case with the expansionism of Nazi Germany and militarist Japan (Snyder 1991b: 283–6; 1991c). In the context of weak motivation and good or dubious opportunity (Table 2.1, boxes one and two), decision-makers are more likely to be rational because they have less incentive to engage in wishful thinking. Furthermore, a challenge can be rational even when it is made in a context of strong motivation and dubious opportunity (Table 2.1, box three) as long as decision-makers understand that it is a long shot. The challenge is irrational when they engage in wishful thinking about the prospects for success. It may be difficult to eliminate the scope for psychological biases by converting a dubious opportunity which contains a little scope for optimism into stark absence of opportunity.

Understanding rational behaviour requires an understanding of culture because culture influences the ends desired and the means used to pursue those ends. Furthermore, while psychological biases are to a great extent a product of the way the human mind works regardless of culture, misperception may also result from failure to comprehend cultural differences correctly.

THE ROLES OF STRATEGIC CULTURE

Decision-makers understand that culture matters, but the motto here can be 'When I hear the word "culture", I reach for my mirror': even though the need to avoid ethnocentrism is acknowledged, mirror-imaging persists. Alternatively and, it will be argued, more frequently, cultural differences are caricatured and exaggerated and the opponent demonised: incomprehension results in the opponent being seen as mad, bad or both. The degree of diversity, factionalism and latitude for choice within any strategic culture also tends to be exaggerated. The term 'strategic culture' was coined by Snyder, who saw it as a 'a set of general beliefs, attitudes and behavioral patterns . . . [which] has achieved a state of semipermanence'.[8] His basic argument was that the shift in US nuclear strategy towards options for using limited numbers of nuclear weapons was incompatible with Soviet strategic culture, which stressed large-scale nuclear use from the outset. Snyder's view of strategic culture was rooted in the idea that a particular strategic approach could persist beyond the existence of the initial conditions which brought it about. To a great extent, culture is about continuity, and the concept of strategic culture draws attention to some of those continuities. However, there was also a tendency among right-wing Western analysts to exaggerate the persistence of strategic patterns and underestimate the potential for change. For example, the characterisation by Gray (1986, especially 85–8) of Soviet strategic culture as being unable to change fundamentally without world war was clearly invalidated by Gorbachev's reforms from 1985 to 1991, never mind the rapid and almost bloodless collapse of Communist power in the Soviet Union in the wake of the failed coup of August 1991. He stated that 'it is safe to assume that Soviet leaders would take any military risk if they could discern no alternative path to save their patrimony' (1986: 85). This is not to criticise Gray for failing to predict the changes but to criticise him for being so unequivocal.

Strategic culture is usually presented as being more about differences in national style, which may be based less on cultural factors than on non-cultural factors such as the demands of geopolitics. Most discussions of strategic culture actually have very little to say about culture (e.g. Segal 1985a; Gray 1986; Jacobsen 1990; Zhang 1993). Snyder has expressed concern that cultural explanations of strategic behaviour risk being too vague in their logic, make cause and effect too distant in time and sequence, exaggerate differences between states, distract the analyst from more concrete causes of behaviour, and are often labels for, rather than analyses of, cross-cultural differences.[9] The concept of strategic culture is valuable for making analysts avoid misperception caused by ethnocentrism, realise the importance of history and of understanding one's opponent, and grasp the important differences between sets of decision-makers.[10] However, this defence of the notion of strategic culture does not deal with the methodological problems identified above. A definition of strategic culture will now be developed and these problems addressed.

The relationship between attitudes, behaviour and culture

Strategic culture has been defined in terms of attitudes and behaviour by some (e.g. Snyder 1977: *v*; Gray 1986: 36; Booth 1990:

121), and only in terms of attitudes by others (e.g. Lord 1985: 271; Segal 1985a: 180; Vertzberger 1990: 272–3; Johnston forthcoming). In line with the broader literature on culture,[11] I prefer to restrict my definition of culture (strategic and otherwise) to attitudes because culture is compatible with a wide range of behaviour. In addition, my objective is to explain behaviour and that behaviour may or may not be influenced by culture, as will be explained below. So, for the purposes of this study, strategic culture is a shared pattern of attitudes regarding military power.

Strategic culture as description and understanding

The concept of strategic culture can have descriptive or explanatory usages.[12] In the former sense, it is the label attached to a description of a pattern of attitudes regarding military power shared by a collectivity of some kind – be it armed services, a particular country or 'the West'. In that sense, every collectivity has a strategic culture, and that strategic culture may be heterogeneous or homogeneous, consistent or inconsistent and formal or informal. Those who are dismissive of the descriptive aspects of strategic culture (Snyder 1990) or political culture (Elkins, Simeon 1979) are coming from the social science perspective which stresses explanation over understanding.[13] My definition of strategic culture in terms of attitudes rather than behaviour has its origin in the social science perspective. In contrast, those who prioritise understanding reject the distinction. According to Clifford Geertz 'Once human behaviour is seen as . . . symbolic action – action which . . . signifies – the question as to whether culture is patterned conduct or a frame of mind, or even the two somehow mixed together, loses sense. . . . The thing to ask is what their import is: what it is . . . that, in their occurrence and through their agency, is getting said' (1973: 10, cf. 15). One should not dismiss the value of strategic culture as description. This was understood by Sun Tzu, who wrote that 'if you know others and know yourself, you will not be imperiled in a hundred battles; if you do not know others but know yourself, you win one and lose one; if you do not know others and do not know yourself, you will be imperiled in every single battle' (Sun Tzu [*c*.400 BC] 1988: 82). The popular maxim 'Know your enemy' is only part of the picture. You need to understand how you differ and how you are similar. You also need to understand your own weaknesses and strengths. Assessments of others can turn out to be outward projections of your own image or demonisations rather than analyses. Description is by no means trivial because it is a vital part of understanding (Geertz 1973: especially 3–30; 1983). Nevertheless, my primary purpose is explanation, and the attitudes-behaviour distinction serves that purpose by separating out what is to be explained from what might help explain it. Actions which are symbolic – and are in Geertz's sense cultural – can have cultural causes, non-cultural causes or, more likely, mixed causes. To define culture in terms of attitudes is not to deny that actions can have cultural significance and meaning: however, the actions themselves are not culture.

Strategic culture as explanation

Strategic culture, seen in explanatory rather than descriptive terms, does a number of overlapping things.[14] First, it serves a cognitive function: it helps the individual make sense of the world. This would include attaching particular weightings to different interests; in other words, it helps to shape the hierarchy of preferences (Douglas, Wildavsky 1982). It is a mindset, a perceptual prism (Fisher 1988). Second, it may be used to legitimise behaviour. This can include masking a gap between professed attitudes and actual behaviour. Alastair Johnston (forthcoming) points out that this perspective is characteristic of left-wing critiques of US foreign policy (for example, Chomsky 1989), which argue that elites promote economic interests under the guise of strategic necessity or the promotion of liberal democracy. Third, it may socialise people into particular perceptions. Thus the manipulators identified in the left-wing critique are themselves manipulated by the system. They believe profoundly that they are actually acting according to strategic necessity or that their actions will promote liberal democracy. Fourth, it may communicate perceptions to others outside the group without socialising them into becoming part of it. Finally, it has an operational or behavioural function: it influences, but does not fix rigidly, the boundaries of choice. It is permissive rather than deterministic. It makes the doing of some things more and others less likely. Certain things are unthinkable – or, to be more accurate, more difficult to contemplate – in ethical terms or in terms of preference hierarchies. They are 'not the way we do things', 'barbaric', 'dishonourable', and so on, although those barbaric or dishonourable things may still occur.

In trying to work out whether or not strategic culture explains a particular piece of behaviour, we need to consider competing explanations. Some prefer to have culture merely as a residual explanation if no other structural or institutional explanation will fit (Elkins, Simeon 1979; Snyder 1990). The preference for non-cultural analyses is based on a search for parsimonious theories which use measurable factors. However, this social science approach tends to end up in complicated multi-factor explanations and subjective measures in spite of the original intentions. As a result, treating culture as one of the possible explanatory variables from the start probably has fewer costs than is often imagined by those with social scientific leanings. When these points are combined with my view of the value of the descriptive approach to analysing strategic culture, my incentives to treat strategic culture as more than just a residual factor are clear.

The impact of strategic culture can be illustrated vividly by contrasting US and Japanese attitudes in the Second World War to kamikaze tactics (a term coined by Japanese-Americans fighting on the allied side) and surrender. The United States did not anticipate Japan's kamikaze tactics due to mirror-imaging: the kamikaze option was not part of US strategic culture and so the United States did not realise that it was part of Japan's strategic culture, although the use of kamikaze aircraft (and boats) against ships can be highly effective.[15] This is not to say that the Japanese were somehow generally more rational in calculating the optimum cost to the enemy for a given expenditure of life. Japanese troops were encouraged to commit suicide or launch certain-death charges rather than surrender, even though prisoners of war tie up significant amounts of an opponent's resources in terms of personnel and supplies. The differing attitudes to kamikaze attacks and surrender are rooted in differing warrior cultures of facing death with equanimity in the Japanese code of *bushido*, and of placing a much greater emphasis on the avoidance of death in the US case. The aim of kamikaze tactics was to keep the spirit and honour of the Japanese Emperor and nation afloat, as well as to sink ships.[16] However, Japanese strategic culture did not simply result in the use of kamikaze tactics: Japan only resorted to them beginning with the Philippines campaign in October 1944. In other words, a particular state of the military balance combined with *bushido* strategic culture to produce the behaviour: neither factor alone could produce it. A more positivist explanation would have to take Japan's strategic culture for granted (unless, of course, the culture was treated as a measurable factor). Furthermore, many Japanese troops preferred to surrender rather than die, and in the end Japan surrendered rather than order mass suicide and a fight to the bitter end. The fact that surrender was not confined to Western troops suggests also that the contrast between the two sides should not be overstated.

STRATEGIC CULTURE AND STRATEGIC CONCEPTS

The discussion of strategic culture suggests the possibility that the concepts used in this study are ethnocentric and therefore inappropriate for analysing the behaviour of the two main non-Western protagonists, the Soviet Union and China. This concern will be shown to be unfounded by examining Soviet and Chinese approaches to the concepts of crisis, deterrence, compellence, the military balance and the balance of interests.[17] I will show that the extent of the differences claimed in the literature is exaggerated. There is no radical incommensurability of perspective; instead, the perspectives overlap sufficiently so that my approach to explaining international crisis outcomes is not simply a 'Western' conception imposed ethnocentrically and inappropriately on other strategic cultures. I take this as sufficient justification to assume, especially in the absence of obvious evidence to the contrary, that the strategic cultures of the other countries such as Iraq and Argentina also overlap in a similar way. This is not to say that there are no differences or that the differences which do exist are of no importance. The aim here is, as Geertz put it, 'cutting of the culture concept down to size, therefore actually insuring its continued importance rather than undermining it' (1973: 4).

Perceptions of the nature of crisis

The Chinese word for crisis (*weiji*) combines danger (*wei*) and opportunity (*ji*), whereas Western definitions emphasise danger. In the auxiliary assumptions often associated with deterrence theory, crises are seen as being the result of a revisionist state trying to exploit an opportunity and which understands that it is taking risks to do so. It then becomes tempting to see the conceptual difference of emphasis as a product of China having been more revisionist territorially and ideologically than the West, which is supposedly status quo-orientated. The United States perceived its actions in Asia in the 1940s and 1950s as purely reactive, defensive and status quo-orientated (Zhang 1993: 279). This perception stemmed from Cold War bias and ignored a glaring example of Western revisionism from that period, namely the invasion of North Korea in 1950, which was unmatched by anything in Chinese behaviour. Even an invasion of Taiwan in that period, if it had occurred, should not be construed as more revisionist than the invasion of North Korea because the Communists would have been acting to reunite their own country. An alternative explanation of the difference in emphasis – which I advance only speculatively to generate a possible line of enquiry – might be that the Chinese concept has its origins in the Taoist emphasis on the importance and interaction of paradoxes and opposites (Cleary 1988). Even if the Western concept of crisis lacks this dialectical element, Western decision-makers have still shown a willingness to exploit opportunities and even create them through destabilisation – that is, the creation of crises. Furthermore, linking danger and opportunity does not necessarily mean that China has been willing to accept danger in order to exploit opportunities. It can also be interpreted defensively – if you are put in a situation of danger (such as the US advance towards China through North Korea), an opportunity may arise (such as the chance to expel the United States from the Korean peninsula completely).

The pitfalls of exaggerating differences and of failing to consider alternative interpretations of possible contrasts can be demonstrated by an examination of Stephen Shenfield's analysis of Soviet views of crisis and crisis management. First, Shenfield claims that Soviet writers on international relations did not use the term 'crisis management' because they rejected 'the manipulation of military signals in crises to achieve favourable outcomes without falling over the brink of war' as 'unrealistic, metaphysical and provocative' (1990: 198; see also Hart 1984). They may have rejected the term, but they did not reject the practice. It should be noted that Schelling, an enormously influential writer on crisis tactics, derived his ideas to a great extent from the behaviour of Stalin and especially Khrushchev. Soviet decision-makers frequently manipulated military signals and thus deliberately engaged in coercive crisis diplomacy. This is demonstrated in Roy Allison's chapter (1990) in the same volume as Shenfield's essay, and by my case studies. Stephen Kaplan identifies 190 incidents (many of which were crises) between 1945 and early 1979 when the Soviet Union used its armed forces for foreign policy purposes. Essentially, the same point can be made about China's crisis behaviour: whatever words it used, it engaged in crisis management such as the use of probes and controlled pressure, which was not only comprehensible to Western analysts but was used by them in the development of their theories. Furthermore, there have been plenty of Western analysts who have rejected fancy theories of crisis management (e.g. Lebow 1987a).

Second, Shenfield claims that in Soviet theory a crisis was an objective condition rather than something perceived subjectively by decision-makers. This point, and the implied contrast with Western theory, is overstated. Shenfield himself cites a 1983 text from the Department of Theory of International Relations of the Soviet Institute of World Economy and International Relations which refers to the crisis phase of international conflict as involving, in Shenfield's words, 'direct threat of military force, objectively *or subjectively* approaching the direct unleashing of armed conflict' (1990: 199–200, emphasis added). In Western analyses, both viewpoints are also examined. For example, the International Crisis Behaviour Project at McGill University in Canada is in the process of analysing hundreds of crises from a systemic behavioural perspective as well as from a foreign policy perceptual perspective (Brecher, Wilkenfeld, Moser 1988; Wilkenfeld *et al.* 1988; Brecher, Wilkenfeld 1989a,b).

Third, according to Shenfield, Soviet theorists defined a crisis as existing when there was a 'direct' threat of war, and the synonym in Soviet military literature was the 'threat period', which is when 'one or more states make direct preparations for war' (1990: 199). While many Western commentators refer to many lesser confrontations as crises, Soviet commentators called these 'conflicts'. This contradicts his claim that the Soviets had a 'razor-sharp distinction between "peace" and "war"' (1990: 202), unless conflicts and crises sit on the razor's edge. Furthermore, Shenfield does not mention the fact that since the beginning of the 1960s some Western theorists, such as Lebow, have felt it necessary to distinguish between crises in general and acute or intense crises 'in which war was perceived as a fairly distinct possibility by policy-makers of at least one of the protagonists' (Lebow 1981: 9). Lebow classifies the Munich crisis, the Berlin blockade and the Cuban missile crisis, but not the Taiwan Straits crisis of 1958 or the Berlin Wall crisis, as acute crises. Those theorists who do not use the crisis/intense crisis labels still take into account the differing degrees of danger from one crisis to another.

Deterrence and compellence

In Russian there are two words for deterrence. *Ustrasheniye* means frightening or intimidation; has pejorative, offensive connotations like the Western phrase 'nuclear blackmail'; and was associated with accusations that the United States sought to establish a first-strike capability. In contrast, *sderzhivaniye* means restraining or keeping in check, has defensive, positive connotations and implies reliance on an assured second-strike capability (Jukes 1975; Trofimenko 1980: 53; Erickson 1982; Kux 1986: 228–35). The line between the two concepts is not clear. Henry Trofimenko, who was head of the Foreign Policy Department of the Institute of the United States and Canada of the Soviet Academy of Sciences at the time he wrote, pointed out that *ustrasheniye* was used in the Soviet Union to denote the Western concept of containment as well as deterrence, which created some confusion in Russian translations of English language material (Trofimenko 1980: 53–4; see also Garthoff 1990a: 24). He condemned containment as an offensive Western strategy designed, as he observed correctly, to bring about the transformation of the Soviet Union (1980: 50; see also Garthoff 1990a: 8, 24–6). This means that Western *ustrasheniye* could have been politically offensive (in the case of containment) as well as defensive (in the case of maintenance of an assured second-strike capability). Predictably, the USSR was always presented as engaging in *sderzhivaniye* rather than *ustrasheniye*. Once the period of *détente* began, Soviet commentaries tended to refer to US strategic policy as *sderzhivaniye* much more often than *ustrasheniye* (Kux 1986: 229; Garthoff 1990a: 25). Some Soviet commentators in the 1980s used the term 'mutual deterrence' (*vzaimnoye sderzhivaniye* or *vzaimosderzhivaniya*) (Kux 1986: 229). Although they did not see mutual deterrence as an acceptable long-term principle for relations between states, they did accept it as a fact for the time being (Kux 1986, 235–54).

There is no clear equivalent in Russian for compellence. This is hardly surprising, as it is a recent English-language neologism, although they could have developed their own equivalent term independently. Here is how Trofimenko used the concept: 'During the first brief stage of America's atomic monopoly, deterrence meant compellence, or coercion of the opponent – through the overt or implied threat of a preventive nuclear strike – to accept the American idea of the world order'.[18] Similarly, he said of the period of US nuclear superiority: 'deterrence in the Dulles interpretation was a clear attempt to compel the Soviet Union to follow a certain type of behavior imposed by the United States through the threat of superior atomic power and retribution for "wrong behavior" ' (1980: 7). This kind of offensive deterrence was designed to influence 'any world event that could undermine the pro-American status quo' (1980: 7). Trofimenko equated deterrence for offensive purposes with compellence (making someone do something), although compellence can be used for defensive purposes. According to Garthoff, the Soviet routine translation of Western references to deterrence as *ustrasheniye* meant that Soviet readers read into those materials an offensive or compellent tone which was absent in the original. And when Soviet writers then rejected the legitimacy of this Western 'deterrence', their writings were interpreted as reflecting the offensive or compellent objective of preventing the West from having a capability to prevent an attack upon itself (1990a: 25–6). However, the way in which both sides perceived the other as offensively motivated and themselves as defensively motivated cannot credibly be attributed primarily to conceptual confusion: the ambiguity of behaviour, the strategic competition between the two and the role of psychological biases are sufficient.

In a similar approach to that of the Soviet Union, the Chinese do not use the term deterrence (*weishe*) in descriptions of their own, French or British nuclear strategies: this they applied only to US and Soviet nuclear strategy. *Weishe* translates as 'to intimidate through strength' or 'to terrorise with military force' (Kux 1986: 497). This is similar to the Soviet notion of *ustrasheniye* (Kux 1986:

496). Chinese sources only referred to *weishe* in order to condemn it as blackmail and as part of a futile and yet unstable US-Soviet competition to establish nuclear superiority (Kux 1986: 498–9). The Chinese attribute paramount importance to people's war (*renmin zhanzheng*) and counter-attack (*baochou*, *baofu* or *huanji*) for war prevention. Although the Chinese would seem to be concentrating on deterrence by denial, using everything from guerrilla war through to strategic nuclear war, there is an implicit element of deterrence by punishment in their theories (Kux 1986: 500–01, 510–11). Overall, Chinese thinking about deterrence is shaped by their strategic history and current preoccupations, but not in a way that would lead one to expect mutual incomprehension in dealing with the outside world. Mutual incomprehension may have occurred, but its roots will not have been conceptual.

The military balance and the balance of interests

Soviet decision-makers thought in terms of a broad concept known as the correlation of forces (*sootnoshenie sil*) (Garthoff 1965: 65–97; Deane 1976; Legvold 1979; Kux 1986: 142–85; Wohlforth 1993). This phrase referred to the direction of the historical flow in the world-wide struggle between socialism and imperialism in economic, social, cultural, moral and military terms. It was the military balance, the balance of interests and much more combined. The Chinese equivalent term for the correlation of forces was promulgated by Mao on 17 November 1957, when he referred to 'the east wind prevailing over the west wind' (quoted in Hsieh 1962: 84; see also 85, 121, 131, 162). This phraseology became standard fare in Chinese foreign policy assessments and pronouncements. In estimating the US-Soviet balance of power, the Chinese have thought primarily in military and economic terms, but have also taken into account issues such as science and technology, the state of relations with other countries, leadership and popular support in a way which seems easily comprehensible to Western minds (Garrett, Glaser 1988; see also Hsieh 1962, Liu 1972, Gelber 1973, Pillsbury 1975, Pollack 1984, Lin 1988).

Western conceptions of the Soviet view of power as having been excessively militarised were inaccurate, according to Robert Legvold: 'in the Soviet mind, military power remains not only a function of other forms of power, economic in particular, but their auxiliary as well – never, as so many analysts in the West surmise, their substitute' (1979: 9). However, equally, one must not understate the importance of military factors in Soviet analyses. The conclusion drawn by Soviet analysts at the beginning of the 1970s in the Brezhnev era that the correlation of forces had shifted in favour of socialism was seen to have been brought about primarily and very narrowly by the growth of Soviet conventional and especially strategic nuclear capabilities (MccGwire 1991: 83). Indeed, Soviet analysts sometimes referred to the correlation of military forces (Garthoff 1990: 100). In the final humiliation, Soviet-style socialism collapsed in 1989–91 due to a failure to understand the economic, ideological and social dimensions of power. While it is also true that Western conceptions of the balance of power can be more static and more narrowly military and economic than this broad notion of correlations of forces and East-versus-West winds, talk about the struggle of the 'free world' against Communism can be based on elements as broad as the correlation of forces. Analysts should be wary of crude characterisations of which side had the more sophisticated or less militarised conception of the balance of power.[19]

Soviet analysts developed an explicit notion of the balance of interests, although it was different from the one used in this study. The expectation that successes during crises or even attempts to bring about favourable outcomes, especially when military force is used, would provoke effective balancing was a basic element of the new thinking in Soviet foreign policy introduced by Gorbachev. Victor Kremenyuk of the Soviet Institute of the United States and Canada stressed that the use of force in the Third World did not bring victory but instead counter-intervention by the other superpower and the raising of the stakes: 'The situation in world politics and the balance of global and regional forces are such that any move by a militarily strong side comes up against adequate resistance from the other side and sources of aid and support are found' (in Akopov *et al.* 1988: 137). Kremenyuk argued that, in an effort to escape this stalemate, the Soviet Union convinced itself that its interventions were just, only to find out that the military option did not work. In this period, both sides revealed their interests by 'declarations or demonstrations', and by rejecting the other side's claims of interests 'out of hand'. Each side tried to pressure the other into respecting its vital interests through threats of force. His alternative was that the United States and Soviet Union should discuss their 'lawful interests' through the mass media as well as diplomatic channels; that they should not define their interests in terms of a zero-sum game; that regional conflicts should be resolved through political means; and that economic aid should be used where necessary. According to Oleg Peresypkin, the Rector of the Diplomatic Academy of the Soviet Foreign Ministry: 'What we are now advocating as a basis for foreign policy is not a balance of forces but a search for a balance of interests' (in Akopov *et al.* 1988: 142; see also Garthoff 1990a: 136–7, 189). The Soviet Union until its collapse made great progress with this approach in areas of political deadlock in US-Soviet relations. In this approach, the balance of interests is a policy of compromise, whereas this study considers the balance of interests as an outcome of a struggle to achieve objectives in a crisis. However, the idea that each side will have different mixes of personal, intrinsic and strategic interests at stake has been comprehensible to and commonplace among Western, Soviet and Chinese decision-makers: it is the normal discourse of their relations. As Kratochwil puts it: 'the national interest requires validation within a discourse that provides a common frame of reference for the conflicting claims of the participants in the international game' (1982: 24). Misperception, even if it occurs, can still be occurring within a mutually comprehensible discourse.[20]

CONCLUSION

Rationality is shaped by strategic culture in that it influences the range of options considered, the hierarchy of preferences adopted, and the weightings attached to interests. Misperception will occur if strategic cultural differences are underestimated, exaggerated or simply misapprehended. Strategic culture refers to a shared pattern of attitudes regarding military power. This descriptive approach to the concept is valuable because, if used properly, it can aid understanding. However, my priority is to find out how, if at all, strategic culture shapes international crisis outcomes. Strategic culture may legitimise strategic preferences, socialise those within a group, communicate with those outside a group, or influence strategic preferences. Strategic culture is unlikely to determine behaviour alone: it will be more likely to influence the range of likely behaviour and create predispositions and inclinations within that range. Behaviour produced by strategic culture is not itself strategic culture, although that behaviour may communicate strategic cultural meaning and have strategic cultural effects. Analysing strategic culture alerts us to differences and helps us to understand those differences; as Geertz put it 'Understanding a people's culture exposes their normalness without reducing their particularity' (1973: 14). While explanation and understanding have different methodological roots, the two perspectives can inform each other. Although the role of culture is worth studying, one should not exaggerate the differences and ignore the similarities between different societies, see a direct link between strategic culture and behaviour, or fail to address possible non-cultural explanations of differences in behaviour.

The elements of my approach to explaining international crisis outcomes are now in place. The next task is to apply those elements to the case studies.

NOTES

[1] Key contributions on rationality and irrationality in deterrence and crisis behaviour include Jervis 1970, 1976, 1982–83, 1984, 1989b; Allison 1971; Janis 1972; Steinbruner 1974, 1976; Janis, Mann 1977; Snyder, Diesing 1977; Snyder 1978, 1991c; Lebow 1981, 1987a, 1989; Jervis, Lebow, Stein 1985; Lebow, Stein 1987a,b, 1989, 1990, 1994; Kull 1988; the 1979 special issue of *World Politics* on the rational deterrence debate; Rhodes 1989; Huth, Russett 1990; and Jervis, Snyder 1991.

[2] For applications of these two rationalities to the possibility of accidental nuclear war see Wiberg 1993 and to perceptions of domino and bandwagon behaviour see Snyder 1991a,b. For a third view of rationality known as 'prospect theory', see Tversky, Kahneman 1979 and Stein, Pauly 1993.

[3] See pp. 22–5, 71 and 249.

[4] Jervis 1985a: 11. For an attempt to develop an alternative, 'cybernetic' model, see Steinbruner 1974, 1976, and for an application of that model to the Cuban missile crisis see Snyder 1978.

[5] See especially Jervis 1976, Janis, Mann 1977, Lebow 1981. Other typologies are possible. In his study of the Gulf crisis, Alex Roberto Hybel

(1993) divides cognitive theories into attribution, schema and cognitive consistency theory. Attribution theory sees decision-makers as trying to find causal relationships: irrationality flows from the limits of the decision-maker's ability to carry out that task. Schema theory posits decision-makers who respond to pressure on their time, energy and mental resources by developing and applying analogies from the past to new situations: irrationality is produced by the application of inappropriate analogies. Cognitive consistency theory expects decision-makers to try to balance their beliefs and values with what they perceive: irrationality is rooted in ignoring perceptions which clash with their beliefs and values.

[6] On heuristics and biases, see especially Kahneman, Slovic, Tversky 1982. On the role of historical analogies in decision-making see Jervis 1976: 217–87; Neustadt, May 1986; Khong 1992; and Hybel 1993.

[7] Gregory M. Herek, Irving L. Janis and Paul Huth (1987), in a study of US presidential decision-making in nineteen crises since World War II, found support for the intuitive view that the better the quality of the decision-making, the more favourable the outcome.

[8] 1977, *v*. In addition to the literature discussed in this chapter, see Gray 1984 and Klein 1991 on the theory of strategic culture; Klein 1988 and Lord 1985 on US strategic culture; Pipes 1977 and Strode 1981–82 on Soviet strategic culture; Ermath 1978 on differences between US and Soviet strategic thought; Shih 1990 on Chinese foreign policy 'psycho-culture'; and Tanham 1992 on Indian strategic culture. For a critique of Shih's book as part of a review article on the study of Chinese foreign policy, see Yu 1994.

[9] 1990. See also the sceptical book review by Scott Sagan (1983).

[10] Booth 1990. Booth – who has done his own share of debunking myths about US strategic culture (1978) – is currently engaged in a project on strategic culture and conflict resolution in the Asia-Pacific region with Russell Trood.

[11] On culture, see Fisher 1988 and Johnston forthcoming. On political culture see Kavanaugh 1972; Elkins, Simeon 1979; Brown 1984; Wildavsky 1985, 1987; Eckstein 1988; Inglehart 1988; Laitin, Wildavsky 1988; and Gibbins 1989.

[12] My approach to strategic culture has benefited greatly from the work of Elkins and Simeon (1979) and Johnston (forthcoming). I use the term 'attitudes' in the same way that Elkins and Simeon refer to 'assumptions'.

[13] On the two approaches, see Hollis and Smith (1990) and see pp. 22–5.

[14] This list integrates the functions of ideology indicated by Adomeit

(1982) and those of strategic culture indicated by Johnston (forthcoming). See also Booth (1987a) on the functions of 'deterrence ideology'. I have not addressed what explains the existence of strategic cultures: that is a different question from what strategic culture explains. Strategic cultures may originate in the interaction of cultural factors, non-cultural factors, or some combination of the two. There is no fundamental reason why strategic culture cannot be monolithic, but the variety and complexity of human experience suggests that the existence of subcultures is likely to be the norm. Similarly, as states are the primary strategic actors, distinctive national strategic cultures may emerge, but strategic culture is not necessarily national: it may be shared by more than one state or by groups within more than one state.

[15] Initially, the Japanese success rate increased tenfold. However, the idea of a ratio of 'one aircraft, one ship' has little basis in fact, and the effectiveness of kamikaze tactics declined dramatically once the allies adjusted their own tactics. Overall, approximately 8,000 kamikaze aircraft were used and sank 36 allied ships, damaged nearly 400 more and resulted in the loss of nearly 800 allied aircraft (Marder, Jacobsen, Horsfield 1990: 398–403, 423–9, 439–41, 444–50).

[16] On *bushido*, see Nitobé 1905. On the role of kamikaze tactics in ensuring that the spirit of Japan lived on, see Marder, Jacobsen, Horsfield 1990: 400. In some ways the Western perception has spread: in a recent study it was found that Japanese and US college students concur in seeing the actions of kamikaze pilots as meaningless and bad, if brave. However, the Japanese still showed a much more positive underlying emotional response to them (Krus, Ishigaki 1992).

[17] One might add to this list the broader concept of rationality. The literature on Western and Chinese thought regarding rationality finds limited rather than radical contrasts. See Biderman and Scharfstein 1989 and Schirokauer 1986. This fits with my conclusions regarding strategic concepts. On related methodological issues see also Yu 1994.

[18] 1980: 11. See also 5–6. The second stage for Trofimenko was the period in which the United States attempted nuclear blackmail with its nuclear superiority (*ustrasheniye*). The third stage represented convergence of US and Soviet views on deterrence as the prevention of attack by the threat of unacceptable retaliation (*sderzhivaniye*). When he wrote, his concern was that the United States was enhancing its war-fighting capabilities (a return to *ustrasheniye*) at the expense of mutual, stable deterrence.

[19] The most careful and extensive comparison of US and Soviet perceptions of power is Wohlforth 1993. The important issue here is less the

definition of the balance of power than perspectives on how it operates. See Wohlforth (1993: especially 153) on the contrasting policy implications for Soviet decision-makers when they assumed that increases in Soviet power tended to divide the Western alliance, and when they assumed that increases in Soviet power tended to unite it.

[20] While strategic cultures can clash within eras (the normal preoccupation of the strategic culture literature), strategic cultures can also be shared and can change from era to era. For example, the notion of national interest in European interstate relations in the early nineteenth century was part of a set of conventions which recognised the legitimacy of the interests of other actors and thus mitigated the effects of international anarchy. It shifted in the late nineteenth century to one based on the 'glorification of unbridled self-interest'; the national interest was seen 'merely as an indication of the preferences of decision makers, preferences that were increasingly conceived in social-darwinistic terms' (Kratochwil 1992: 5, 22). This shift may have contributed to the outbreak of World War I, in part by helping to produce a European strategic culture which embodied what Snyder has called the 'ideology of the offensive' (1984).

Part II

CASE STUDIES

Chapter Four

THE BERLIN BLOCKADE, 1948–49

With respect to Germany as a whole, just as with respect to Berlin, the Russians will probably continue to insist on unreasonable advantages, because without unreasonable advantages they cannot hope to maintain any influence at all.

Policy Planning Staff, US State Department (*FRUS 1948* 2: 1245)

THE FAILURE OF SOVIET PRESSURE TO EXTRACT CONCESSIONS

At the end of the Second World War, Germany was divided into four zones controlled by the United States, Britain, France (henceforth referred to as the allies) and the Soviet Union. After the Soviet Union and the allies failed to agree on a joint policy on the future of Germany, the allies began to develop a separate policy with other Western European countries. When the Soviet Union refused to co-operate with the introduction of a new all-German currency, the allies introduced it in their own zones of Germany on 20 June 1948. While the Soviets had been interfering with access to West Berlin since March 1948, the currency reform triggered on 24 June 1948 a complete Soviet closure of ground access to the sectors of Berlin controlled by the Western allies. West Berlin was an enclave located 100 miles inside the Soviet zone of Germany which had to have all of its food and fuel brought in by the Western allies by land and water.

The primary Soviet objective was by no means clear. Stalin could have been trying to force the West out of West Berlin or trying to lever concessions on the future of Germany. He could have been hoping that the West would abandon its plan for a separate West German state and instead negotiate the establishment of a neutralised, unified, demilitarised state; or he could have been seeking guarantees that a new West German state would not join any military alliances or have nuclear weapons (Adomeit 1982: 67–77, 121–33; Taubman 1982: 187–92; Tusa, Tusa 1988: 94, 106, 204–07). There was a great deal of uncertainty in the West about Soviet objectives (*FRUS 1948* 2: 972–3, 984–5). Stalin maintained – and Western decision-makers eventually believed – that his main area of concern was the future of Germany and not the control of Berlin (*FRUS 1948* 2: 999–1005, 1013–14). Soviet policy towards Germany more generally was riven with contradictory impulses and desires (Ulam 1974: 440–2; Adomeit 1982: 121–33; cf. Fish 1991: 221n). Perhaps Stalin was pursuing all three objectives, and which one was most important to him might have varied according to which looked the most attainable. This ambiguity makes it unclear whether the main Soviet operational objective was to deter further moves towards the establishment of a West German state or to compel the abandonment of existing plans on that question. Similarly, by increasing the risk of war, the Soviets could have been said to have been trying to deter the West from mounting or continuing to mount a resupply effort, or to compel the West to withdraw from West Berlin. Elements of deterrence and compellence were present. The case falls into the 'immediate' category because it is clear that the allies were actively preparing for actions to which the Soviet Union objected, because the allies did not want to do what the Soviet Union sought to compel them to do, and because the Soviet Union engaged in specific actions designed to increase the risk of war. It is also a 'direct' case in that the Soviet Union principally required that the allies undertake certain actions and not undertake others. However, even here there is an element of overlap with the extended category in that the subject of the bargaining was Germany. The basic thing we can be clear about is that the Soviet Union increased the risk of war with the intention of securing diplomatic concessions.

The outcome was unambiguous in that the Soviet Union achieved none of the objectives discussed. A separate West German government was established with no concessions made on the nature of its armed forces or foreign policy orientation, the Western allies remained in control of their zones of Berlin, and the Soviet

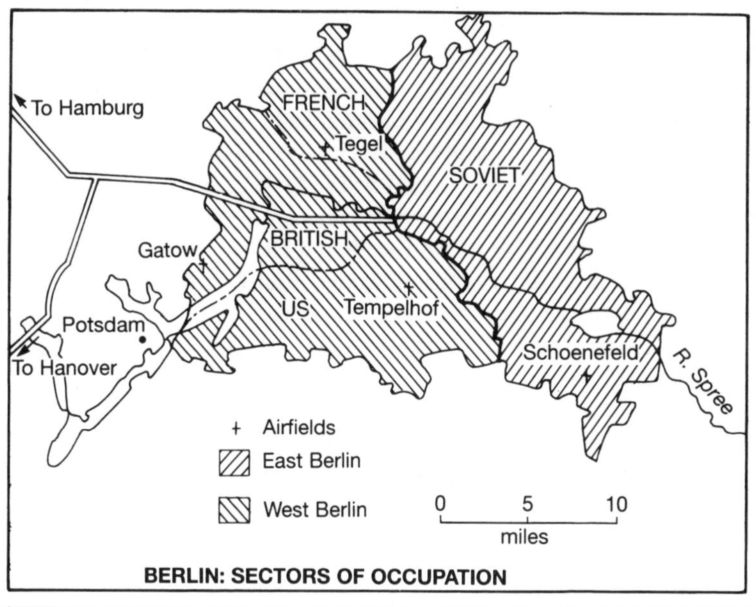

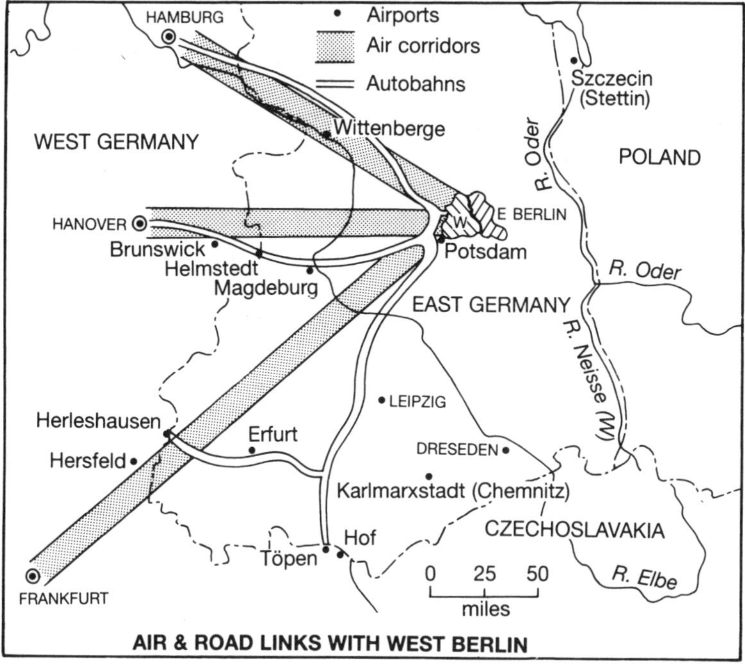

4.1 The Berlin crises, 1948–49 and 1958–62

authorities reopened ground access after the airlift helped the West Berliners to survive the winter. The underlying problems remained unresolved – the existence of a Western enclave in Soviet-controlled territory and the role of what became West Germany in Europe – and tension rose twice more under Stalin's successor, Khrushchev. While Western military expenditure did not increase after the blockade, there were many negative consequences for the Soviet Union – hardening of images of Communist aggressiveness and immorality (in trying to starve out the West Berliners), and beliefs that one could only negotiate with Communists from a position of strength; accelerated discussions of Western defence integration including the United States; the weakening of the left in France; and strengthened anti-Sovietism in Yugoslavia (Adomeit 1982: 173–7). The final resolution came in 1989, with the collapse of Communism in Eastern Europe and the reunification of Germany as a market democracy.

THE MILITARY BALANCE AND MUTUAL FEAR OF WAR

When the Soviet Union blockaded West Berlin, the main Western response was the airlift, which ensured that the city had enough supplies to get through the winter. West Berlin was located deep inside Soviet-controlled territory, and it is clear that the Soviet Union had local superiority in conventional forces. In addition, the Western allies believed that the Soviet Union had short-term conventional military superiority in Europe as a whole (Adomeit 1982: 138–41; Evangelista 1982–83). If they had tried to relieve West Berlin by an overland attack, they would have been risking a wider war in Europe which they expected to lose in the short term, although they might have prevailed in a general war of attrition (Adomeit 1982: 143).

In early July, shortly after the beginning of the blockade, the governments of the United States and Britain agreed that three groups of US B-29 bombers should be moved to Europe. The B-29 was famous for being the aircraft used to drop atomic bombs on Hiroshima and Nagasaki. The fact that Truman had ordered the dropping of atomic bombs in the past may have increased the credibility of his implicit nuclear threat. Sixty of these bombers were deployed in late July. Although officially on a routine training mission, middle-ranking government officials indicated that they were nuclear-capable (that is, able to deliver nuclear weapons) and implied that they were actually carrying nuclear weapons. In reality, they were not nuclear-capable (*FRUS 1948* 2: 924, 927–8, 966; Shlaim 1983: 228, 236–40; Betts 1987: 24–5). At the time of the dispatch of the B-29s, the nuclear stockpile of the United States stood at only around fifty unassembled bombs. The US Air Force was short of bombers, trained crews, bombs, teams to assemble bombs, air bases, targeting information and long-range fighter escorts. The US Joint Chiefs of Staff expected the Soviet Union to suffer fewer than three million dead from a nuclear attack, and the Harmon Report concluded in May 1949 that the Soviet Union could not be defeated with atomic weapons alone (Etzold, Gaddis 1978; Adomeit 1982: 141–2; Rosenberg 1982: 28–9; 1983: 14; Betts 1987: 28–9). As the crisis continued, the United States expanded significantly its nuclear capabilities in terms of military contingency planning, the transfer of control of nuclear weapons from the civilian US Atomic Energy Commission (AEC) to the military, and preparation of aircraft and crews for nuclear missions (Betts 1987: 30). The United States had a pure nuclear monopoly during this crisis, in that no other state in the world possessed nuclear weapons. There were various rumours and Soviet claims that the Soviet Union had nuclear weapons before 1949, but these were not taken seriously by top US decision-makers (*FRUS 1948* 2: 895, 1196–7; Adomeit 1982: 136; Prados 1986: 18–20; Betts 1987: 31).

The bombers were sent to show resolve, to compensate for conventional inferiority, to deter war, to prepare for war should it occur, and to increase the perceived risk of war in order to encourage the Soviet Union to lift the blockade. British Foreign Minister Ernest Bevin wanted the bombers not because he thought that they would be of much military value but to show determination (*FRUS 1948* 2: 924). Similarly, General Lucius D. Clay, the US Military Governor in Germany and Commander-in-Chief of the US European Command, wanted the bombers for 'immediate psychological purposes', although Lieutenant General Curtis Le May, Commander of the US Air Force in Europe, wanted them for operational purposes (*FRUS 1948* 2: 709; Betts 1987: 25, 29; Shlaim 1983: 239).

What effect did the implicit US nuclear threat have on the Soviet Union? The fact that the Soviet Union did not lift its pressure on West Berlin for another nine months suggests that the threat was not very effective. However, the Soviet Union did not escalate even when it became obvious that the airlift was resupplying West Berlin successfully (Shlaim 1983: 240; Betts 1987: 30). Some analysts state that the US nuclear monopoly 'undoubtedly' (Bundy 1988: 384) or 'almost certainly' (Adomeit 1982: 137, 143) prevented the Soviet Union from escalating. Stalin was certainly aware of risks he was taking and of the potential of nuclear weapons (Holloway 1994). In May 1948, the Soviet Union protested about a speech by the Commander of Strategic Air Command (SAC), General George Kenney, in which he talked about plans for ringing the Soviet Union with bases and using atomic bombs on the large cities of the Soviet Union and especially Moscow (*FRUS 1948* 4: 886–8). Stalin set in motion a large-scale effort to break the nuclear monopoly of the United States as soon as possible (Holloway 1994), and in an interview in September 1946, Stalin accepted that the Western nuclear monopoly 'does create a threat' (quoted in Adomeit 1982: 134). There is a substantial possibility that Bundy and Adomeit state their conclusion too baldly. Indeed, the Soviet Union might have been restrained primarily by a desire to avoid a conventional war. To Stalin, West Berlin was not worth war, conventional or nuclear (Holloway 1994: 259). Stalin said that the value of nuclear weapons was limited because, among other things, nuclear threats only work against leaders with weak nerves and the outcome of a general war would still depend on conventional forces (Adomeit 1982: 134–7). Furthermore, in a general war, it looked likely that the Soviet Union would succumb to the United States' strategic invulnerability, naval superiority, and industrial and technological lead (Adomeit 1982: 143). If Western leaders had been forced to choose between their nuclear capability and their conventional capability, I am sure they would have chosen the latter.

This would be an immediate military deterrence success if the Soviet Union had considered seriously the use of force to stop the airlift from succeeding but had not done so due to allied threats to respond with force (Huth, Russett 1990: 484–5; forthcoming). However, it is unlikely that Stalin ever considered this seriously (Lebow, Stein 1990: 368–9). It is more persuasive – unless evidence to the contrary emerges from former Soviet archives – that escalation was prevented by general deterrence. Both sides were highly averse to war, and each knew that the other side felt the same way. As Walter Bedell Smith, US Ambassador to the Soviet Union, put it on 16 September 1948: '[The] Kremlin discounted completely the possibility that we might actually force the issue to [the] point of hostilities, just as we estimated no similar intention on their part, and . . . their belief has been reinforced during [the] protracted course [of the] Moscow talks' (*FRUS 1948* 2: 1161; see also 1194). Similarly, the British position in late April was that they would not be prepared to initiate the use of force to maintain their position in Berlin and would only use force in response to a 'clear organized act of war' (*FRUS 1948* 2: 899–900). This mutual aversion to war helped reduce the sense of crisis, although it did not eliminate it. Indeed, the perception of crisis was maintained by perceptions of the interests at stake and the manipulation of crisis tactics.

INTERESTS AND CRISIS TACTICS

The personal interests of Stalin were not particularly at stake in this crisis. His control of power in the Soviet Union was undisputed, and, in the course of the Berlin blockade, the political balance in the Politburo remained virtually unchanged (Adomeit 1982: 144–52). The Soviet Union was in a difficult position in pursuing its intrinsic interests with regard to Germany. There was little potential for a Communist revolution in Germany as a whole; the decisive weakening of German power demanded a degree of cooperation from the Western allies which looked unlikely to be forthcoming; the division of Germany would result in the bulk of the country joining an anti-Soviet alliance; and a neutral Germany would probably be a capitalist, pro-Western state (Adomeit 1982: 121–33; Wohlforth 1993: 74–5). With no good options, the Soviet strategy basically amounted to avoiding any risk of the loss of the Eastern German zone, while putting pressure on West Berlin in the hope of getting some concessions on the future of the rest of Germany or getting control of West Berlin.

The Policy Planning Staff of the US State Department was aware of the difficulties the Soviet Union faced:

> If the continuation of the present deadlock threatens us with the loss of Berlin, it threatens them with the loss of Germany itself. . . . If. . . they cannot get an abandonment of the western German arrangements, our withdrawal from Berlin would be the next best thing. It is imperative, however, in Russian eyes, that one or the other of these objectives is achieved: if not the second, then the first. This line of conduct is motivated on their part by defensive considerations of the most serious nature.
>
> (*FRUS 1948* 2: 1242–3)

Similarly, General Clay recognised the Soviet intrinsic interest in trying to 'liquidate this remaining "center of reaction" east of [the] Iron Curtain' (*FRUS 1948* 2: 885; see also 879, 949, 1209). The Policy Planning Staff's (PPS) assessment indicates that both sides were highly motivated because both were struggling to avoid incurring a loss. Soviet resolve was reinforced by another point, as the PPS observed: 'With respect to Germany as a whole, just as with respect to Berlin, the Russians will probably continue to insist on unreasonable advantages, because without unreasonable advantages they cannot hope to maintain any influence at all' (*FRUS 1948* 2: 1245). In other words, if the Soviet Union failed to make a gain it would incur a loss. It would have been less strongly motivated if failure to make a gain involved no loss from the starting point.

The United States and Britain were concerned more about strategic interests in terms of dominoes than the intrinsic interest of West Berlin or even Germany. Robert D. Murphy, the US Political Adviser for Germany, indicated to Secretary of State George C. Marshall on 26 June 1948 his worries:

> [The] presence in Berlin of Western occupants became a symbol of Western resistance to eastern expansionism. It is unquestionably an index of our prestige in central and eastern Europe. As far as Germany is concerned, it is a test of US ability in Europe. If we docilely withdraw now, Germans and other Europeans would conclude that our retreat from western Germany is just a question of time. [The] US position in Europe would be gravely weakened, and like a cat on a sloping tin roof.
>
> (*FRUS 1948* 2: 919–20)

Many similar statements by British and US officials are on record (*FRUS 1948* 2: 886, 925, 968–9, 982, 1050, 1060, 1062, 1241–2;

FRUS 1949 3: 709). The domino thinking of the United States was promoted by the *coup* in Czechoslovakia in February 1948 by the Czech Communist Party, which overthrew the elected government (Macdonald 1991: 122–3).

In spite of the idea discussed in Chapter Two that the defender of the status quo might feel unable to compromise, General Brian H. Robertson, British Military Governor for Germany and Commander-in-Chief of the British Section of the Control Commission for Germany, suggested on 2 April 1948 that the potential for compromise on West Berlin be explored. Murphy and General Clay believed that the West should not look too eager to make concessions and believed that there would be little point in compromise on Berlin if the Soviet actions were, as Murphy put it, 'part of a larger and more ambitious program' (*FRUS 1948* 2: 888; see also 936–8, 956–67). On 25 June, Clay proposed to his superiors a compromise involving economic assistance to East Germany in response to guaranteed access to West Berlin. As the West would still retain a separate currency in West Berlin, he believed the deal would not involve a loss of prestige (*FRUS 1948* 2: 917–18). Clay soon proposed compromising even further. On 4 August Clay indicated in a telegram that 'there is obviously no other course of action left open to us except to accept in principle the Soviet proposal' for a lifting of the blockade in return for a withdrawal of the Western currency from Berlin (*FRUS 1948* 2: 1012; see also 929–30, 940, 1020). Clay believed talks on currency reform would be a face-saving way for the Soviet Union to compromise (*FRUS 1948* 2: 956–7), but by mid-August it looked as if the Soviets were in no hurry to come to an agreement and seemed to be stalling so that winter would undermine the airlift (*FRUS 1948* 2: 1046, 1227–8).

The Soviet Union seemed to have a good opportunity to act due to the vulnerability of West Berlin as an isolated enclave. It was difficult to force concessions on the future of the allied zones of Germany because the Soviet Union was not willing or able to reassure the West of the limits of its ambitions and dispel its fears of domino effects. The West was more willing to make concessions on West Berlin itself than on the future of the Western zones of Germany because it seemed that West Berlin was a special case from which the knock-on effects would be less damaging. The Western willingness to make concessions was also linked to the vulnerability of the city. Although the West was generally quite optimistic about its airlift capabilities (*FRUS 1948* 2: 982, 1060, 1284; but see also 917, 918–19, 924, 1048), the PPS believed that maintenance of the Western position in West Berlin was going to rely on the psychological resilience of the city's population as much as on logistics (*FRUS 1948* 2: 1242).

In this context, crisis tactics played a central role. The West had the initial advantage that it was defending the territorial status quo. The point of the Soviet blockade was to make the territorial status quo untenable by cutting the surface supply routes to West Berlin. In order to hinder the airlift, the Soviet Union harassed allied aircraft. For example, on 4 September 1948, Marshal Vasily D. Sokolovsky, the local Soviet military Commander-in-Chief, indicated that extensive Soviet air manoeuvres which would include the air corridors to Berlin would begin on 6 September and last for several days (*FRUS 1948* 2: 1121). The idea was that allied fear of unintended escalation would make them back down. As it turned out, allied determination to distinguish between incidents as opposed to clear organised acts of war helped to draw the sting from this tactic. As a result, the burden of the first use of force lay with the Soviet Union. There were rumours that the Soviet Union might use barrage balloons to block the flight-paths of allied aircraft. The value of this tactic is that it would have switched the burden of the first use of force back onto the allies. Its weakness is that the allies would only have been destroying objects rather than engaging in combat. In response to the rumour, Britain decided that it would only approve shooting down the balloons on the basis of a joint US-UK decision (*FRUS 1948* 2: 936; see also 956). Robertson was not to be allowed to act on his own initiative (*FRUS 1948* 2: 940). Thus tight control was being exercised over the local military commander to try to avoid uncontrolled escalation.

The allies debated the value of an attempt to breach the surface blockade. Murphy and General Clay believed that armed convoys could be sent overland to Berlin through the Soviet zone because the Soviet Union did not want war (*FRUS 1948*, 2: 957–8). In contrast, Smith thought the risk of war to be substantial (*FRUS 1948* 2: 969; cf. 971). On 28 July the Joint Chiefs of Staff judged that the risk of war was excessive for such an operation to be used as anything other than a last resort, but began contingency planning for the operation as requested by Secretary of Defence James

Forrestal (*FRUS 1948* 2: 994–5). In the end, the success of the airlift made a surface probe unnecessary.

IDEOLOGICAL HOSTILITY COMBINED WITH RATIONAL DECISION-MAKING

The basic Cold War hostility between East and West combined with the vulnerability of West Berlin meant that a crisis over the city was a significant possibility. The Stalinist line assumed that the 'impending crisis of capitalism' was heralded by imperialist expansion in the search for new markets. In such conditions, this line predicted that there would be revolutionary opportunities which could be exploited, as suggested by the successful Communist take-over in Czechoslovakia in early 1948. Militant tactics, from strikes and demonstrations to kidnaps, were used by Communists in West Berlin. Overall, the pressure on Berlin fitted the broader ideologically-based thrust of Soviet policy in Europe (Adomeit 1982: 114–21, 328–34). While strategic cultural factors in the form of Soviet ideology made the crisis more likely and influenced some of the details of its conduct (such as the style of the Communist disruption in West Berlin), the basic conduct and outcome of the crisis was unaffected. Stalinist ideological tenets about the inevitability of war between Communism and capitalism contrasted with Soviet crisis diplomacy which stressed the avoidance of war and the potential for a return to cooperation (Adomeit 1982: 112–14). The careful tactical behaviour of both sides shows that their management of the crisis was not undermined by psychological biases, although strategic cultural factors exacerbated the tensions between them. Stalin saw the capitalist camp as powerful and implacably hostile and yet also vulnerable to pressure (Taubman 1982; Wohlforth 1993): this fed the impulse to probe, but to probe carefully. When the Soviet blockade met with vigorous Western opposition, talks began with the Soviet Union on a possible compromise. Smith, in a report to Marshall, stated that '[the] fact that Stalin made [a] proposal not too much out of line with our own implies that they also are feeling [the] pinch and that, in conformity with standard Bolshevik tactics when opposition to direct action [is] encountered, [they] are trying the more circuitous route' (*FRUS 1948* 2: 1010). The idea that Stalin was conforming to some distinctive Bolshevik strategic culture in talking about a possible compromise after meeting resistance is unconvincing. Using an indirect approach when a direct one is unsuccessful sounds like unremarkable rational behaviour. Even with an indirect approach the Soviet Union failed to prevent the West from going ahead with its plans for a separate West German state, failed to force the West to recognise East Germany and failed to compel the allies to withdraw from West Berlin.

The Soviet challenge to West Berlin was in part provoked by the failure of Western decision-makers to make clear their commitment to remaining in their sectors of the city. The allied indecision was a product of their being in the psychologically uncomfortable position of feeling that they had to defend their position in West Berlin, but also believing that there was a substantial possibility that it might not be defensible. Soviet pressure on West Berlin in the months before the blockade (including what is known as the 'baby blockade' of April 1948) did not result in a full assessment of the situation (Fish 1991: 198–202). No good options appeared to exist in a potentially dangerous situation, and so Western policy-makers engaged in what is known as 'defensive avoidance', which involves procrastination, attempts to attribute responsibility for the situation to others and 'bolstering' (that is, exaggeration of the chances for their policy to succeed and a failure to take sufficiently seriously the warnings inherent in actions such as the baby blockade) (Janis, Mann 1977: 57–8, 74, 197–233).

Once the blockade had begun, some officials expressed dissatisfaction with the extent and even the existence of the allied commitment. Smith said to the Policy Planning Staff on 28 September 1948 that 'we should never have let ourselves get into an exposed salient like Berlin . . . From the political point of view, Berlin has become the important symbol it now is largely because we ourselves have made it so' (*FRUS 1948* 2: 1194). Similarly, Pierre de Leusse, Chief of the German-Austrian Section at the French Foreign Ministry was reported by the US Ambassador as saying that 'a serious error had been committed by the Western powers when the Berlin crisis first arose by overstressing the importance of remaining in Berlin and announcing that we would remain there at all costs' (*FRUS 1948* 2: 916–17). These officials did not explain what should have been done for the people of West Berlin, but their point seems to have been that the interests of those people must be subordinated to the interest of avoiding large-scale war. However, they did seem to believe that, once the commitment was made, there was no turning back.

CONCLUSION: FAILED BUT RATIONAL PRESSURE

The United States had a pure but weak nuclear monopoly. The Soviet Union had local and short-term conventional superiority, but had reason to be concerned about the likely outcome of a general war. As neither side wanted war, conventional or nuclear, over West Berlin, they were both constrained by fear of war, which reduced the importance of their respective military advantages. In the end, there is no clear link between any measure of the military balance and the outcome of the Berlin blockade, although the military balance did influence the tactical conduct of the crisis in terms of the role of the blockade and the burden of the first use of force. The apparent vulnerability of West Berlin to blockade, the uncertainty of the Western commitment to it and the Soviet superiority in the local and short-term conventional military balance all worked in favour of the Soviet Union, and encouraged the West to consider making concessions. However, the West rejected the Soviet framing of the Berlin question as *sui generis* (and thus without wider implications should the West make concessions). Instead, it reinforced its bargaining position by making it clear that it felt its strategic interests to be threatened (Jervis 1970: 109–11). In the end, the outcome of the crisis was decided by the success of the Western airlift and Stalin's unwillingness to escalate beyond a non-violent blockade because the stakes were not high enough to justify the risks. The potential for uncontrolled escalation was limited by the caution on both sides and by tight control of local commanders. The Soviet Union rationally probed a vulnerable Western half-commitment and hoped to gain leverage from this probe. The outcome and broader consequences for the Soviet Union were rather negative, but this was not sufficiently obvious at the time to make putting pressure on the West irrational. The West, which had got itself into this situation through the psychological bias of defensive avoidance, responded rationally by firming up its commitment and defeating the Soviet blockade tactic.

Chapter Five

THE US INVASION OF NORTH KOREA, 1950

> With China and Korea separated by one river, with 1,000 *li* [500 km] of common frontier, we can under no circumstances allow American imperialism, already proved to be China's most fierce enemy, to occupy Korea . . . and threaten the security of China.
>
> *New China News Agency*, 1 November 1950 (quoted in Friedman 1971: 240)

> we should enter the war; we must enter the war; entering the war will have great benefits; the harm inflicted by not entering the war would be great.
>
> Mao Zedong, telegram to Zhou Enlai, 13 October 1950 (quoted in Christensen 1992: 153. See also Mao's telegrams 1992: 72)

During the Sino-Japanese struggle for control of Korea in the late nineteenth century, the United States pursued a hands-off policy. In 1905 it accepted the idea that Korea could be a protectorate of Japan in the hope that Japanese imperial ambitions would be appeased, and in 1919 stood aside when the Japanese crushed a Korean nationalist uprising. Towards the end of the Second World War, the United States, Britain and China agreed that Korea should become independent after a five-year trusteeship run jointly by the Soviet Union, Great Britain, China and the United States. Upon the Japanese surrender in 1945, the United States ended up in control of the southern half of the Korean peninsula while the Soviet Union controlled the northern half. As in the case of Germany, East-West conflict over the future of the country resulted in its division at roughly the half-way point of the 38th parallel, a line that had no ethnic or geographical salience. UN-supervised elections took place in the southern half alone in June 1948, as a result of which Syngman Rhee was elected President, and the Soviet Union established the North Korean state under President Kim Il Sung.

On 25 June 1950, North Korean forces invaded South Korea and soon took the capital, Seoul, but by 30 September UN forces, led by the United States and composed mostly of US troops, had driven the North Koreans back to the 38th parallel. China tried to deter the UN forces from invading North Korea. In spite of the Chinese threats, the United States decided that China would not enter the war, and the attack went ahead. This decision is the main concern of this chapter. South Korean forces crossed the parallel on 1 October and on 7 October US forces followed when the UN General Assembly voted in favour of this attempt to reunify Korea by force. The Chinese began to mobilise, increase their assistance to North Korea, and warn the UN forces not to approach or cross the Sino-Korean border, which is demarcated by the Yalu River and, in the east, the Tumen River. On 8 October, Mao Zedong, Chairman of the Chinese Communist Party (CCP), ordered the People's Liberation Army (PLA) to enter the war on the side of North Korea, and PLA forces began to clash with those of the United Nations later that month. UN forces took the North Korean capital, Pyongyang, on 19 October and reached part of the Yalu on 26 October. In spite of limited attacks by Chinese forces across the Yalu from 27 October onwards, the UN Supreme Commander General Douglas MacArthur declared that China would not enter the war and began a broad push towards the Yalu. On 25 November China and North Korea launched a large-scale offensive which drove the UN forces back into South Korea and which almost resulted in the reunification of Korea under Communism. Seoul fell to Chinese and North Korean forces on 14–15 March 1951, and one month later General MacArthur was replaced by General Matthew Ridgway. By 20 May the UN forces were able to start driving the Communist forces back and by mid-November were holding a line slightly north of the 38th parallel.[1] They were all back more or less where they had started: the North Korean invasion of South Korea and the US invasion of North Korea had come to naught. The war became stalemated and dragged on until an armistice was signed on 27 July 1953.

The United States did not believe that crossing the 38th parallel

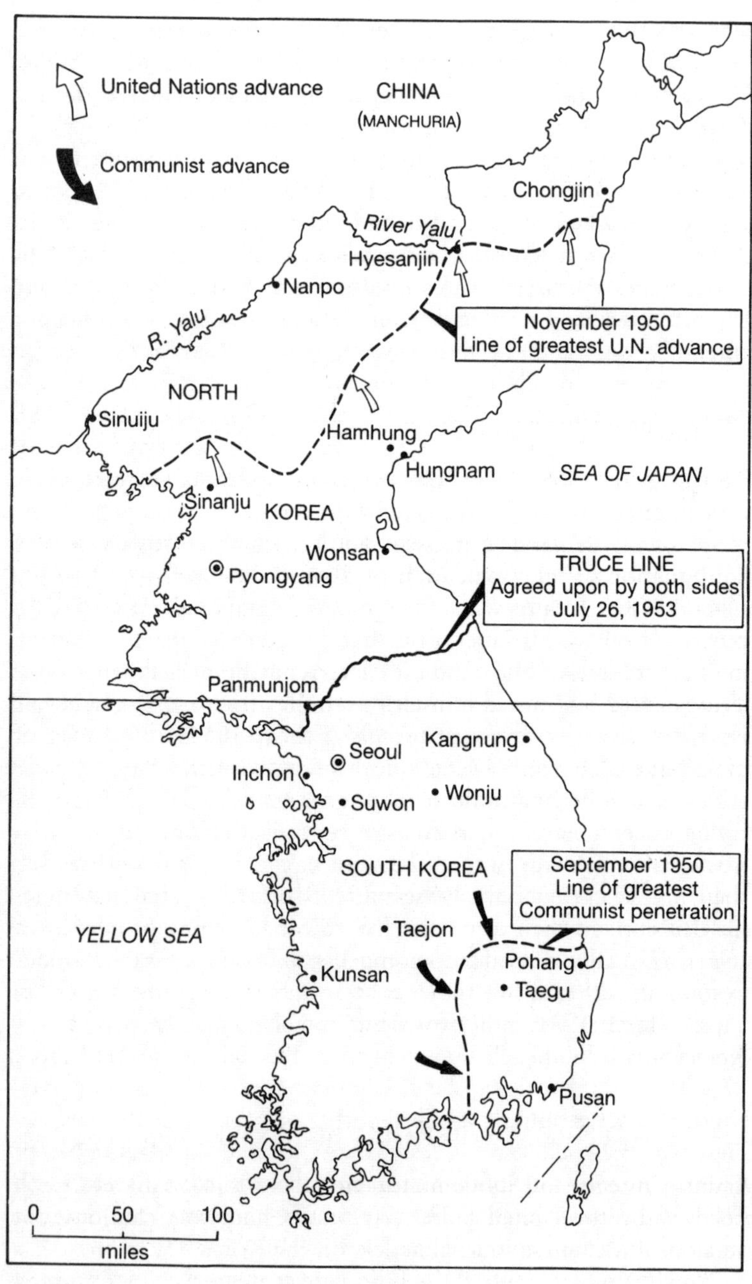

5.1 The US invasion of North Korea, 1950

would result in large-scale Chinese counter-intervention. This belief was rooted in a number of factors considered below: China's deterrence shaded into compellence; the United States dismissed China's threats as bluffs; the United States believed that, even if China was not bluffing, it would be able to win the resulting war without too much difficulty; and the United States undervalued the interests China had at stake and did not take its fears seriously. Misperception was driven by psychological biases produced by President Harry S. Truman's domestic political vulnerability and the perceived long-term costs of not eliminating the North Korean threat.

DETERRENCE SHADES INTO COMPELLENCE

This was an example of Chinese failed extended deterrence of attack, but there is still an element of overlap with compellence (in terms of the demand to 'cease doing') in that the advance was a continuation of the momentum of driving the North Koreans out of South Korea, and was a crossing of a notional rather than a physically obvious frontier. This made it easier for the US decision-makers to ignore the Chinese deterrent threats. Furthermore, Truman had committed himself to reunification before China had issued most of its deterrent threats (Lebow 1981: 150–1). Thus, after some time, while Chinese decision-makers may have believed that they were trying to deter the United States, they were actually trying to compel Truman to reverse a decision he had already made but which was in the process of being carried out. However, the Chinese started making their threats before Truman had made his decision, so the case should be classified as one of deterrence which gradually shaded into compellence. China's task was made even more difficult by the fact that the United States thought China's threats – whether for deterrent or compellent purposes – were actually bluffs.

THREATS PERCEIVED AS BLUFFS

China's threats and its commitment to North Korea were never believed by the United States. At first, China was cautious: the version of a Chinese journal article on the Korean War broadcast to North America omitted the following sentences: 'North Korea's enemy is our enemy. North Korea's defense is our defense. North Korea's victory is our victory' (quoted in Whiting 1960: 84–5). As September wore on, the Chinese threats became more explicit (Whiting 1960: 106–11; Ridgway 1967: 44). China made it clear that an invasion of North Korea would be unacceptable, and it openly increased its troop levels on the Sino-Korean border between July and September from 180,000 to 320,000 (a process reported widely in the Western press) (Whiting 1960: 106–11). Nevertheless, Truman authorised the crossing of the 38th parallel by UN forces on 27 September on the condition that 'there has been no entry into North Korea by major Soviet or Chinese Communist Forces, no announcement of intended entry, nor a threat to counter our operations militarily in Korea' (*FRUS 1950* 2: 781). However, he also added that military operations should continue if there was covert use of Soviet or Chinese forces; they should also continue if major Chinese units were used openly south of the 38th parallel as long as the prospects for military success were 'reasonable' (*FRUS 1950* 2: 781). Truman then handed judgement on these issues over to MacArthur, who was both popular and politically powerful; the only area Truman reserved control over was action against China itself (Whiting 1991: 103). Leaving these judgements in the hands of the military commander in the field was a major abdication of responsibility.

Chinese Foreign Minister Zhou Enlai stated on 30 September that China would not 'supinely tolerate seeing their neighbours being savagely invaded by imperialists'. Mao decided on 2 October to send forces to Korea, on the proviso that the Soviet Union would supply air support (China had no air force) and war materials. When Stalin would not send part of his air force, Mao decided on 13 October to press on regardless (Hao, Zhai 1990: 108–12). On 2 October, Zhou made it clear to K. M. Panikkar, Indian Ambassador to China, that China did not want war but would fight if the United States entered North Korea (Panikkar 1955: 110). Panikkar was the main intermediary between the two governments because the United States had refused to recognise Communist China and had supported the claim of the defeated Nationalists to speak for all of China. Panikkar communicated Zhou's position to US Secretary of State Dean Acheson, but Acheson's response was that Zhou's words 'were a warning, not to be disregarded, but on the other hand, not an authoritative statement of policy' (Quoted in Hao, Zhai 1990: 103n). James R. Wilkinson, the US Consul General in Hong Kong, argued in telegrams on 2 and 5 October to John Foster Dulles, then Consultant to Acheson, that the assistance promised by Zhou probably meant diplomatic and material support, and that Zhou's reference to a 'prolonged war of resistance' by the 'Korean people' implied that China would not intervene militarily (*FRUS 1950* 7: 852; see also 912–13). On 4 October at a meeting with British and US officials at the United Nations, Acheson stated his belief that the fact that China was making its threats privately through Panikkar enabled it to disavow those threats if necessary and that China was therefore bluffing (*FRUS 1950* 7: 868). As late as 14 November, Alan G. Kirk, the US Ambassador to the Soviet Union, was able to report to Acheson that '[the] Chinese Communist Government has not yet made any formal statement, to our knowledge, committing itself to [the] defense of [North] Korea' (*FRUS 1950* 7: 1154).

Perhaps the invasion of North Korea could have been deterred if Chinese forces had been stationed near the 38th parallel (Huth 1988b: 144; see also 145–7). This would have made it impossible for the United States to dismiss the Chinese threats as bluffs. Huth speculates that China may have been unable to deploy such a force due to possible logistical problems but notes that Chinese forces entered North Korea a week after the US forces entered it (1988b: 146–7). A plausible alternative explanation is that China was worried about making a commitment which would risk provoking the United States into making war on China itself. There is no record that such an option was discussed: it may not have helped anyway, due to US willingness (indicated above) to fight Chinese forces.

MILITARY OVER-CONFIDENCE

The United States had local conventional military superiority: this enabled it to occupy all of North Korea. China's short-term conventional superiority was demonstrated by the fact that, when US forces reached the Yalu River, it was able to drive them out of North Korea and take most of South Korea. China's task was eased by MacArthur's over-confidence: he put little effort into precautions against a possible counter-attack. MacArthur had reassured Truman at the Wake Island conference on 15 October that China would not intervene, and that, if it did, US air power would ensure victory (*FRUS 1950* 7: 953; see also 944). Much of the US foreign policy bureaucracy was discredited due to the successful Communist revolution in China in 1949: it was seen as partly to blame for the 'loss of China'. One of the consequences was that dissension from MacArthur's extremely optimistic line was not tolerated (Lebow 1981: 153–64, 223).

Although Stalin did not try to extend nuclear deterrence to China or North Korea, the Chinese leadership drew some comfort from Soviet development of nuclear weapons in 1949. China was aware of the threat from the nuclear forces of the United States, but showed no signs of being unduly alarmed by them (Hao, Zhai 1990: 8). According to Panikkar, General Nieh Jung-chen, acting Chief of Staff of the PLA, said to him on 25 September that China would have to do something to prevent the United States from approaching the Sino-Korean border and that:

> We know what we are in for, but at all costs American aggression has to be stopped. The Americans can bomb us, they can destroy our industries, but they cannot defeat us on land . . . They may even drop atom bombs on us. What then? They may kill a few million people. Without sacrifice a nation's independence cannot be upheld . . . China lives on farms. What can atom bombs do there? Yes, our economic development will be put back. We may have to wait for it.
>
> (Quoted in Panikkar 1955: 108)

China also believed that the value of US nuclear weapons would be limited by the small size of the US stockpile (Hao, Zhai 1990: 8). Regardless of this mixed expression of concern and confidence, no explicit or implicit nuclear threats were issued by the United States in order to prevent China's entry into the war. Later in the war, as the US forces were in headlong retreat due to the weight of the Chinese offensive, Truman casually made a vague nuclear threat on 30 November at a press conference. The threat was quickly retracted and the Chinese attacks continued (Betts 1987: 33–6; Bundy 1988: 231–2; Hayes 1991: 11–12). According to a CIA espionage source in December 1950, the Chinese were 'absolutely confident' that the United States would not go nuclear over the war in Korea, and the Soviet spy, Donald Maclean, had access to documents showing that Truman had assured British Prime Minister Clement Attlee that he would not use nuclear weapons in Korea (Betts 1987: 35–6). However, the CIA source seems too unequivocal. As indicated in the comments by General Nieh, China did not rule out entirely the possibility of escalation. Ironically, if the US nuclear monopoly over China was influential at all, it may have been influential in a way which was counter-productive to US interests. China may have been inhibited from deploying a credible conventional deterrent near the 38th parallel in part by the nuclear risk of such a move, and so the United States ended up fighting a costly war which ended in stalemate. Then again, as in the case of the Berlin blockade, this is speculation, and fear of war of any kind on Chinese territory may have been enough to prevent China from making the deployment. Fear of escalation may also have influenced the extent to which China was prepared to make clear threats to prevent UN forces invading North Korea. Domestic economic and political weakness made it doubly reluctant to commit itself outside its borders (Gurtov, Hwang 1980: 25–34).

US decision-makers believed they had an opportunity to reunite Korea. They were encouraged to see it as a good opportunity for two reasons. First, as Loy S. Henderson, the US Ambassador to India, argued in a telegram to Acheson on 4 October, failure of the United Nations to enter North Korea would result in either a costly, indefinite commitment to protect South Korea (the outcome which materialised and which exists to the present day) or a withdrawal at some point which would allow North Korea to conquer South Korea.[2] Second, Truman was very vulnerable domestically and was badly in need of a resounding victory somewhere, anywhere (Lebow 1981: 172–84, 214, 222–3; Whiting 1991: 113–14). The administration was being criticised for failing to anticipate the North Korean attack, and even for encouraging it by a weak Far Eastern policy. The reunification of Korea would be a great victory, but China would have to be prevented from intervening. Hence there was a very substantial incentive to take risks in order to exploit an opportunity, avoid long-term costs and protect Truman's personal interests.

UNDERVALUATION OF CHINESE INTERESTS AND FEARS

China was motivated primarily by a sense of threat to its strategic interests. Hans Engen, a member of the Norwegian Permanent

Delegation to the United Nations with good Soviet and US contacts, stressed Soviet fears for their territory as a consequence of the UN advance past the 38th parallel, and their fear of the domino effects in Europe and Asia of the overthrow of a Communist state by the West (*FRUS 1950* 7: 909–10). The possibility that China also felt such domino fears is considered in National Intelligence Estimate NIE–2 of 8 November.[3] Such fears were present, but the main Chinese concern was the strategic interest of defending Chinese territory. Although Kirk was sceptical, he reported to Dulles on 29 September that Panikkar believed that the Chinese had decided to intervene should the UN forces cross the 38th parallel. According to Kirk, Panikkar argued that the decision was based upon the belief that 'the basic aim of [the] US, if its forces enter North Korea, is to carry [the] war to Manchuria and China in order to return Chiang Kai-Shek [Jiang Jieshi] to power in China'.[4] Jiang was the leader of the Nationalists, who had lost the Chinese civil war and had retreated to the island stronghold of Taiwan. The strategic threat of preventive war also represented a threat to the personal interests of the Chinese leadership in maintaining their position. Mao felt there was no alternative but to fight the United States. The opponents of war in the CCP leadership argued that the United States was enormously powerful militarily and economically whereas China and its Communist government were weak. However, Mao's view was that confrontation with the United States was inevitable, the United States could invade China any time it wished on a pretext if it controlled all of Korea, and China could not afford long-term deterrence on a 1,000-mile border. In addition, he believed that the superiority of the UN forces' firepower could be undermined by Korea's mountainous terrain, China's shorter lines of communication, China's larger numbers and the poor co-ordination of UN forces (Chow 1960: 116–18; Gurtov, Hwang 1980: 29–30, 59–61; Peng 1984: 474; Hao, Zhai 1990: 104–81; Christensen 1992).

Statements of concern by China resulted in attempts to reassure it that the aims of the United Nations were limited to the reunification of Korea.[5] However, the credibility of those attempts was undermined by many of the words, actions and assumptions on the UN side. For example, Henderson argued on 6 October in another telegram to Acheson that 'hesitation or equivocation at this time in the face of threats of Commie China might tend to by Edmund O. Clubb, Director of the Office of Chinese Affairs in the State Department, of the possibility that China might have its own perspective did not rise above caricature. In a memorandum on 4 October 1950 he concluded that the United States was dealing with 'hypersensitive and already embittered, xenophobic Orientals' (*FRUS 1950* 7: 865). Ironically, on this basis, Clubb should have argued that US efforts to reassure China were not likely to succeed. The kind of virulent hostility towards China expressed even by supposed experts was commonplace in the United States at the time (Friedman, Selden 1971).

Many US officials pointed out that China did not intervene at the optimum moment in terms of the maximum vulnerability of the UN forces. For example, Kirk argued in a telegram to Dulles on 29 September 1950 that China was unlikely to intervene because the '[m]oment for armed intervention was logically when UN forces were desperately defending [the] small area [of] Taegu-Pusan, when [an] influx of overwhelming numbers [of] Chinese ground forces would have proved [the] decisive factor' (*FRUS 1950* 7: 822; see also 1155). MacArthur communicated the same view to Truman on 15 October (*FRUS 1950* 7: 953; see also 944). The US analysis gave primacy to the state of the military balance and the availability of an opportunity, when the Chinese intervention was actually determined by the balance of interests based or maximum fear of loss.

The US intelligence assessment was on firmer ground in perc the primary Chinese objective once it did enter the war. Ac to NIE-2/1 of 24 November – the day before the mai offensive – prepared by the CIA to explain the initial lim intervention which began on 27 October:

> There has been no suggestion in Chinese propag statements that the Chinese support of North Korea objective such as protecting power plants, establishing a bu on the border, or forcing the UN forces back to the 38th Paral. fact, none of these objectives has been mentioned by the Chinese. A Chinese formulations have been in terms of the necessity of bringing about a withdrawal of foreign forces from Korea.
>
> (*FRUS 1950* 7: 1221–2)

This hit the nail on the head, and it followed that such an objective could only be achieved by a massive offensive rather than the

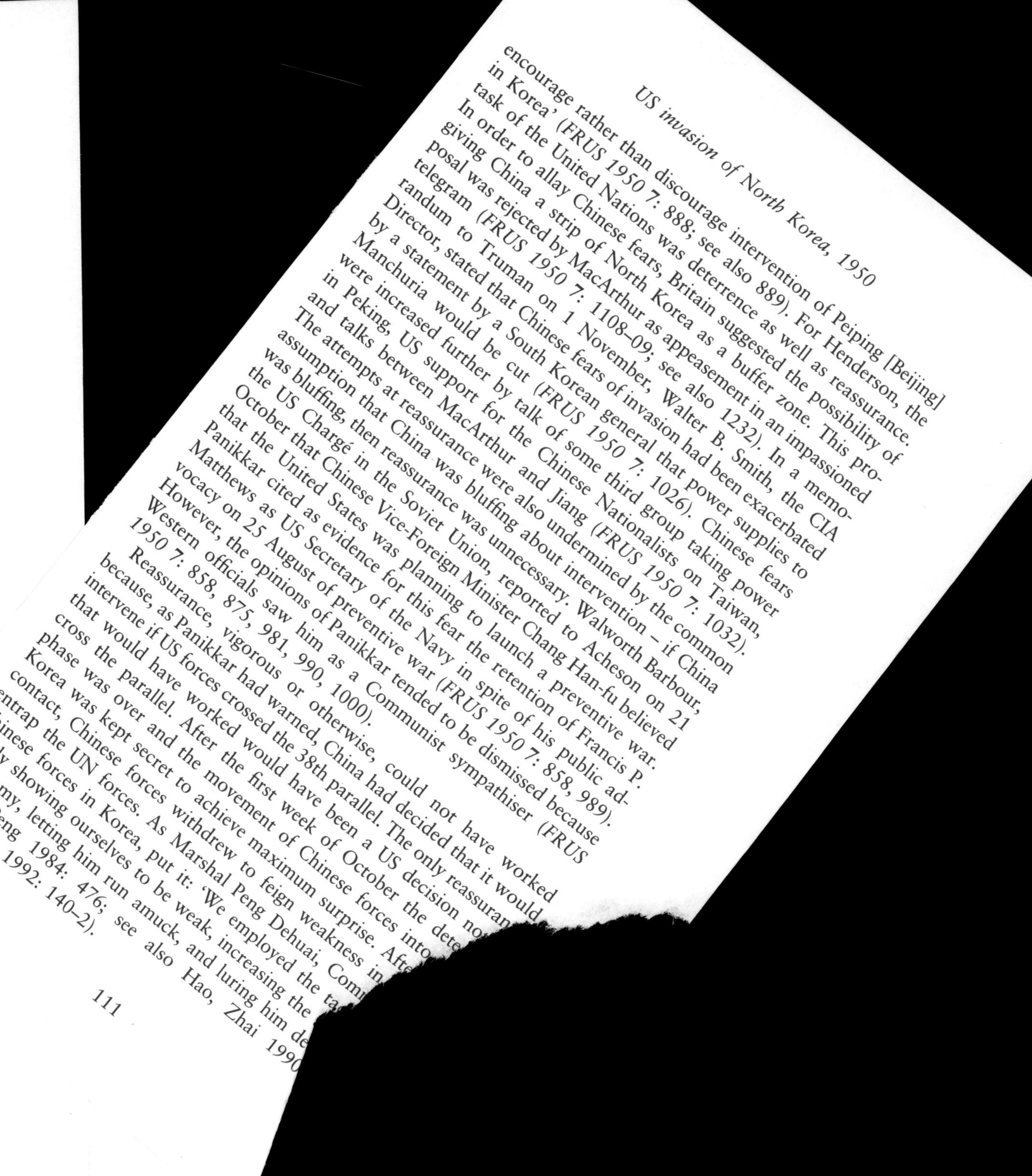

US invasion of North Korea, 1950

encourage rather than discourage intervention of Peiping [Beijing] in Korea' (*FRUS 1950* 7: 888; see also 889). For Henderson, the task of the United Nations was deterrence as well as reassurance.

In order to allay Chinese fears, Britain suggested the possibility of giving China a strip of North Korea as a buffer zone. This proposal was rejected by MacArthur as appeasement in an impassioned telegram (*FRUS 1950* 7: 1108–09; see also 1232). In a memorandum to Truman on 1 November, Walter B. Smith, the CIA Director, stated that Chinese fears of invasion had been exacerbated by a statement by a South Korean general that power supplies to Manchuria would be cut (*FRUS 1950* 7: 1026). Chinese fears were increased further by talk of some third group taking power in Peking, US support for the Chinese Nationalists on Taiwan, and talks between MacArthur and Jiang (*FRUS 1950* 7: 1032).

The attempts at reassurance were also undermined by the common assumption that China was bluffing about intervention – if China was bluffing, then reassurance was unnecessary. Walworth Barbour, the US Chargé in the Soviet Union, reported to Acheson on 21 October that Chinese Vice-Foreign Minister Chang Han-fu believed that the United States was planning to launch a preventive war. Panikkar cited as evidence for this fear the retention of Francis P. Matthews as US Secretary of the Navy in spite of his public advocacy on 25 August of preventive war (*FRUS 1950* 7: 858, 989). However, the opinions of Panikkar tended to be dismissed because Western officials saw him as a Communist sympathiser (*FRUS 1950* 7: 858, 875, 981, 990, 1000).

Reassurance, vigorous or otherwise, could not have worked because, as Panikkar had warned, China had decided that it would intervene if US forces crossed the 38th parallel. The only reassuran that would have worked would have been a US decision no cross the parallel. After the first week of October the dete phase was over and the movement of Chinese forces into Korea was kept secret to achieve maximum surprise. Afte contact, Chinese forces withdrew to feign weakness in entrap the UN forces. As Marshal Peng Dehuai, Com Chinese forces in Korea, put it: 'We employed the ta posely showing ourselves to be weak, increasing the the enemy, letting him run amuck, and luring him de areas' (Peng 1984: 476; see also Hao, Zhai 1990 Christensen 1992: 140–2).

limited operations which had taken place up to that point.[6] Then again, the Chinese formulations could be taken as an expression of a wish which could not be fulfilled, rather than an operational objective. On 28 November, Acheson argued in a telegram that, because the Chinese intervention had been prepared over a long period, 'two offensives ran into each other'. According to Acheson, 'this point removes any question that the Chi[nese] were merely reacting to the UN offensive' and 'clearly reveals an intention to attempt to destroy UN forces in NK' (*FRUS 1950* 7: 1250; see also 1069–70, 1264). Acheson's aim was to deny that the crossing of the 38th parallel by UN forces provoked the Chinese intervention; this claim was the basis of a substantial number of US Cold War historical studies (discussed in Friedman 1971: 228–31). However, the evidence shows that China would not have attacked the UN forces if they had not invaded North Korea. Once North Korea was attacked, China was determined to drive the UN forces off the Korean peninsula entirely: only in that sense did two offensives run into each other. There was some dissent – especially from Marshal Peng – about whether trying to drive the US off the peninsula entirely would be too risky, but Mao was adamant (Whiting 1991: 115–16; Christensen 1992). The Chinese decision to enter the war was tied closely to the invasion of North Korea both chronologically and in terms of the content of the verbal and military threats made.

CONCLUSION: IRRATIONAL INVASION, RATIONAL COUNTER-ATTACK

Psychological biases were central to the consistent misinterpretation by US decision-makers of the significance of the fact that China did not intervene when UN forces had been driven back to the Pusan perimeter. They pointed out that China did not intervene at the optimum state of the military balance. When China did intervene on a large scale, the two-month delay from the initial crossing of the parallel allowed US decision-makers to retain their belief that the intervention was not caused by their crossing of the 38th parallel. Acheson argued on 28 November that China was not responding to the US offensive but was waiting for the optimum time to launch its own offensive to expel UN forces from the peninsula (*FRUS 1950* 7: 1250; see also 1069–70,

1264). In other words, the initial misperception that China was motivated by the military balance rather than the balance of interests between peace and war was not corrected by the realisation that China was not bluffing about intervention. Instead, the new information was interpreted in a way which allowed the decision-makers to adhere to their initial belief.

The fact that China was engaged in extended deterrence rather than direct deterrence and to some extent was engaged in compelling the reversal of a decision already made and in halting a forward military movement already under way contributed, but only in small degree, to the outcome of the crisis. US decision-makers were greatly encouraged by their local military superiority to exploit what they saw as an opportunity. They should have placed much more weight on the Chinese ability to change that picture in the short term, but did not do so because they dismissed the possibility of Chinese intervention and because MacArthur placed excessive faith in US air power. The nuclear balance was a permissive rather than a motivating factor – that is, the absence of a Chinese nuclear capability made the advance into North Korea more acceptable to US decision-makers, but consciousness of their nuclear capability did not contribute significantly to their decision. Both sides had a great deal at stake but a rational decision-maker should have seen the crucial importance of Chinese strategic interests, which China was prepared to defend. The lack of direct contacts between Chinese and US representatives, and reliance on intermediaries, especially Panikkar whom the US regarded as suspect, did not help but probably was not central. In spite of arguments to the contrary (Orme 1987), the crossing of the 38th parallel was an irrational act. The United States ignored a Chinese deterrent threat which was clear, communicated and backed up by a sufficient military capability, because Truman was driven by the objective of silencing his domestic critics by means of a foreign policy success (Lebow 1981, 1987). This motivation was reinforced by the fact that Truman had committed himself to the reunification of Korea and had done so publicly before China had issued most of its threats. US decision-makers concentrated on their own interests and did not take sufficiently seriously Chinese fears for their interests. A gamble can be rational: the irrationality lay in Truman's belief that the military weakness of North Korea offered him a good opportunity rather than a dubious one.

NOTES

[1] Brodie (1973: 85–97, 105) argued that the United States should have driven north once again at this point to reunify Korea again because of the weakness of the Chinese and North Korean forces.

[2] *FRUS 1950* 7: 871–3. The decision of the United States to intervene to prevent the fall of South Korea in June 1950 was undoubtedly influenced by domino fears. The parallel with divided Germany was obvious, the Munich appeasement analogy was fresh and West European governments had indicated that they would measure the general resolve of the United States by its reaction to the Korean crisis (Larson 1991: 96–8). Once the Chinese began to drive the UN forces out of North Korea, domino fears were again prominent among US decision-makers (for example, *FRUS 1950* 7: 1324, 1326, 1369). Domino fears played much less of a role in the decision to invade North Korea, although Henderson argued in his 4 October telegram to Acheson that failure of the United Nations to enter North Korea would 'represent capitulation to threats of aggression' (*FRUS 1950* 7: 871–3). The threats in question were China's intervention threats.

[3] *FRUS 1950* 7: 1104–05. National Intelligence Estimates (NIEs) are authoritative interdepartmental assessments of foreign policy issues circulated at the highest levels of the US government under the auspices of the CIA, with the State Department providing some of the economic and all of the political elements. Special Estimates (SEs) (also known as Special NIEs) are the same as NIEs, except that they are prepared under more time pressure, such as during a crisis.

[4] *FRUS 1950* 7: 822. For similar statements by other US officials, see *FRUS 1950* 7: 829, 914, 915, 1152.

[5] *FRUS 1950* 7: 784, 874–5, 885, 956, 987, 1029, 1068–9, 1074, 1118, 1121, 1123, 1156, 1158, 1161, 1164–5, 1173–4, 1213–15, 1221, 1244–5.

[6] Karl L. Rankin, the US Chargé in China, argued to Acheson on 6 November 1950 that China had not entered the war in strength because it thought the North Koreans would win; delayed entry gave it more time to prepare and shorter lines of communication; fighting on or near the Chinese border gave China's actions greater domestic and international legitimacy; and the best way to counter UN successes, increase Communist prestige and maximise US losses would be to inflict a crushing military defeat (*FRUS 1950* 7: 1069–70). On 17 November, John P. Davies of the Policy Planning Staff concluded that China had delayed its entry into the war in order to undermine the UN military campaign by making the UN

action look aggressive and the Communist action defensive (*FRUS 1950* 7: 1179). China did not think the North Koreans would win, but all the other factors identified by Rankin and Davies did play a role (Hao, Zhai 1990; Christensen 1992; Paul 1994).

Chapter Six

THE TAIWAN STRAITS CRISIS, 1954–55

> [T]here were still other advantages in holding on to these islands – notably as a jumping-off point for a Nationalist invasion of the mainland. Indeed, it was precisely this threat which made the Communists so anxious to capture the islands.
>
> Summary of remarks by Admiral Arthur W. Radford, Chairman of the Joint Chiefs of Staff, at a US National Security Council meeting on 9 September 1954.
>
> (*FRUS 1952–54* **14**: 592)

Communist China and the United States were soon to confront each other again after the Korean War, this time in the Taiwan Straits. The Nationalist Chinese, who had been defeated in 1949 in the Chinese civil war, held the main island of Taiwan 120 miles from the mainland. It also held a number of groups of small islands. The ones which were to become central to the crisis of 1954–55 were the sixty square miles of the Jinmen islands, two miles from the mainland and which dominated access to the mainland port of Xiamen, and the twelve square miles of the Mazu islands to the north, ten miles out from the mainland port of Fuzhou. The Nationalists also held the Penghu islands thirty miles west of Taiwan in the Straits, and the Dachen islands (composed of Yijiangshan, Upper Dachen, Lower Dachen and a few smaller islands) just off the Chinese coast and 200 miles north of the Straits. President Truman had been prepared to let Taiwan fall as anticipated to Communist China until North Korea attacked South Korea in June 1950, at which point he sent the US Seventh Fleet to protect Taiwan as a precautionary measure. When Communist China (the People's Republic of China or PRC) entered the Korean War, Truman agreed to assist Taiwan (as the Republic of

China or ROC as it has generally become known) militarily under the terms of their Mutual Defence Assistance Agreement of February 1951.

On a number of occasions in August 1954, Chinese leaders called for the liberation of Taiwan (*FRUS 1952–54* **14**: 550, 565). On 3 September 1954, China began to shell Jinmen and to augment its military capabilities opposite Taiwan. The shelling continued for months and from November China also began aerial bombing of Dachen. On 18 January 1955 China successfully invaded Yijiangshan (George, Smoke 1974: 285). President Dwight D. Eisenhower, who succeeded Truman in January 1953, persuaded the Nationalist leader Jiang Jieshi to withdraw from vulnerable Dachen and signed with Taiwan a Mutual Defence Treaty on 2 December 1954, which they had been in the process of negotiating before the shelling began. He also sent US forces to help resist a possible invasion of the other islands and secured the passage through Congress of the Formosa Resolution on 25 January 1955, which committed the United States to the defence of Taiwan and the Penghus, including, if necessary, defence of other unspecified Nationalist-held islands (George, Smoke 1974: 285–6; Gordon 1985: 638; Chang 1988a: 102–05). In spite of the actions of the United States, the Chinese attacks and military build-up continued. In March, comments by the President and others in his administration on the possible need for the use of nuclear weapons resulted in much public opposition in the United States to his support for Taiwan. The following month, China ceased the attacks and on 20 April Chinese Foreign Minister Zhou Enlai stated that he did not want war with the United States and offered negotiations, which began in Geneva a few months later (George, Smoke 1974: 291–2; Chang 1988a: 117–18).

A further crisis occurred in the Taiwan Straits in 1958, and China and Taiwan have still not recognised each other. China has continued to state that it has not renounced force (*The Guardian*, 11 October 1991). In April 1991, the ruling Guomindang (GMD) in Taiwan declared that it recognised the existence of China's control of the mainland and proposed reunification as a liberal democracy (*Keesing's* 1991: 38146–7). It has also tried to manipulate fear of a Chinese attack in order to head off the declaration of independence sought by Taiwan's main opposition party (*The Guardian*, 29 November 1991; *The Economist*, 11 January

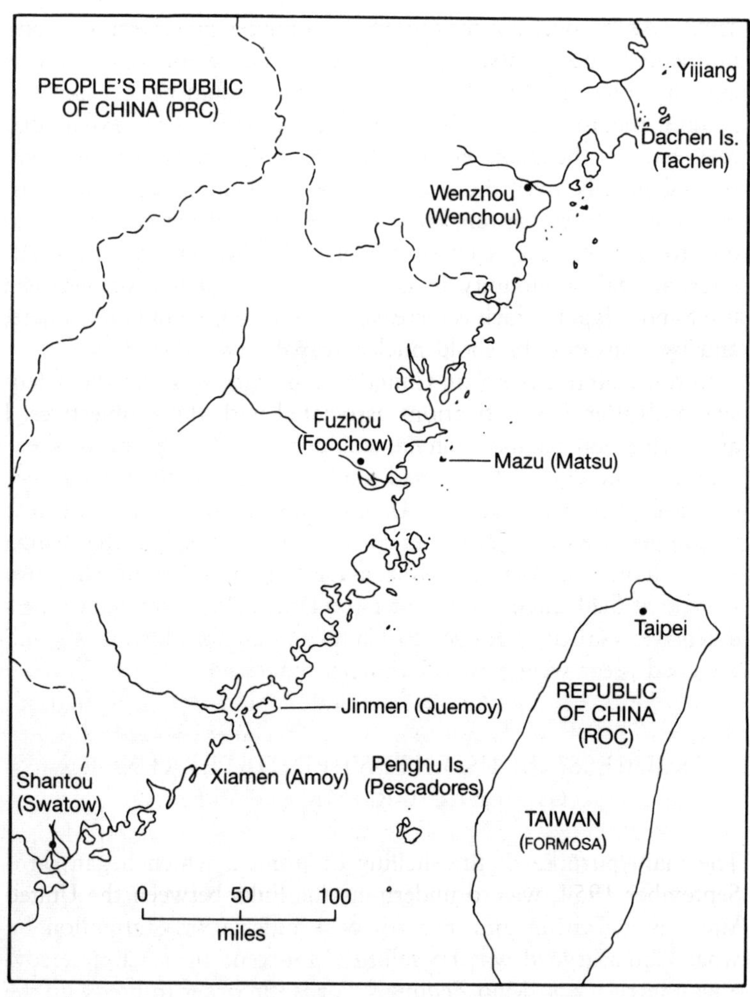

6.1 The Taiwan Straits crisis, 1954–55

1992). As US decision-makers may no longer perceive their commitments to be so interconnected due to the end of the Cold War and the collapse of the Soviet Union, they would be less likely to commit themselves to Taiwan in a future crisis to the extent that they had in the past. Furthermore, Sino-US relations have improved greatly over the years, while the United States has distanced itself from Taiwan. However, China is likely to be restrained due to the negative reaction which could be expected from the international community in general, by fear of tension between itself and a Japan which is increasingly active in the military sphere, and by Taiwan's threshold nuclear capability.

In this chapter, I explain China's main objectives and the defensive and offensive motivations associated with those objectives. I argue that, on balance, China would have invaded the offshore islands if the United States had not made its extended deterrence commitment. I show that the US commitment was heavily nuclear to compensate for weakness in conventional forces, but that China would have been deterred by a much less vigorous effort. I also show that the United States understood but underestimated China's defensive motivations, stressed China's offensive motivations and attached great weight to US strategic interests.

SUCCESSFUL US EXTENDED DETERRENCE – GENERAL OR IMMEDIATE?

The main purpose of the shelling of Jinmen, which began on 3 September 1954, was to undermine the links between the United States and Taiwan and also to focus international attention on what China argued was US military intervention in Chinese sovereign territory. In Mao Zedong's words: 'In order to break up the collaboration between the United States and Chiang Kai-shek [Jiang Jieshi], and keep them from joining together militarily and politically, we must announce to our country and to the world the slogan of liberating Taiwan' (quoted in Zhang 1993: 193). In contrast, the bombardment of Yijiangshan which began on 1 November and the invasion on 18 January were not intended to have any diplomatic effects; nor was the occupation of Dachen on 14 February after the ROC withdrawal (He 1990: 226–7).

The defensive motivation for trying to break up US-ROC links was that China believed, reasonably but mistakenly, that the United States was intending to support an ROC invasion of the mainland (Zhang 1993: 189–224). Jiang was partly concerned to retain the offshore islands as outposts against Communist Chinese attack, but mainly wanted to use them as springboards for an invasion of the mainland (Gordon 1985; Chang 1988a: 120). Although Jiang toyed with the idea of a unilateral attack on China, his main hope was a war in which the United States fought on his side against China (Gordon 1985: 641–2). The United States sought to reassure China and convince Jiang that it would not support an attack on the mainland by his forces. However, the attempts to reassure China were undermined in 1953 by Eisenhower's references to 'unleashing' Jiang, by the fact that he encouraged Jiang to increase his military presence on the offshore islands, and by Chinese knowledge of CIA operations on the mainland (George, Smoke 1974: 269–70, 275, 279). China wanted to avoid war with the United States over the islands, as it might have escalated to war on the mainland and an attempt to topple the Communist government with the help of Jiang (George, Smoke 1974: 292; Chang 1988a: 117–18).

The offensive motivation for trying to undermine US support for Taiwan is that it would have made more practical an invasion of the offshore islands in the near future and, after some time, Taiwan itself. The effectiveness of US general extended deterrence in the Taiwan Straits is not in doubt. As General Fu Tso-i, a Vice-Chairman of the Chinese National Defence Council, said to a meeting of the Chinese People's Political Consultative Conference in February 1956: 'Premier Chou [Zhou] has pointed out that the main reason why Taiwan is still not liberated is the American armed occupation of Taiwan and intervention in China's internal affairs'. He went on to say that 'We are actively preparing for the liberation of Taiwan with war if necessary, but in the meantime are still endeavoring to liberate it by peaceful means' (*New China News Agency*, 3 February 1956; see also Kalicki 1975: 128–30). China did not want to have its territory divided in the same way that Korea and Vietnam had been divided into North and South (He 1990: 224–6). In October 1958, towards the end of the next Taiwan Straits crisis, Mao decided that it would be better to leave the islands in Jiang's hands so that it would be less likely that the links between the two Chinas would be broken (He 1990:

231–41; Lebow, Stein 1990a: 354; 1990b: 38–40). In contrast, the view that China had no intention at all to invade the offshore islands and that the US deterrent threats were unnecessary is much more debatable in the 1954–55 case.

The question of whether this was successful immediate extended deterrence (or, as some might see it, a partial success, as some force was used by China) hinges on whether China intended to invade the offshore islands very soon after undermining the US commitment to Taiwan. It is very plausible that it would have done so. In 1949, an attempted Chinese invasion of Jinmen was repelled with heavy Chinese losses (Kalicki 1975: 134). Before the United States committed itself to Korea, the general expectation was that China would take not only the offshore islands but also Taiwan by force. In 1950, China had expressed that intention and was judged by the United States to have deployed the capability to be able to act upon it (Whiting 1960: 21–2: Huth, Russett 1990: 487). The planned invasion of 1950 seems to have been discouraged by the diversion of Chinese attention to the war in Korea and by the US deterrent commitment (Huebner 1987). Mao approved a plan in late 1952 to seize all of the offshore islands, but suspended it when the Korean armistice was signed in 1953. In January 1954, the Chinese leadership approved a plan to take the Dachen islands. In June, the United States and ROC responded strongly to China's military build-up with one of their own. Mao was absolutely determined to avoid combat with US forces, but ordered the shelling of the Dachens, which began in early July, and continued preparations to invade Yijiangshan and Dachen (Zhang 1993: 195–9). China shelled Jinmen in September to undermine the US-Taiwan link, test US intentions and distract attention from Yijiangshan, which was to be the first target. The 18 January 1955 invasion met no US opposition, and so attention turned to Dachen. Although China had bombed Dachen on 10 January, due to the presence of US forces it did not invade as the Taiwanese troops withdrew. Lebow and Stein go too far in summarising the work of He Di, who has also had access to important Chinese sources, in the following manner: 'He Di . . . argues that in 1954 the PRC had *no* plans for invading either Quemoy [Jinmen] or Matsu [Mazu]' (1990b: 40n; emphasis added). Actually, He argues that 'The August 1954 battle plan evidently did not not call for an *early* attack on either Jinmen or Mazu' (He 1990: 224;

emphasis added). China did intend to attack both if US support for Taiwan was undermined after taking Yijiangshan and Dachen. The Chinese approach was to move, in a phrase used at the time, 'from small to large, one island at a time, from north to south, and from weak to strong' (quoted in He 1990: 223). Similarly, Shu Guang Zhang, who has studied PRC sources extensively (1993: 224), states that 'there was no indication that the Chinese leaders were planning to attack Jinmen or Mazu through the end of 1954. The Zhedong Front Command concentrated on seizing Dachen' (1993: 216). This is fully compatible with his judgement, based on those PRC sources, that, after the occupation of Dachen on 14 February, China decided not to invade the other islands, including Jinmen and Mazu, due to 'the immediate and conceivable danger of US military action' (1993: 220; see also 224). Overall, this is a probable case of immediate extended deterrence. Far from undermining links between the United States and Taiwan, the crisis resulted in a strengthening of those links, symbolised by vigorous US threats; on the other hand, Yijiangshan was lost, Dachen island abandoned and Jinmen bombarded.

NUCLEAR THREATS TO COMPENSATE FOR CONVENTIONAL WEAKNESS

Although Eisenhower intended to use force if necessary to defend the offshore islands, he felt unable to make a categorical public commitment because he thought it might be opposed domestically and by his allies, and because he did not want to give Jiang an incentive to provoke war (*FRUS 1955–57* **2**: 238–40, 243–7, 270–2, 307–09, 418–22, 445–6; Huth 1988b: 108–09). In September 1954, Eisenhower, Secretary of State John Foster Dulles, Chairman of the Joint Chiefs of Staff Arthur W. Radford, Chief of Naval Operations Admiral Robert Carney and Far East Commander-in-Chief General John E. Hull were of the view that the offshore islands could not be held without the use of nuclear weapons (*FRUS 1952–54* **14**: 604, 610, 611; *FRUS 1955–57* **2**: 336–7, 347, 349, 370, 390, 400, 410, 459; Betts 1987: 55; Bundy 1988: 277). The key passage is in NSC 5501 of 6 January 1955 on Basic National Security Policy:

> As the fear of nuclear war grows, the United States and its allies must never allow themselves to get into the position where they must choose between (a) not responding to local aggression and (b) applying force in a way which our own people or our allies would consider entails undue risk of nuclear devastation. However, the United States cannot afford to preclude itself from using nuclear weapons, even in a local situation, if such use will bring the aggression to a swift and positive cessation, and if, on a balance of political and military considerations, such use will best advance U.S. security interests. In the last analysis, if confronted by the choice of (a) acquiescing in Communist aggression or (b) taking measures risking either general war or loss of allied support, the United States must be prepared to take those risks if necessary for its security.
>
> (*FRUS 1955–57* **2**: 356)

The last point makes little sense: defence of islands such as Jinmen and Mazu was predicated on fears for allied morale, whereas this policy statement implies a willingness to risk losing allied support in order to defend them. The policy statement says that this may be necessary for US security, but it does not explain the connection. General Matthew Ridgway, then US Army Chief of Staff, argued that an attack on the mainland would be necessary to interdict assault forces. He believed that this would provoke general war with China, including the use of nuclear weapons, and he argued that this would be seen in the eyes of the world as US aggression (*FRUS 1952–54* **14**: 608). However, he believed the islands could be defended without nuclear weapons if more conventional forces were deployed (*FRUS 1955–57* **2**: 408; see also 400). The United States increased its conventional (and nuclear) capabilities in the region in January and February 1955 (*FRUS 1955–57* **2**: 102, 250, 268; George, Smoke 1974: 288; Huth 1988b: 109). Nevertheless, Dulles said on 10 March that nuclear weapons would still be required for the defence of the offshore islands, although he feared the likely effects on public opinion (*FRUS 1952–54* **14**: 650; Betts 1987: 57; Chang 1988a: 106).

The peak of US concern came in mid-March, when US decision-makers became concerned that China might attack before Taiwan had maximised its defensive capabilities on the offshore islands (Eisenhower 1963: 477; George, Smoke 1974: 290). Admiral Carney predicted that China would attack the offshore islands by

15 April (George, Smoke 1974: 291; Chang 1988a: 112). On 15 March, Eisenhower was told of the opinion of Admiral Felix Stump, Commander-in-Chief Pacific (CINCPAC), that the combined Taiwanese and US conventional forces could defend the islands as long as China did not deploy large amounts of its airpower. Stump indicated that he thought that the United States would be forced to use nuclear weapons to avoid defeat if China did enhance its local air capabilities. He thought that after about 25 March, it would take an all-out amphibious, artillery and air attack to defeat the Nationalists alone, and that such an attack would not occur in less than four weeks against Mazu and less than eight against Jinmen. He believed that in the intervening ten days, as defences were being built up, a Chinese amphibious attack using tactical surprise might succeed (*FRUS 1955–57* **2**: 366–7; Eisenhower 1963: 477; Kalicki 1975: 150; Betts 1987: 58). However, as late as 25 April 1955, Jiang was told that Radford could not guarantee the defence of the offshore islands without nuclear weapons, and Radford claimed that the use of nuclear weapons would 'undoubtedly' be necessary (*FRUS 1955–57* **2**: 512–13).

As shelling and military preparations by China continued, Dulles on 8 March and Eisenhower on 16 March indicated at press conferences that tactical nuclear weapons would be used if necessary against China (*FRUS 1955–57* **2**: 336–67; Betts 1987: 59; Chang 1988a: 106; Huth 1988b: 111). Eisenhower also had a series of tactical nuclear weapon tests announced publicly (Betts 1987: 59). Eisenhower claimed that he was serious about using nuclear weapons if necessary (Betts 1987: 58–9). However, he saw this as a rather unlikely circumstance (Bundy 1988: 278–9), and Dulles tried to reassure the British government on this point (*FRUS 1955–57*, **2**: 88–9). The US nuclear threats represented what Bundy calls 'stop-gap' deterrence for ten more days from the reporting of Stump's views to Eisenhower. By 25 March the Nationalists had completed their fortifications of the offshore islands, which made the islands safe from all but a very large attack (Kalicki 1975: 149–51; Bundy 1988: 277), and the United States had demonstrated its commitment to the offshore islands through the active role of US air and naval forces in the vicinity. The possibility of being forced back onto the nuclear option encouraged Eisenhower to move cautiously and avoid using conventional force (Bundy 1988: 284–7).

At the time that China chose to de-escalate, the local military balance favoured the United States and Taiwan because of US naval and aerial superiority, which would have been able to foil an amphibious Chinese attack (Huth 1988b: 112–13), although China was capable of taking the offshore islands by force if it was faced only by ROC forces without US backing (*FRUS 1952–54* **14**: 356, 413, 416; Kalicki 1975: 132–3, 135). In contrast, the short-term military balance was probably favourable to China. The view of General Ridgway on 14 September 1954 was that China had enough junks and small craft to move 50,000 troops with artillery plus some follow-on forces at short notice, and enough aircraft to establish local air superiority without warning (*FRUS 1952–54* **14**: 606–08).

China showed itself to be aware of and worried about the nuclear danger it faced (Zhang 1993: 213–16, 220–2, 224). In January 1955, the Chinese authorities began to explain to the population the danger of US nuclear attack (Hsieh 1962: 32–3; Chang 1988a: 108). China responded to the US nuclear threats by condemning what they saw as Eisenhower's view that nuclear weapons could be used 'without massacring civilians' (quoted in Betts 1987: 59). Huth believes that the US nuclear threats during this crisis 'may have had a deterrent impact' and 'may have been perceived as credible by PRC policymakers'. Fairly clear threats had been made, aircraft capable of executing tactical nuclear attacks had been deployed to Taiwan, tactical nuclear attacks would have been effective in preventing China from invading the offshore islands, China had no nuclear weapons of its own, the Soviet Union had not issued extended nuclear deterrence threats to cover China, and the situation fitted US declaratory policy that massive retaliation could be expected when the United States lacked adequate conventional options (Huth 1988b: 113–14). Zhang puts it even more strongly: 'The Chinese forces would have tried to take Jinmen, Mazu, and the other offshore islands if Beijing leaders had not been concerned about the nuclear threat' (1993: 224).

The United States tried to highlight the differences between China and the Soviet Union in order to split them. Gordon Chang is quite dismissive of the importance of the Soviet Union in US calculations (Chang 1988a: 108–10, 117–18). However, if it came to a general war with China, the United States expected to have to fight the Soviet Union as well (*FRUS 1955–57* **2**: 275–6;

Eisenhower 1963: 464; Brands, Jr. 1988: 128–9, 136–7, 139–41, 143; Zhang 1993: 216–18). Eisenhower even said at an NSC meeting that he would *prefer* to have general war with the Soviet Union as well because otherwise the Soviet Union could help China without having to fight the United States. In those circumstances, he said, he would 'want to go to the head of the snake' (*FRUS 1952–54* **14**: 617; see also 621). Although Dulles tried to get the Soviet Union to restrain China (*FRUS 1952–54* **14**: 366), Eisenhower stated on 27 January 1955 that he was certain the Soviet Union was trying to drag the United States into a general war with China (*FRUS 1955–57* **2**: 137).

PERCEPTIONS OF INTERESTS

During the Taiwan Straits crisis of 1954–55, the United States correctly understood the political costs to China of not achieving its offensive goals with regard to territory. To a lesser extent it understood but did not take seriously Chinese defensive motivations, especially with regard to possible US support for an invasion of the mainland. The Special National Intelligence Estimate (SNIE) of 4 September 1954 estimated China's motivations in terms of sovereignty, honour, the recapture of integral parts of China, the need to consolidate control of all of China, the need to free its coastal shipping lanes, the need to recapture the offshore islands before the United States formally guaranteed their security, and the need to break up the alliance between the United States and Taiwan (*FRUS 1952–54* **14**: 566–8; see also 291). According to another US intelligence report, a PRC failure to recapture the offshore islands 'would have important political and psychological effects in the Far East, particularly because it would constitute "loss of face"', and added that 'the US, through its guarantee, would have made face in the Orient' (*FRUS 1952–54* **14**: 571). From this perspective, a failure by China to make a gain would result in a loss rather than a neutral outcome, and the avoidance of a loss by the United States would constitute a US gain. As a result, the advantage of the United States in defending the territorial status quo will have been at least partly undermined. On 12 September 1954, Harold E. Stassen, Director of Foreign Operations, implied at an NSC meeting that the clear perceptibility of the status quo would help the United States: 'the whole world knows that we have been on those islands' (*FRUS 1952–54* **14**: 619). The problem is that the key US decision-makers were not at all keen on getting the territorial status quo legitimised through the UN because, while it might have restrained China, it would have required that the United States – which had not recognised the Communist Chinese government – accept Communist Chinese control of the mainland (*FRUS 1952–54* **14**: 612).

The offshore islands were perceived by the United States to be of little intrinsic value to either the United States or Taiwan. Their strategic value was both concrete and abstract. Their concrete strategic value was linked to the fact that, according to the Joint Chiefs of Staff, they were militarily useful but not vital for the defence of the main island of Taiwan (*FRUS 1952–54* **14**: 240), and they were seen as crucial to any hopes that the Nationalists would be able to invade the mainland. The United States was more concerned with abstract strategic interests in terms of possible domino effects in Taiwan and elsewhere (*FRUS 1952–54* **14**: 348, 514, 533, 535, 556–7, 569–71, 599–600, 618, 619). The commitment to the offshore islands was intended to demonstrate US resolve. As SAC Commander General Thomas Power put it: 'If we were willing to stand up and risk war for some so-called useless rocks, what better proof could we give of our determination to stand up to a more serious incident' (quoted in Futrell 1980: 306). There were many statements by US decision-makers regarding the political and psychological importance of the offshore islands to Taiwan (*FRUS 1952–54* **14**: 234, 244, 616, 622). At one point Dulles said that he did not think that the loss of the offshore islands would seriously damage the Nationalist government or Nationalist military morale in the long run (*FRUS 1952–54* **14**: 591), but this was very much the exception.

There were some US expectations of balancing in Asia in response to Chinese gains, should they occur. According to an NSC Staff Study presented to the NSC on 6 November 1953: 'Throughout most of the area there is fear of Chinese expansionism which, provided Western support continues, can be expected to produce increased efforts against Communism rather than ostrich-like immobility' (*FRUS 1952–54* **14**: 299). In addition, the detailed assessment of the prospects until mid-1955 in the NIE of 10 February 1954 concluded that China probably believed that the

United States would respond to the use of force anywhere in Asia with attacks up to and including nuclear weapons, and that the United States would not launch an unprovoked attack. Nevertheless, the report did conclude that many opportunities remained for subversion of Asian countries, to which the US would find it difficult to respond (*FRUS 1952–54* **14**: 395). Overall, the main US tendency was to make domino assumptions.

The US attempt to extend deterrence to cover the offshore islands was made more difficult by its own provocative behaviour, and that of Taiwan. China not only felt threatened by Taiwan but was actually suffering losses in terms of guerrilla attacks, propaganda and intelligence activities, restrictions on the use of its coastline, and symbolic damage (George, Smoke 1974: 276–9). John M. Allison, the US Ambassador to Japan, was aware of at least one aspect of US provocation. On 16 August 1954 he argued in a telegram to the State Department that manoeuvres planned for the Seventh Fleet in the vicinity of the offshore islands were misconceived: 'If our purpose is, through [a] show of strength, to deter Communist attack on Formosa I think it will fail. This will be looked upon as mere aggravation and might well inspire counteraction we hope to avoid in [the] off-shore islands' (*FRUS 1952–54* **14**: 523). Dulles, in his response of 20 August, dealt with a number of issues but simply ignored this central point (*FRUS 1952–54* **14**: 545–7). A lengthy NSC Staff Study presented to the NSC on 6 November 1953 stated that:

> Peiping's foreign policies . . . are not motivated purely by an aggressive urge. The psychology of fear plays an important role. Peiping suffers from traditional Chinese suspicion and fear of the outside world and is keenly conscious of the ideological hostility of the West. The difficulties inherent in the defense of its extensive frontiers have therefore made Peiping doubly sensitive to the development of potentially hostile military powers or coalitions in the Far east, particularly based in Japan.
>
> (*FRUS 1952–54*, **14**: 291)

Chinese perceptions of a threat emanating from Taiwan were justified. This is indicated by the statement by Admiral Radford at an NSC meeting on 9 September 1954 that the offshore islands were worth defending as a springboard for a Nationalist invasion of the mainland. He even stated explicitly that this was the main reason China wanted to capture the islands (*FRUS 1952–54* **14**: 592; see also 482–3, 612).

Although the United States was acting provocatively, Eisenhower said on 22 May 1954 at an NSC meeting that he did not want a public US commitment to holding any of the offshore islands because it would be 'too big a commitment of US prestige and forces' (*FRUS 1952–54* **14**: 428). He was also aware that its allies such as Britain would be disquieted and not reassured by such a commitment, due to their fear of a wider war, and he did not want to give Jiang a means of provoking general war (Huth 1988b: 108–09). In effect, the United States was committed to fighting for the offshore islands but did not make its commitment as clear as it might for reasons of alliance management. Taiwanese Foreign Minister George K. C. Yeh drew a parallel with the way in which China committed itself to the defence of North Korea but did not deploy troops at the 38th parallel (*FRUS 1952–54* **14**: 550). The supposed danger of the widespread uncertainty about the US position was stressed by the Indonesian Ambassador to the United States (Chang 1988a: 121; *FRUS 1955–57* **2**: 121). In fact, China was fully persuaded that the United States' commitment was credible.

The United States considered blockading China as a way of preventing its military build-up. The Special Estimate (SE-27) of 5 June 1952 concluded that a blockade would be risky and escalatory (*FRUS 1952–54* **14**: 59–62). On 4 February 1953, Admiral Radford indicated that he did not want hasty action taken and stated his concern about the vulnerability of Hong Kong to retaliation (*FRUS 1952–54* **14**: 142–3). Nevertheless, detailed planning was undertaken by the United States and Taiwan (*FRUS 1952–54* **14**: 144–5, 148–56, 160–2, 218–19). SE-37 of 9 March 1953 predicted Soviet and Chinese Communist military action against a blockade, but did not expect the Soviet Union to begin general war (*FRUS 1952–54* **14**: 149). The most dangerous development in the consideration of the blockade tactic came in April 1955. At that time Eisenhower offered to blockade the 500-mile stretch of the coastline of China along the Taiwan Strait in order to coerce China into renouncing the liberation of Taiwan if Jiang would withdraw from Jinmen and Mazu. Jiang turned down the secret offer (Chang 1988a: 98, 114–16, 121; *FRUS 1955–57* **2**: 504, 510–17). If the blockade had been implemented, the potential for escalation – and for dissension domestically and among the allies of the United States – was substantial, because the United States would have been acting against Chinese shipping in Chinese territorial waters. The United States also considered various combinations of blockade and bombardment (*FRUS 1952–54* **14**: 148–56), but in the end was careful not to use force against the mainland. China did use force in its shelling and invasion of minor islands, but these acts were clearly distinguishable from the initiation of war.

The proposal at the United Nations to neutralise the offshore islands (*FRUS 1952–54* **14**: 693) might have been seen as a reasonable compromise to get out of a dangerous situation, especially as US leaders knew that Taiwan and the Penghus were different in that they had been Japanese-held rather than Chinese-held in the past. However, there were a number of problems. First, compromising on the status quo during a crisis is something leaders do not like to do, mainly for fear of the effect on their bargaining reputation. Second, US and Taiwanese decision-makers were concerned that the springboard for a return to the mainland would have been lost. Third, China might take the islands by force after neutralisation. Dulles believed that the proposal would be opposed by China and Taiwan, and that it would be vetoed by the Soviet Union. His preferred approach was for Taiwan to keep quiet while the United States made positive noises so that China would look bad when it refused to co-operate (*FRUS 1952–54* **14**: 693–6). Needless to say, the neutralisation proposal came to nothing.

CONCLUSION: CHINESE PRESSURE BACKFIRES BADLY

In this crisis, China's objective was to undermine US-Taiwanese links. The defensive motivation was to forestall a possible US-Taiwanese invasion of the mainland in the not too distant future. It overestimated US willingness to support such an invasion: this miscalculation was encouraged by the fact that some in the United States were inclined towards it, even if it was not US policy. The United States' efforts to reassure China on this point were undermined by its own ambivalence; indeed, the United States was not keen on having the status quo ratified through the United Nations mainly because it still entertained vague hopes of supporting a

Nationalist return to the mainland. The offensive PRC motivation was to open the way for the capture of the offshore islands as part of its preparations to capture Taiwan. China chose to probe and if possible undermine the US commitment to the defence of the offshore islands. If the United States had not responded, it is hard to believe that China would not have invaded the islands. It had the capability, the declared intention and the past record of invading other Nationalist-held islands. China's behaviour was rational on the question of there being a reasonable chance of success – as measured, for example, by a US willingness to encourage the Nationalists to withdraw from other vulnerable islands. However, their surprise at the vigour of the US deterrent and especially nuclear threats shows that they were not as in control of the situation as they thought.

The United States was correct in thinking that deterrence was required but overestimated how much deterrence would be necessary. China was determined to avoid any combat with US forces and sought to proceed extremely cautiously. A limited, symbolic US commitment to the offshore islands would have been sufficient to deter China. The shock of the seriousness and extent of the US nuclear threat reinforced China's desire not to go to war with the United States but appears to have been deterrent overkill. The United States inaccurately believed that the vagueness of its deterrent commitment might tempt China to attack. The US commitment to defending the offshore islands was not explicit, in order to keep Jiang under control and to reassure its West European allies. It chose to commit itself explicitly to the defence of Taiwan and the Penghus, and left vague its position on the other islands. US decision-makers were generally of the view that they could not press the Nationalists to withdraw from the offshore islands because it would have had a disastrous effect on their morale. However, the fact that they offered to blockade the Chinese coastline in return for a withdrawal suggests that they thought the blockade would maintain their morale. The Nationalists turned down the offer, probably because they thought their presence on the offshore islands was more likely to bring about the Sino-US war they wanted. Indeed, perhaps the most remarkable aspect of the crisis is the fact that US decision-makers were willing to use nuclear weapons and risk general war over the offshore islands rather than concede them along with Yijiangshan and Dachen.

Chapter Seven

THE BERLIN CRISIS, 1958–62

> Khrushchev is losing East Germany. He cannot let that happen. If East Germany goes, so will Poland and all of Eastern Europe. He will have to do something to stop the flow of refugees. Perhaps a wall. And we won't be able to prevent it. I can hold the Alliance together to defend West Berlin, but I cannot act to keep East Berlin open.
>
> President John F. Kennedy, comments to adviser Walt Rostow, August 1961.
>
> (Quoted in Beschloss 1991: 265)

In the wake of the Berlin blockade of 1948–49, the Western zones of Germany had become the Federal Republic of Germany (FRG or West Germany) and the Soviet zone had become the German Democratic Republic (GDR or East Germany), but there was no peace treaty and Berlin still had military occupation status. In 1955, West Germany joined the North Atlantic Treaty Organisation (NATO) and the Soviet Union established the Warsaw Treaty Organisation (WTO or Warsaw Pact). On 27 November 1958, Khrushchev argued in a diplomatic note that the United States, Britain and France justified their presence in Berlin on the basis of the wartime Potsdam agreements. In his view, they had broken the Potsdam agreements by, among other things, setting up a separate West German state, and had therefore lost their right to be in Berlin. On these grounds, he did not feel bound by the provisions of Potsdam. He objected to the rearming of Germany and the use of Berlin for 'intensive espionage, sabotage, and other subversive activities'. Khrushchev demanded that 'the three Western Powers return to a policy in German affairs that would be pursued jointly with the USSR and in conformity with the spirit and principles of the Potsdam Agreement'.[1] He explained that this would mean the simultaneous withdrawal of the two Germanies from their respective alliances, limits on their armed forces, and a peace treaty involving recognition of East Germany by all parties. He proposed that Berlin become a demilitarised free city – that is, one not controlled by any state, but one with full control over its own political, economic and social system, so that it could be based on capitalism if its occupants so desired. He argued that this solution would be a concession by East Germany, and stated that, if the Berlin question was not resolved within six months, he would sign a separate peace treaty with East Germany, hand the administration of all of Berlin over to the East German authorities, and assert as final the existing borders.[2] The Western (including West German) response was essentially that the Soviet Union had no legal basis upon which to end the rights of access to Berlin by the Western powers; that 93.1 per cent of West Berliners participated in free elections on 7 December 1958, 98.1 per cent of whom voted for political parties which preferred the status of the city based on occupation law over any other arrangement in the context of a divided Germany; and that the free city solution was unacceptable because it did not guarantee the democratic rights of the two million people of West Berlin. Western reluctance to sign a peace treaty was based upon their refusal to accept the legitimacy of the East German state. In particular, West Germany claimed the right to be the sole representative of all the German people.[3]

After talks with the West, Khrushchev withdrew his ultimatum but renewed it on 10 June 1959 at the Geneva conference of foreign ministers through his Foreign Minister Andrei Gromyko, who stated that the Western powers could exercise their occupation rights for one more year.[4] Khrushchev once again withdrew the ultimatum on 27 September at the Camp David summit with Eisenhower. Other than forcing the West to more discussions on the future of Berlin and Germany as a whole than it desired, no other significant Soviet objectives were achieved. Khrushchev did not carry out his threats, and waited to see how Eisenhower's successor, John F. Kennedy, would respond to pressure after he took office in January 1961. The episode with Eisenhower is often seen as a separate crisis, but it can also be regarded as the first round in an extended crisis.

At the Vienna summit with Kennedy in June 1961, Khrushchev

restated the demands and threats made to Eisenhower. In particular, he demanded an immediate peace treaty and agreement on internal German questions between the two German governments within six months. US-Soviet talks took place intermittently to a background of military confrontation and Soviet harassment of ground, water and air access to Berlin. The United States reacted in a limited fashion when work began on the Berlin Wall on 13 August to make total the travel restrictions which had begun to be imposed from October 1960 in order to stop the flood of refugees from East Germany to the West through West Berlin. On 17 October Khrushchev announced that he did not require a peace treaty to be signed by the end of 1961. Although he denied that there had ever been a deadline, this was the lifting of the deadline. The military confrontation peaked with a tank confrontation at one of the Wall's crossing points known as Checkpoint Charlie. On 22 October, four US tanks escorted a US diplomat into East Berlin so that he did not have to comply with the new demand that he show his passport (which would have implied recognition of the legal authority of East Germany). On 25 October, General Lucius D. Clay, Kennedy's special representative in Berlin, moved ten tanks near the Wall at Checkpoint Charlie. Khrushchev responded by deploying ten tanks directly opposite them and contacted Kennedy secretly. They agreed that the Soviet Union would withdraw its tanks and that the United States would do the same immediately afterwards. The withdrawals occurred on 28 October. Khrushchev believed incorrectly that the West was about to knock down the Wall: he knew (although Kennedy did not) that Clay had secretly ordered combat engineers to practice knocking down a mock-up of the Wall (Garthoff 1991). Soviet pressure continued into 1962 until the Cuban missile crisis, as Khrushchev fished for concessions in the wake of the otherwise moderate reaction in the West to the Berlin Wall (Adomeit 1982: 302–07; Beschloss 1991: 294–5, 399–400). Through the *détente* process of the 1970s, the West, including West Germany, did recognise the East German state, but this took place through inducements rather than threats. West Berlin continued in its occupied status until the collapse of Communism in East Germany in December 1989, the tearing down of the Berlin Wall and the reunification of Germany as a democratic, capitalist state.

In this chapter, I classify the case as one of failed Soviet compellence, examine the use of military threats by both sides to create risk and demonstrate resolve, argue that the balance of interests favoured the East over East Germany and the West over West Berlin, and propose that the outcome of this crisis is best understood in conjunction with an analysis of the outcome of the Cuban missile crisis.

SOVIET COMPELLENCE: ON BALANCE, A FAILURE

If the main Soviet objective in this crisis is seen as an attempt to force the abandonment of West Berlin, then this is a clear case of failed Soviet compellence. However, the main Soviet objective was a resolution of the German question, and the pressure on West Berlin – combined with a belief that the correlation of forces had shifted in favour of the socialist states – was a lever to achieve it. The Soviet Union wanted *de jure* recognition of East Germany, the abandonment of Western hopes of German reunification, acceptance of existing borders and a guarantee that West Germany would not be allowed to acquire nuclear weapons. NATO was talking about sharing nuclear weapons with a rearmed Germany, and there was the possibility that co-operation could break down and West Germany could end up with an independent nuclear capability (Trachtenberg 1991: 180–91). East Germany was politically and economically unstable at the time. In the early 1950s US policy-makers did not believe that Europe could be stable if Germany was divided, and so they sought reunification (Trachtenberg 1991: 173–80). Especially bearing in mind the uprising in East Germany in June 1953, the Soviet Union and the East German government wanted reassurance that, in an escalating East German crisis, a nationalist West German government would not intervene and drag the West in with it (Trachtenberg 1991: 179–80).

On balance, Soviet compellence failed. The West did not recognise East Germany formally, did not rule out the possibility of West German access to nuclear weapons and, on the secondary objective, did not withdraw from West Berlin. The failure to achieve these objectives, and the failure to show the world that the much-vaunted shift in the correlation of forces in favour of socialism would produce Western concessions, damaged Khrushchev's political standing (Beschloss 1991: 294–5, 351–2). Nevertheless, the fact that the Western powers also effectively ceased to assert their rights to a say in the future of East Germany was treated by Khrushchev as a success (Adomeit 1982: 300–02). Indeed, it represented *de facto* recognition. In addition, Khrushchev was able to stabilise East Germany by physically preventing its citizens from leaving. The crisis helped reconcile US decision-makers to the division of Germany. By the late 1950s they were becoming more willing to accept the status quo, even if they were not wholly reconciled to it, as their main priority became keeping West Germany as part of the Western alliance: this view became firmer under Kennedy (Trachtenberg 1991: 173–80, 226–31). As indicated by Kennedy's comments quoted at the beginning of this chapter, there was some understanding of the primarily defensive Soviet motivations (see also Trachtenberg 1991: 172–3, 232).

MILITARY THREATS, RISK AND RESOLVE

Khrushchev engaged in a campaign of threats and what became known as 'rocket rattling'. In stunning blows to US belief in its technological superiority and its military security, the Soviet Union launched an ICBM in August 1957, put the satellite Sputnik in orbit in October 1957 and claimed to be mass-producing ICBMs (Horelick, Rush 1966). During the 1958–59 phase of the crisis, Eisenhower pressed on with most of his planned reduction of 30,000 in US army personnel. He justified this by arguing that the Soviet Union was bluffing, that Soviet conventional superiority was too great to be overcome, and that if war did occur it would be an all-out nuclear war in which his planned build-up of intercontinental nuclear forces would compensate for conventional weakness (Betts, 1987: 85–9; Bundy 1988: 370–4). While not being too blunt in order to avoid causing alarm in the United States and Western Europe, he did indicate that any Soviet attempt to use force with regard to Berlin would result in unrestrained nuclear war (Betts 1987: 89–91). For the same reason – that escalation would be rapid and total – Khrushchev stressed that the West would have to be mad to use force over the Berlin question, but that the Soviet Union was prepared to go nuclear should war come (Heidelmeyer, Hindrichs 1963: 195; Betts 1987: 84, 90–1;

Wohlforth 1993: 158). In May 1960, the commander of the Soviet air force returned Soviet long-range strategic aircraft (which normally flew without nuclear weapons on board) to their bases in case he was ordered to load them with nuclear weapons in response to the US world-wide nuclear alert at the time of the Paris Summit in May 1960. However, the US alert was over quickly and the Soviet aircraft returned to their normal patrolling (Blair 1993: 23). At the time, the Soviet Strategic Rocket Force (SRF) was not equipped with functional ICBMs.

When Kennedy succeeded Eisenhower, he engaged in vigorous military efforts to demonstrate his resolve. In March 1961, he ordered the US nuclear bombers to a very high level of alert. On 25 May 1961, he decided to request an extra $3.4 billion for conventional forces (Kaplan 1984: 297; Betts 1987: 95). Khrushchev triggered the second round of the crisis on 4 June by reissuing the demands he had made of Eisenhower. During that month, Soviet and East German forces carried out extensive manoeuvres in East Germany, and in early July, Khrushchev announced the suspension of his planned troop cuts and an increase of around one-third in military spending (Adomeit 1982: 239–41). Kennedy responded strongly in a televised speech to the nation on 25 July in which he indicated that US nuclear forces had been strengthened, civil defence upgraded and the scrapping of 270 B-47 bombers delayed (Betts 1987: 103; Trachtenberg 1991: 219). He also announced his planned increase in conventional spending, an increase in military personnel of 200,000, preparations to call up the reserves and an extension of the draft (Kaplan 1984: 297; Betts 1987: 102–03). This worried Khrushchev sufficiently to make him seek to cool the atmosphere. In early August he appealed against the creation of 'a war psychosis' and reassured the West that he had no intentions whatsoever of blockading West Berlin, impeding access to it or even infringing upon 'any lawful interests of Western Powers' there (quoted in Trachtenberg 1991: 219, 233).

However, Khrushchev did not abandon his military show of resolve. On 11 August, two days before the Wall went up, he spoke at length about the risk of nuclear war but also asserted that there need be no war (Bundy 1988: 365–6). Shortly after work on the construction of the Berlin Wall began on 13 August, Soviet conscripts had their term of service lengthened, the Warsaw Pact for the first time officially announced its intention to meet and in early October announced officially – again for the first time – that it would be holding manoeuvres (Adomeit 1982: 242–4). The Soviet Union had begun civil defence efforts in July, restarted nuclear testing in August, and announced in September its intention to test-fire ICBMs into the Pacific (Betts 1987: 107–08). However, its ICBMs and Intermediate Range Ballistic Missiles (IRBMs) were not mated with their warheads, its bombers were not on alert, and nearly all of its nuclear missile-carrying submarines were in port (Kaplan 1984: 295).

An even bigger shock than Kennedy's tough line hit Khrushchev in the autumn, as the superiority in nuclear forces he had claimed was publicly exposed as being completely untrue. In his election campaign, Kennedy asserted repeatedly that there was a substantial 'missile gap' in favour of the Soviet Union, but soon after he was elected, increasing scepticism developed about this claim. In the summer of 1961, estimates inside the Kennedy administration of the number of Soviet intercontinental ballistic missiles (ICBMs) still varied wildly between 300 and fewer than ten (Kaplan 1986: 286–8; Prados 1986: 117). Finally, after much searching with spy satellites, the CIA concluded in September that the Soviet Union had a mere four SS-6 ICBMs, with sites for twenty SS-7s and SS-8s being built but not expected to be operational before some time in 1962 (Kaplan 1984: 289). This was made public and also seems to have been communicated directly to the Soviets in early October (Betts 1987: 104). In September and October, US officials made a concerted effort to stress the enormous scale of the US nuclear forces, although they still accepted the vulnerability of both sides (Betts 1987: 104–06). At the same time, the Kennedy administration reassessed the overall conventional balance in Europe and found that while the Warsaw Pact had something like 175 divisions to NATO's 26, the Warsaw Pact divisions were only about one-third as capable as those of NATO (Wohlforth 1993: 177). Kennedy's perceptions of the strength of the West's position improved dramatically.

The exposure of the reality of the strategic nuclear balance took much of the wind out of Khrushchev's sails. He fell back on stating many times that a war in Europe would escalate rapidly, and asserting that the vulnerability of Western Europe would restrain the West (Adomeit 1982: 251–2; Betts 1987: 106–07). On 17 October, Khrushchev gave notice of multi-megaton nuclear tests, which took place within days.[5] He also said that he no longer required a peace treaty by the end of the year (Adomeit 1982: 214; Betts 1987: 106, 108), but the pressure on West Berlin continued into 1962 when the Cuban missile crisis became the focus of confrontation.

Whether or not Kennedy thought himself actually prepared to go nuclear during a conventional conflict over West Berlin we do not know (Betts 1987: 99–100; Bundy 1988: 375–8; Beschloss 1991: 258–9). Although some US civilian analysts thought that an effective first strike – that is, an attack which would reduce to an acceptable level the Soviet capability to retaliate – was feasible, this was not the view of the top US decision-makers. Even on the assumption that the Soviet Union's forces would not be on alert (and thus not be ready to fire before they were destroyed) at the time of the attack, the plan expected that around thirty million Western Europeans and between two and fifteen million US citizens could be killed by the Soviet IRBMs and intercontinental bomber aircraft likely to survive the first strike (Kaplan 1984: 294–5, 299–300, 306; Betts 1987: 99, 101–02; Beschloss 1991: 255–6). Kennedy's conception of the role of conventional forces was that they should buy time for negotiations before nuclear use and should engage the Soviet forces on a large enough scale to make threats of nuclear use look more credible (George, Smoke 1974: 426–47; Kaplan 1984: 298; Bundy 1988: 374–5; Trachtenberg 1991: 216–17).

Khrushchev admitted in a speech on 11 August that the Soviet Union had feared US superiority in the past:

> There was a time . . . when American Secretary of State Dulles brandished thermonuclear bombs and followed a position of strength policy with regard to the socialist countries . . . This was bare-faced atomic blackmail, but it had to be reckoned with at the time because we did not possess sufficient means of retaliation, and if we did, they were not as many and not of the same power as those of our opponents
> (Quoted in Trachtenberg 1991: 220–1)

The issue of nuclear superiority was important to Khrushchev. He thought he could use it as a diplomatic lever if he claimed to have it, and he was worried when he was seen not to have it (see also Betts 1987: 120). However, nuclear danger – that is, the absolute high costs of nuclear war rather than the relative ability of either side to inflict costs – may have been more important in restraining Khrushchev from blockading West Berlin or signing a separate peace treaty with East Germany and thus handing over control of access to a government which might be much less restrained in taking action against West Berlin (Bundy 1988: 159, 364–5, 449; see also Garthoff 1989: 159, 211). The value of US nuclear superiority did seem to be limited by the fact that the Soviet Union's nuclear retaliatory capability appeared to be sufficient to inflict a degree of damage that Kennedy would find unacceptable (Bundy 1988: 379–80). Although the United States had superiority in numbers of warheads, it did not have superiority in terms of a high confidence first-strike capability or in terms of sufficient damage limitation.

Khrushchev did not end the pressure on West Berlin. He seemed to be hoping that although Soviet strategic nuclear capabilities were now known to be drastically inferior to those of the United States, the Soviet intercontinental and European theatre nuclear forces would be sufficient to deter US nuclear use should the crisis escalate. In the mean time, he was planning to deploy missiles in Cuba in order to even up the nuclear balance, at least partly with the intention of improving his bargaining position in yet another round of the Berlin crisis (Garthoff 1989: 21, 46, 49). Indeed, during the Cuban missile crisis US decision-makers were worried about the possibility of a move against West Berlin to counter the US blockade of Cuba (Garthoff 1989: 54, 56, 61, 72, 195–201).

Overall, the costs of war would be high, and, as I will now explain, the balance of interests on both sides favoured peace over war. The fear of war was manipulated by both sides in order to avoid losses and, to a lesser extent, to make gains.

THE BALANCE OF INTERESTS: FAVOURABLE TO THE EAST OVER EAST GERMANY, FAVOURABLE TO THE WEST OVER WEST BERLIN

In 1958–62, as in 1948–49, the Soviet Union tried to make Western concessions (or its own retreat) easier by stressing its intrinsic interests and by stressing the uniqueness of the situation, by using East Germans for many of the harassment activities and for building the Wall, and by referring to 'technical' difficulties hindering free movement. The West resisted this and emphasised the strategic interests at stake (Jervis 1970: 191–2, 204–05, 209–13). Intrinsic interests were very important to the Soviet Union and East Germany during this crisis. In particular, the viability of East Germany was being threatened by economic crisis. Large numbers of skilled workers were migrating to the West, East Germany was very short of investment capital, investment in heavy industry completely overshadowed consumer industry investment, and accelerated collectivization of agriculture plus poor harvests had caused a downturn in agricultural production (Adomeit 1982: 184–5, 232–6). These problems were more of a threat to the personal interests of the East German leader Walter Ulbricht than to Khrushchev, and East Germany was consistently more confrontational than the Soviet Union (Slusser 1973: 355–6; Adomeit 1982: 271–2). Khrushchev dominated the Politburo and had confidence in his authority. Nevertheless, he felt under pressure from his domestic political opponents and from China in their rivalry to lead the Communist world. His economic policies were in trouble, his policy of arms cuts and his reductions in tension with the West seemed to be failing to produce any returns. As a result, he curtailed his conventional force reductions, emphasised heavy industry and took a more confrontational foreign policy line (Adomeit 1982: 256–71, 273–4; Lebow, Stein 1994: 51–66). Adomeit argues that Khrushchev was more highly motivated than Stalin to take risks over Berlin because he had issued a number of ultimatums over Berlin and had failed to carry out intervention threats over the Middle East in 1956, 1957 and 1958 and the Taiwan Straits in 1958. As a result, Adomeit argues that his prestige was on the line (Adomeit 1982: 292–3). However, it is not obvious that backing down from the blockade in 1949 involved a smaller loss of prestige. Furthermore, as Khrushchev was in the habit of making empty threats and yet had not sustained critical damage to his prestige, there is no reason to believe that this crisis was any different. Indeed, the fact that the deadline was vague and postponable means that he had essentially backed away from trying to achieve his objectives a number of times.

Khrushchev was fundamentally persuaded that the correlation of forces had shifted in favour of the Soviet Union, that the West basically understood this, and that he could cash that power not only for loss avoidance but also for diplomatic gains (Wohlforth

1993: 164–5; Beschloss 1991: 238–9). The optimism in Soviet strategic culture at the time encouraged Khrushchev to believe that the West could be compelled to recognise East Germany and perhaps even withdraw from West Berlin. By the time of the Berlin crisis, Khrushchev had rejected Stalin's view that war between the capitalist and socialist states was fatalistically inevitable. His ideological position stressed a shift from military competition and confrontation to *détente* and economic co-operation as a way of defeating the West. He believed that the capitalist states could be made to realise that, while working people would suffer greatly in what would be a nuclear war, 'capitalism would be swept away and destroyed by the peoples' as Khrushchev put it (quoted in Adomeit 1982: 222; see also 220–5). There was a powerful sense of optimism in the Soviet camp about its ability to catch up with and overtake the West economically in a few years, while remaining militarily secure (Legvold 1979: 7–8; Adomeit 1982: 226–7; Wohlforth 1993: 138–83). The optimism of Soviet strategic culture in this period, coupled with the threat to the stability of East Germany and with the opportunity of the vulnerability of West Berlin, made a policy of exerting pressure very desirable. The failure of Khrushchev to see that the challenge was not compatible with his aim of economic co-operation with the West and a reduction of arms competition shows that he did not fully consider the potential costs as well as the potential benefits of pressure on the West. He also suffered from motivated bias in his excessive optimism about the potential for squeezing concessions from the West after freedom of movement between the two parts of Berlin was ended.

The Soviet Union may have worried that a failure to support the East German government would have a domino effect in the rest of Eastern Europe by encouraging popular opposition (Adomeit 1982: 238). In order to justify the crisis to the Soviet public and lesser officials who had been kept in the dark about the great problems facing East Germany, Khrushchev claimed in *Pravda* in August 1961 that he dare not delay a peace treaty further, in spite of the danger of war, because the West would see such a delay as a 'strategic breakthrough and would at once broaden the range of their demands . . . [They would] demand liquidation of the socialist system in the German Democratic Republic, try to annex the lands restored to Poland and Czechoslovakia under the Potsdam

Agreement and finally attempt to abolish the socialist system in all countries of the socialist camp' (quoted in Adomeit 1982: 270–1; see also Slusser 1973: 112). Ulbricht pushed for the building of the Berlin Wall in order to prevent the East German domino from falling (Adomeit 1982: 272–3; Beschloss 1991: 266–7). The move was made tentatively and with some trepidation because East Germany and the Soviet Union were worried about the potential for a violent reaction from the people of East Germany or West Berlin, or from Western governments (Adomeit 1982: 285–7, 293). To some extent, the allies were relieved because their main concern was the possibility of another blockade and because the flow of refugees to the West was inconvenient (Adomeit 1982: 287–91; Beschloss 1991: 273). Kennedy concluded that the building of the Wall showed that Khrushchev had no intention of seizing the whole of Berlin (Beschloss 1991: 278; Trachtenberg 1991: 221). Nevertheless, there was still a sense of crisis in the United States as it was still possible that the Wall was an interim step before further pressure on West Berlin. It also increased the sense of crisis amongst those such as Dean Acheson, drafted in by Kennedy to advise him on the crisis, who saw it as threatening to end their hopes of a reunified Germany and who wanted to use force to tear the Wall down (Trachtenberg 1991: 221–2).

The United States did not react strongly to the building of the Wall, although it did protest and sent 1,500 US troops to West Berlin to show resolve and bolster the morale of the West Berliners (Slusser 1973: 136–7; Beschloss 1991: 277, 285). Kennedy perceived the sending of the troop convoy to be the most dangerous episode of the crisis (Adomeit 1982: 210–11, 291). The main point is that the allies were not prepared to use force to remove the barbed wire and wooden barriers set up initially or the Wall built later. Even if they were, all the East Germans needed to do was re-establish the barbed wire on their own side of the sectoral line so that the allies would have had to encroach onto East German territory to remove it (Adomeit 1982: 293–4; Beschloss 1991: 282). Both sides were careful not to use force against each other, although shots were fired by East German police over demonstrators in the French sector on 25 August, people trying to flee were shot, and aircraft were harassed (Adomeit 1982: 211).

The ending of freedom of movement between East Germany and West Berlin represented a breach of the legal status quo, but as the West had no confidence in its ability to enforce its rights, it accepted the situation. The West concentrated on the issue of access to West Berlin, and not on Western rights in Berlin as a whole (Jervis 1970: 187–8, 196–7). As Adomeit puts it: 'It is in the light of this limitation of interests to West Berlin that a significant *change* in the status quo could appear to the West as mere *confirmation* of the status quo' (1982: 304–05). The West's acceptance of this change was probably helped by the fact that it was clear that East Germany was trying to defend its vital interests when it built the Wall. In that action, the balance of interests favoured the Communist side. However, in their efforts to pursue their secondary objective of compelling the West to withdraw from West Berlin, they were threatening vital abstract strategic interests of the West. Acheson argued that the Soviet Union was primarily testing the general resolve of the United States, while Soviet specialists such as Llewellyn Thompson, US Ambassador to the Soviet Union, and W. Averell Harriman, a former US Ambassador to the Soviet Union, argued that Khrushchev was mainly (although not solely) interested in protecting Communist interests in Eastern Europe (Beschloss 1991: 242–4; Jervis 1991: 22–3). The judgement of the Soviet specialists is more persuasive in this case.

The balance of interests favoured the Soviet Union and East Germany in the building of the Berlin Wall due to the clear threat to their intrinsic interests and to the personal interests of Ulbricht posed by the inability of East Germany to control its border. However, the balance of interests favoured the West in its resistance to concessions on the future of West Berlin and West Germany because of the perceived threat to intrinsic and strategic interests involved in such concessions. Furthermore, the burden of the first use of force – which is heavy when both sides are highly averse to war – was upon the West to resist the building of the Wall, and upon the East to force concessions regarding West Berlin and West Germany.

CONCLUSION: A CRISIS TO CLARIFY THE STATUS QUO

The Soviet Union was strongly motivated to consolidate Communist rule in East Germany after the suppression of the attempted uprising in June 1953. East Germany did not even control its own borders until the building of the Berlin Wall. Soviet and East German decision-makers also felt threatened by US-West European co-operation, West European economic success and integration through the formation of the EEC, successful West German integration into this system, the rearmament of Germany and possible German access to nuclear weapons. The fact that West Germany had declared it would not recognise East Germany or its borders and instead intended to continue to pursue reunification was very threatening to the Communist leaders. In putting pressure on West Berlin, Khrushchev's main objective was to resolve the German question by clarifying the status quo and hence dispel Western hopes of German reunification. He was partly able to achieve this through unilateral measures to stabilise East Germany. However, the Soviet Union failed to compel the West to recognise East Germany formally, or to achieve its secondary objective of bringing about a withdrawal from West Berlin. The building of the Wall helped to stabilise East Germany and the presence of West Berlin as a Western show-case was tolerated. The balance of interests favoured the West with regard to West Berlin because of the extent of the interests at stake. As in the blockade crisis, the Soviet Union had local and short-term conventional superiority. On both occasions the nuclear balance favoured the United States, although in different ways. In 1948–49 the United States had a nuclear monopoly but only a tiny nuclear capability, whereas in 1958–62 the United States had nuclear superiority but the Soviet Union had the capability to strike the United States and destroy much of Western Europe. As long as the Soviet Union did not blockade access to West Berlin or take it over, the risks of war remained relatively controllable (Beschloss 1991: 242–3, 294). Awareness that perceptions of Soviet nuclear and overall conventional superiority were exaggerated was a set-back for Khrushchev's strategy of diplomatic pressure, but that set-back also made him feel the need to deploy missiles in Cuba.

NOTES

[1] Document reproduced in Heidelmeyer, Hindrichs 1963, pp. 180–210.

[2] *Ibid.*, pp. 180–210.

[3] *Ibid.*, pp. 212–32.

[4] *Ibid.*, p. 257.

[5] A megaton is equal to the explosive power of one million tons of TNT. A kiloton is equal to one thousand tons of TNT. The atomic bomb dropped on Hiroshima had a 12.5 kiloton yield, and the one dropped on Nagasaki a 22 kiloton yield. As the accuracy and number of warheads have increased, their yield has been generally reduced from tens of megatons to hundreds of kilotons. On the partial reversal of this trend in the United States under President George Bush, see Ball 1990.

Chapter Eight

THE CUBAN MISSILE CRISIS, 1962

President Kennedy: 'It's just as if we suddenly began to put a major number of MRBMs in Turkey. Now that'd be goddam dangerous, I would think.'

McGeorge Bundy: 'Well, we *did*, Mr. President.'[1]

In December 1958, while the Berlin crisis was still under way, Fidel Castro led a revolution which overthrew the US-backed dictatorship of Fulgencio Batista. The hostility of the United States to Castro's left-wing policies and pro-Soviet stance led Castro to develop quickly a close relationship with the Soviet Union. Khrushchev decided, in consultation with Castro, to deploy nuclear forces secretly in Cuba, ninety miles from the coast of the United States, with a substantial number of Soviet conventional forces, including Surface-to-Air Missiles (SAMs), patrol boats, interceptor aircraft and forty-two Il-28 light bomber aircraft to help protect the missiles from attack and Cuba from invasion. Khrushchev's idea was to present the United States with a *fait accompli* of operational missiles, but US intelligence discovered the attempted deployment. The planned Soviet deployment was twenty-four SS-4 (Soviet designation medium-range R-12) Medium-Range Ballistic Missile (MRBM) launchers with two missiles each and sixteen SS-5 (Soviet designation medium-range R-14) Intermediate Range Ballistic Missile (IRBM) launchers with two missiles each. The SS-4s had a maximum range of 1,020 nautical miles, which would have allowed them to hit US Strategic Air Command (SAC) bases on the west coast, while the SS-5s could reach Washington and New York from Cuba due to their maximum range of 2,200 nautical miles (Betts 1987: 111; Garthoff 1989: 36–7). The

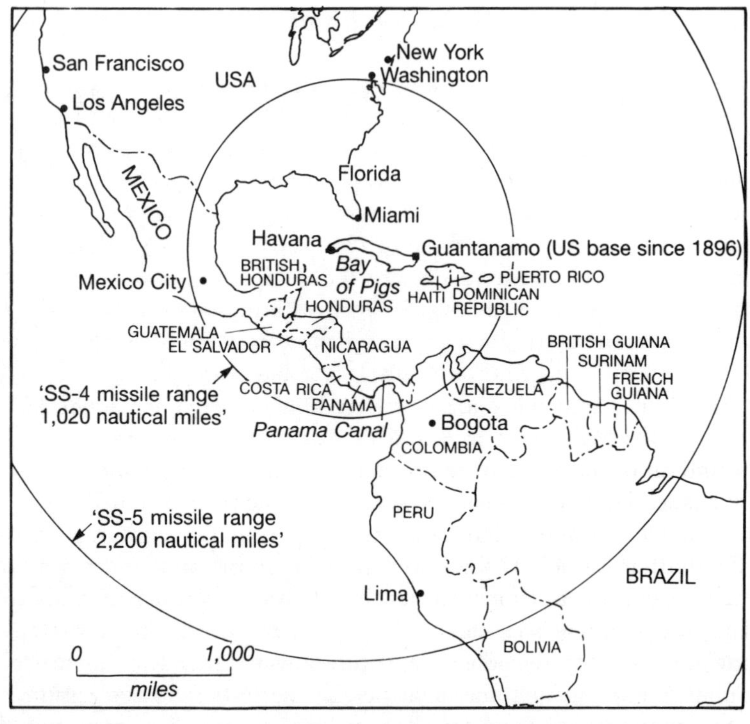

8.1 The Cuban missile crisis, 1962

Soviet Union planned to send forty warheads, one per launcher. The US decision-makers did not perceive time pressure in terms of when missiles would become operational because they assumed from the start that some were operational. Instead, as Lebow and Stein argue, the time pressure they faced was deciding on options and building support for those options within the administration before the crisis became public knowledge and pressure built up for the immediate use of force (1994: 106–07, 335–6). Kennedy chose a naval blockade to prevent the completion of the deployment and to pressure Khrushchev into withdrawing those missiles which had already reached Cuba. When he announced publicly on 22 October his intention to establish a blockade, he called it a 'quarantine', as a blockade is an act of war under international law. Of the forty-eight SS-4 and thirty-two SS-5 missiles, six SS-4s and all of the SS-5s were prevented from reaching Cuba by the blockade. Twenty warheads may have reached Cuba, but there is reasonable certainty that none were ever mated with missiles (Garthoff 1989: 37–42). Six launchers for short-range (sixty kilometre) Luna tactical nuclear weapons were also present in Cuba. The United States became aware of the launchers on 29 October, but did not know whether there were any warheads for them in Cuba. According to some accounts, in the days before the crisis the Soviet General Staff gave Soviet field commanders discretion to use these weapons in response to US invasion of Cuba without further authorisation from Moscow if communications had been disrupted, but, once the crisis began, Khrushchev insisted that the Luna missiles could only be fired on his instructions (Lebow, Stein 1994: 294–5). However, it appears that the General Staff order was 'neither signed nor sent' (Blair 1993: 109–10).

On Friday 26 October, Khrushchev offered in a letter to declare that 'our ships, bound for Cuba, will not carry any kind of armaments', and he implicitly offered to remove the missiles by saying that if the United States promised not to invade Cuba or support an invasion, 'the necessity for the presence of our military specialists in Cuba would disappear' (Kennedy-Khrushchev correspondence 1992: 44). He made this offer because he believed – inaccurately – that the United States was about to invade Cuba and possibly attack the Soviet Union (Burlatskiy 1992: 11; Lebow, Stein 1994: 136–40, 304–05, 308–09). Before receiving a reply, Khrushchev sent another letter on Saturday 27 October offering, under UN supervision, to 'remove those weapons from Cuba which you regard as offensive'. In return, the United States should promise publicly to 'evacuate its analogous weapons from Turkey', also under UN supervision, and promise not to invade Cuba, not to support an invasion and not to intervene in its domestic affairs (Kennedy-Khrushchev correspondence 1992: 48–9). He sent the 27 October letter because, in order to avert war, he wanted to make explicit his commitment to removing the missiles and because he believed – inaccurately – that references to a possible missile trade in the European and US press were a signal from Kennedy that he was interested in such a deal (Lebow, Stein 1994: 130–6).

The United States misinterpreted the 27 October letter as evidence of a new, harder Soviet line because they focused on the demand for removal of the Turkish missiles and because Soviet diplomats in New York were reported to be burning sensitive documents in preparation for war, a Soviet ship was heading for the blockade perimeter, the missile sites in Cuba were still being built as quickly as possible and a US U-2 spy plane was shot down over Cuba (Lebow, Stein 1994: 293–4, 297, 301–04). On 27 October, Kennedy and his Executive Committee (Ex Comm) of the National Security Council (NSC), which managed the crisis, decided to ignore Khrushchev's letter of 27 October and to reply instead to his letter of 26 October. Kennedy's letter offered to end the blockade and 'give assurances against an invasion of Cuba' if the Soviet Union ceased construction of the missile sites immediately and agreed to remove the missiles under UN supervision. The issue of the Turkish missiles was ignored in the letter (Kennedy-Khrushchev correspondence 1992: 50–2). However, Kennedy agreed secretly with key members of the Ex Comm – Secretary of State Dean Rusk, Secretary of Defence Robert McNamara, Attorney General (and brother of the President) Robert Kennedy, National Security Adviser McGeorge Bundy, Special Counsel to the President Theodore Sorensen, Under-Secretary of State George Ball, Deputy Secretary of Defence Roswell Gilpatric and former Ambassador to the Soviet Union Llewellyn Thompson – that the missiles in Turkey would be removed, but not as part of a public deal (Lebow, Stein 1994: 122). This concession was never discussed in the Ex Comm, and, as far as the watching world was concerned, no deal had taken place. It was communicated by Robert Kennedy directly to the Soviet Ambassador Anatoliy Dobrynin and confirmed by Khrushchev in a confidential letter on 28 October (Kennedy-Khrushchev correspondence 1992: 60–2). Khrushchev could use the concession for face-saving purposes only within a small circle in the Soviet government and armed forces. Even more secretly, Kennedy also prepared the option of making the deal public if necessary to avoid war, but in the end he did not have to offer this concession.[2] At Rusk's suggestion, Andrew Cordier of Columbia University was primed to ask, if necessary, UN Secretary General U Thant to propose the public trade. This was done without the knowledge of any of the other members of the Ex Comm: its surviving members only found out at a conference in Moscow in 1989. The United States insisted, as it had from the start of the crisis, that 'offensive weapons' included the Soviet Il-28 bombers, which were capable of delivering nuclear weapons (Kennedy-Khrushchev correspondence 1992: 77–8). The blockade and nuclear and conventional alert continued until 20 November, when the Soviet Union agreed to remove the Il-28 bombers (Garthoff 1989: 97, 114–15).

In this chapter, I argue that the outcome of the crisis can be characterised as successful US compellence with only limited concessions to the Soviet Union; that fear of war undermined the value of US military superiority; that Kennedy's perception of high stakes was reinforced by motivated bias; and that Khrushchev's motivated bias, which led him to underestimate Kennedy's interests, was gradually dispelled as the crisis progressed. Overall, I argue that the balance of interests, including mutual fear of war, provides the best explanation of the outcome of the Berlin crisis of 1958–62 as well as the Cuban missile crisis.

SUCCESSFUL US COMPELLENCE – WITH LIMITED CONCESSIONS

The main objective of the United States in this crisis was to compel the Soviet Union to undo its deployment. The United States was not satisfied with deterring the completion of the deployment: it insisted on the dismantling and removal of what had been deployed. The Soviet Union complied, and so this was a case of successful compellence for the United States. A revisionist line on the outcome of the crisis is that, even if compellence did succeed, it was not a defeat for the Soviet Union but an essentially equal compromise because it is claimed the Soviet Union achieved important objectives and the United States had to make important concessions (Burlatskiy 1992; Lebow, Stein 1994). This argument will be refuted by an examination of the three main objectives usually attributed to the Soviet deployment, namely, the protection of Cuba from US invasion, redressing the strategic nuclear balance and more generally improving the Soviet diplomatic position relative to the United States. I will also examine the outcome of Khrushchev's attempt to save face by seeking a trade of US missiles in Turkey and Italy for the missiles in Cuba.

Khrushchev claimed in his memoirs that the main objective of his missile deployment had been to protect Cuba. The United States had, after all, been trying to destabilise Cuba and assassinate Castro, and in April 1961 sponsored the abortive Bay of Pigs invasion by Cuban exiles (Khrushchev 1971: 498–500). The Soviet Union was convinced that the United States was intending to invade Cuba using its own forces to make sure of overthrowing Castro, and Soviet intelligence was convinced that an invasion would take place in September or October 1962 (Lebow, Stein 1994: 27–32). This was a misperception as no such invasion was planned, although US military exercises made it look as though an invasion was likely (Lebow, Stein 1994: 24–7). As the Soviet missiles were not due to start becoming operational until mid-October and as Khrushchev did not intend to announce their presence until after the November US congressional elections (Lebow, Stein 1994: 63), it is hard to believe that his primary aim was protecting Cuba. Even if we accept his claim at face value, he achieved only partial success. Kennedy's pledge not to invade Cuba in future was never formalised due to Castro's refusal to allow on-site inspection and verification of the withdrawal of the missiles and bombers. The pledge included the conditions that 'offensive weapons' would not be reintroduced,[3] and that Cuba must not commit any 'aggressive acts against any of the nations of the Western hemisphere' (Garthoff 1989: 124–9; *The Guardian*, 8 January 1992; Brenner 1992: 25; Schlesinger, Jr. 1992: 7). Castro was furious with the deal, as he saw the US non-invasion pledge as worthless (Lebow, Stein 1994: 345). The scale of the deployment suggests something well beyond the defence of Cuba (Lebow 1983: 432), and the political costs involved in removing the missiles suggest that the non-invasion pledge was not much of a gain. Bearing in mind that Khrushchev had given Kennedy false assurances in order to trick him into believing that missiles would not be deployed in Cuba, it is hardly surprising that Castro did not believe Kennedy. This may also explain why Khrushchev continued to try into December to have Kennedy's pledge formalised (Brenner 1992: 25–6; Kennedy-Khrushchev correspondence 1992).

The objective of redressing the strategic balance was important to Khrushchev (George, Smoke 1974: 462; Garthoff 1989: 21–4; Burlatskiy 1992: 9). The United States had a short time previously publicised its nuclear superiority, and thus undermined Khrushchev's diplomacy of nuclear threats over the future of Germany. Khrushchev had shown by his rocket-rattling his belief in the importance of the strategic balance. He feared political intimidation by the United States and even a nuclear first strike (Lebow, Stein 1994: 36–42). Khrushchev stated that 'In addition to protecting Cuba, our missiles would have equalised what the West likes to call "the balance of power"' (Khrushchev 1971: 494). The removal of the missiles from Cuba was a serious blow to his attempt to take a short cut to improving the nuclear balance while the Soviet Union developed a large ICBM force. The Soviet Union achieved nuclear parity with the United States by the mid-1970s. The ICBM build-up under Khrushchev and the man who succeeded him in October 1964, Leonid Brezhnev, might be interpreted as a response to the Cuban missile crisis, but the decision to launch a build-up occurred before the crisis and Soviet resolve to compete in strategic arms was simply reinforced (MccGwire 1980; Trachtenberg 1985: 160; Garthoff 1989: 133–4; MccGwire 1987: 24–6, 361–2).

A third objective of the deployment was to provide the basis of a wide-ranging diplomatic initiative in which the United States would have to treat the Soviet Union as an equal. This would allow Khrushchev to try to resolve foreign policy issues such as the future of Germany and West Berlin, and to reinvigorate his stalled domestic policies by shifting resources from the military to the agricultural and industrial sectors (Taubman 1992: 15; Lebow, Stein 1994: 50–66). Domestic opposition to his economic policies and his pursuit of *détente* with the West had forced him into taking a much tougher foreign-policy line in 1960. Khrushchev was planning to propose a US-Soviet summit with a broad agenda in

November, after he had revealed the presence of the missiles (Garthoff 1989: 48; Taubman 1992: 15–17). In spite of the crisis, Khrushchev raised the issue of *détente* in his letter of 27 October at the peak of the crisis and elaborated upon it in his subsequent letters to Kennedy, who stalled on or ignored the broader Soviet agenda until 14 December, when the Cuban issue had been resolved (Kennedy-Khrushchev correspondence 1992; Burlatskiy 1992: 11–12; Taubman 1992: 16). No great progress was made: the hot line agreement of June 1963 was no more than an improvement in communication systems; the status of West Berlin remained unchanged; the nuclear arms race continued; the Partial Nuclear Test Ban treaty of August 1963 sought to ban atmospheric tests when both sides were shifting to underground testing; and a UN Resolution in September 1963 banned the emplacement of weapons of mass destruction in space (which they were not planning to do) (Taubman 1992: 16–17). Nevertheless, tensions were reduced.

In an effort to salvage something from the crisis, Khrushchev proposed a trade of the missiles in Cuba for the fifteen US Jupiter IRBMs in Turkey and the thirty US Jupiter IRBMs in Italy. The symbolism for the Soviet Union of the Turkish missiles was increased because the process of handing them over to the Turkish armed forces was under way just as the blockade was announced. The US Government was unaware of this coincidence (Garthoff 1989: 28–9, 71, 342). Kennedy had wanted the missiles to be phased out, but had not ordered it (Garthoff 1989: 71, 86; Lebow, Stein 1994: 123–5). The United States agreed to the trade and the missiles were removed by 25 April 1963. However, this was a very one-sided trade. First, as the missiles had been deployed through NATO, they would only be removed after the United States had gone through all the necessary NATO procedures so that it would not look as though Turkey (and Italy) had been in any way sold out. In contrast, the Soviet missiles were removed from Cuba against Castro's will. Second, while Kennedy accepted that this trade could be explicit between the two sides, he insisted that the trade could not be made public. Third, Kennedy was removing obsolete missiles while Khrushchev was removing missiles he valued. Fourth, whereas Kennedy insisted that the Soviet Union could not deploy missiles in Cuba in future, Khrushchev acknowledged that the United States could immediately replace the missiles in Turkey and Italy with more modern ones (Khrushchev 1974: 512).

It is true that the United States made limited concessions, but the Soviet Union conceded much more. The outcome was not, as Lebow and Stein claim, 'an accommodation that safeguarded the interests of both and permitted Khrushchev to retreat with minimal loss of face' (1994: 313; see also 110, 140–1, 320, 362–3). It was an outcome designed to ensure the maximum humiliation of Khrushchev compatible with the avoidance of war. Khrushchev justified the outcome to the Politburo by referring to it as 'our Brest Litovsk' (quoted in Zubok 1992: 22). This is a reference to the desperate decision by Lenin to sign a peace treaty in 1917 with Germany, which conceded vast tracts of territory in order to extract the Bolsheviks from their involvement in World War I. The claim of Fedor Burlatskiy, who was a member of the International Department of the CPSU Central Committee at the time of the missile crisis, that Khrushchev did not lose face is untenable (1992: 11). As Lebow and Stein admit: 'His capitulation in the face of American military pressure was a humiliating defeat for the Soviet Union and its leader. Soviet officials confirm that it was one factor in his removal from power a year later. For many years, Americans portrayed the crisis as an unalloyed American triumph' (1994: 352). Bearing this in mind, it is not the case that 'His decision to withdraw the missiles was conditioned almost as much by the expectation of gain as it was by the fear of loss' (Lebow, Stein 1994: 5–6). Khrushchev admitted that his prestige and self-esteem suffered because of the crisis outcome, and that the continuation of the blockade into late November and the US demand that the Il-28s be removed made it even worse (Taubman 1992: 17). More importantly: 'Khrushchev's larger failure was to get results from the crisis commensurate with its risks. And this in turn was the reason for his embarrassing eagerness to credit the crisis with providing the impetus for broader diplomatic progress' (Taubman 1992: 17). Khrushchev sought to gather crumbs of comfort, but they were just that – not half a loaf.

If the outcome of the crisis is seen as an equal compromise, then it could be explained in terms of mutual fear of war and mutual reassurance. However, as the outcome favoured the United States, we must look for factors in the crisis which favoured the United

States. One obvious factor was US military superiority, although its usefulness was limited by mutual fear of war.

US MILITARY SUPERIORITY AND MUTUAL FEAR OF WAR

On 22 October, the day that the blockade was announced, US forces were put on a Defence Condition (DefCon) Three alert world-wide – the first alert of all US commands since the Korean War – with US forces in Western Europe on a lower level in deference to political sensitivities there. DefCon One indicates imminent conventional or nuclear war, DefCon Two indicates full combat readiness, DefCon Three indicates increased combat readiness with war unlikely, and DefCons Four and Five different levels of normal peacetime readiness (Kruzel 1977; Sagan 1985, 1993; Blair 1987, 1993). Previously covert preparations in all arms of the conventional forces for either airstrike or invasion were conducted openly. Unknown to the President, the Navy used small depth-charges to force Soviet submarines to surface and withdraw from the area on 23 and 24 October (Sagan 1985: 112–17). On 24 October, the United States went to its highest-ever[4] alert, DefCon Two, which, roughly speaking, doubled the forces on alert compared to DefCon Three. It included one-eighth of the B-52 bombers armed and airborne, 1,479 nuclear bombers on alert, 182 ICBMs on alert, all Polaris nuclear missile submarines, with a total of 112 missiles, heading out to sea, and many of its nuclear forces throughout Europe and the Pacific in a high state of readiness. This added up to 2,952 warheads on alert (Sagan 1993: 62–5). Britain's Bomber Command, apparently without any political authorisation, put its sixty Thor IRBMs (formally under dual key with the United States, whereby the missiles could only be launched with the authorisation of both Britain and the United States) and around 175 nuclear-armed V-bombers on the highest possible alert status (Scott 1991). General Thomas Power, the SAC Commander-in-Chief, issued the US alert orders on open channels. This has generally been interpreted as an independent initiative taken without the knowledge of his superiors, and as a breach of procedures in not sending it in code. Supposedly his aim was to make the alert completely obvious to the Soviet Union (Sagan 1985: 108–10; Garthoff 1989: 60–2, 69; Lebow, Stein 1994: 341). However, it appears that such orders were actually routinely broadcast on open channels until 1972, and the contents of Power's message emphasised heavily the importance of calmness, caution, avoidance of mistakes and reference to higher authorities for advice (Sagan 1994: 68–9).

For many years the consensus in the West was that the Soviet Union did not respond with a nuclear alert of its own (Bracken 1983: 220; Trachtenberg 1985; Betts 1987: 120; Lebow 1987a: 67; Garthoff 1989: 65). This had been interpreted as evidence of the importance of US nuclear superiority: the Soviet Union dared not respond for fear of provoking a pre-emptive strike (Trachtenberg 1985; Betts 1987: 120–2). Richard Neustadt and Graham Allison claimed in their 'Afterword' in Robert Kennedy's posthumously-published memoir *Thirteen Days* that, on 24 October, Soviet strategic forces went on 'full alert' (1971: 113; see also Kaplan 1981: 54). However, subsequently Allison took the position that their claim was inaccurate.[5] The Soviet Union announced a nuclear alert on 24 October, but on 25 October the CIA intelligence summary indicated no evidence of such an alert.[6] One Soviet academic article refers to 'an alert throughout the Soviet and other WTO Armed Forces' on 25 October 1962 (Sergeev *et al.* 1987: 13). As Bruce Blair points out, Khrushchev's reference in his 12 December 1962 speech to a full Soviet nuclear alert during the Cuban missile crisis has generally been dismissed as rhetoric (1993: 24, 289n). Soviet nuclear forces appear to have been put on an intermediate level of nuclear alert on 24 October. SAC intelligence picked up the alert, identified its intermediate level correctly and also identified correctly the cancelling of the alert on 21 November.[7] Strategic bombers were stood down, so that they could be ready for a mission at short notice. Some may have been loaded with nuclear bombs but none were airborne (Blair 1993: 24–5). Soviet Strategic Rocket Forces (SRFs) may also have been ordered to go to the highest level of alert and mate warheads with missiles at the height of the crisis, but then told within hours to go back to the intermediate alert level (Sagan 1993: 144–5). The Soviet Union and the rest of the Warsaw Pact cancelled their alert on 21 November, the day after the cancellation of the US alert and the lifting of the blockade.[8]

The Soviet Union had deployed 144 surface-to-air (SAM) missile launchers and forty-two MiG–21 interceptor aircraft to defend the missiles on Cuba from air attack. The US Air Force could not guarantee the destruction of all of the missiles in a single attack, but an airstrike option for 29 or 30 October was prepared (Garthoff 1989: 18, 49–50, 86, 160). Given more time or a larger attack than the one planned, it is probable that the Air Force could have destroyed all of the missiles. The United States also made contingency plans for an invasion of Cuba, possibly in the wake of an airstrike on the Soviet missiles. It prepared 140,000 troops, 579 combat aircraft and 183 ships for an attack, should it become necessary.[9] The United States underestimated the size of the Soviet force in Cuba and would thus have been faced with a tougher task than expected had they invaded. Cuban and Soviet fears of an invasion increased as the crisis progressed, but Kennedy became gradually more certain that he did not want to invade Cuba as his desire to avoid escalation increased (Allyn, Blight, Welch 1988–89: 144–7; Lebow, Stein 1994: 103, 120, 292, 305).

The local and short-term conventional military balances favoured the United States in its attempt to compel the Soviet Union to remove its missiles from Cuba. The nuclear balance also favoured the United States. In terms of warheads available for a single-salvo attack (that is, without reloading missile launchers or additional missions by bombers), the United States had around 3,000 warheads on ICBMs, submarines and bombers capable of hitting the Soviet Union, while the Soviet Union had around 250 warheads for a single-salvo attack on the United States (Garthoff 1989: 208). These figures exclude the theatre nuclear capabilities of both sides. The Soviet Union could do little in a first strike to reduce the US retaliatory capability, and the United States had nuclear forces capable of striking the Soviet Union from Western Europe and the Far East. While a US Air Force planner estimated that a US first strike would be between 90 and 100 per cent effective, this might have left the Soviet Union around twenty-five warheads to drop on US cities (Garthoff 1989: 160). Furthermore, as in the Berlin crisis, the Soviet Union also had the capability to inflict vast damage on Western Europe should general war occur. In October, US intelligence thought the Soviet Union had between sixty and seventy-five operational ICBM launchers. The real Soviet figure was somewhere between twenty and forty-four. If the ninety-seven Soviet short-range submarine-launched ballistic missiles (SLBMs) are excluded due to their extreme vulnerability, the planned deployment of forty IRBMs and MRBM launchers in Cuba would have multiplied the Soviet single-salvo capability by two or three times (Betts 1987: 116; Garthoff 1989: 202–03, 206–07; Lebow, Stein 1994: 292, 394–5n).

Kennedy seems to have been comforted to some degree by nuclear superiority and Khrushchev discomfited by nuclear inferiority. The political importance of the nuclear balance is suggested by the fact that the Soviet Union chose to deploy the missiles in the first place (Betts 1987: 109, 122). However, both leaders made it clear to each other that they understood that nuclear war would be a disaster, and that any conventional combat had to be avoided due to the potential for escalation. The mutual fear of war of any kind was much more important than US military superiority. Bundy believes (somewhat impressionistically) that US conventional superiority in the Caribbean was more important than the nuclear balance, nuclear danger made both sides cautious, US nuclear superiority made the Soviet Union a little more cautious than the United States, and the basic outcome would probably have been unaffected by strategic parity (1988: 440, 446–9). Garthoff concurs with Bundy, but speculates that the threat of an airstrike might not have been enough to make Khrushchev back down and that the prospect of an invasion of Cuba was the more important aspect of the conventional military balance (1989: 159–61, 189).

An alternative interpretation, first articulated by Bernard Brodie and later by Paul Nitze and then Betts, is that if the outcome was determined by US conventional superiority, then it is difficult to explain why the Soviet Union did not cancel out this advantage by reciprocal pressure on West Berlin (Betts 1987: 120). US decision-makers were worried about this possibility but went ahead with the blockade of Cuba anyway. The conventional balance favoured the Soviet Union over Berlin in the 1958–62 crisis, but the Soviet Union did not achieve a favourable outcome and did not respond to the blockade on Cuba with pressure on West Berlin. Betts suggests that, if the leaders on both sides were cautious to a similar degree and if the balance of interests did not favour the United States, then it follows that the most likely explanation is US superiority in the nuclear balance (1987: 114–15, 120). He argues that the balance of interests favoured the Soviet Union, in that the United States was faced with the burden of the first use of force in order to prevent completion of the missile deployment and

Table 8.1 *'Nuclear superiority decisive' matrix*

	Berlin	*Cuba*
	Favourable to	
Nuclear balance	US	US
Conventional balance	USSR	US
Burden of the first use of force	US	USSR
Crisis outcome	US	US

ensure the removal of the forces already in Cuba. This perspective is illustrated by Table 8.1. From an early stage in the crisis, the use of force to destroy the Soviet missiles in Cuba looked like a very messy option. For example, on 16 October, Secretary of State Dean Rusk expressed his worries that 'about six' unspecified governments could be overthrown in Latin America due to a Communist reaction to an airstrike on missiles in Cuba, and the United States could find itself isolated with 'the alliance crumbling'.[10] McNamara sounded determined but still emphasised the escalation likely to follow limited military action: 'If you carried out an air strike, this might lead to an uprising such that in order to prevent the slaughter of . . . the free Cubans, we would have to invade to . . . reintroduce order into the country. And we would be prepared to do that.'[11] McNamara also stated that 'You have to put a blockade in following any . . . limited action', and concurred as Robert Kennedy said 'Then we're gonna have to sink Russian ships . . . Then we're gonna have to sink . . . Russian submarines'.[12] Bundy also pointed out the escalatory potential of the blockade: 'You have to make the guy stop to search him, and if he won't stop, you have to shoot'.[13] Betts' point that the burden of the first use of force placed upon the United States was very heavy, in spite of its conventional superiority and because of its nuclear vulnerability, is undoubtedly accurate; indeed, fear of war undermined the value of US nuclear as well as conventional superiority.

The argument that the importance of US nuclear superiority in the Cuban crisis is indicated by the fact that the Soviet Union did not impose a reciprocal blockade on West Berlin is unconvincing, because the deployment of nuclear missiles in Cuba was much more provocative than the maintenance of an allied presence in West Berlin. Only if NATO had attempted to deploy nuclear missiles in West Berlin secretly and there had been no Soviet blockade in response would the parallel be convincing. The threat perceived by the United States to its interests from failure to prevent the Soviet Union from retaining missile bases on Cuba was much greater than the threat perceived by the Soviet Union to its interests from failure to make the West recognise East Germany or withdraw from West Berlin. In the Berlin crisis, the Soviet Union's stabilisation of East Germany through the building of the Wall meant that much of the motivation for forcing the West out of West Berlin or securing recognition of East Germany had dissipated. In addition, Betts takes too narrow an approach in arguing that the side faced with the burden of the first use of force has the balance of interests against it. I argue below that a broader approach suggests that, especially when one takes into account psychological factors, the balance of interests favoured the United States and not, as Betts maintains, the Soviet Union.

KENNEDY'S PERCEPTION OF HIGH STAKES, REINFORCED BY MOTIVATED BIAS

Kennedy's approach of using the Ex Comm apparently to promote free discussion of the pros and cons of various options has been applauded as a model of rational crisis decision-making. However, Lebow argues persuasively that this ignored the fact that the Ex Comm actually had a very narrow remit: to discuss the relative utility of coercive means to have the missiles withdrawn before they became operational. The Ex Comm functioned in practice primarily to provide rationalisations for Kennedy's policy preferences: he excluded the possibility of a non-coercive solution from the start, and the Ex Comm opted for a blockade, followed by force if necessary, only once he had made it clear that was his preference (Lebow 1981: 297–303). A whole range of additional less-than-rational elements of Kennedy's approach to the crisis have also been pointed out by Snyder (1978). Kennedy denied trade-offs by framing war avoidance and preserving prestige as consonant rather than conflicting values; played down the risk of war by arguing that it was a necessary risk to avert a greater risk of war later; overstressed the certainty of the domino effects that would follow a less than totally favourable outcome; and failed to look seriously at other viewpoints. Kennedy's secret decision to reject the fragile consensus built up in the Ex Comm by deciding on an explicit missile trade if the Soviet Union did not back down may have been based on rational criteria, but we cannot know as no record of his reasoning appears to have survived. We can only presume that his primary concern was war avoidance, which suggests that in the end he did recognise the trade-off between that and preserving prestige. This secret decision also dispels further the myth that the Ex Comm was at the heart of the decision-making process. Decision-making can be rational when it is not collegial, but it would be dangerous to assume that the top decision-maker thought through all the issues when colleagues were either kept in the dark or did not explore basic issues for themselves.

Kennedy was motivated by a strong sense of potential loss domestically and in foreign policy terms; he was fixated with the Munich analogy and, especially at the outset of the crisis, saw Khrushchev as motivated by aggressive opportunism based on the belief that he was weak (Lebow, Stein 1994: 94–102). US decision-makers feared serious domino consequences and feared that the Soviet Union would move against West Berlin, and they believed that they had more at stake than the Soviet Union. The SNIE of 20 October 1962 concluded that the public withdrawal of the Soviet missiles from Cuba would inflict costs on the Soviet Union in its relations with Castro and would 'cast doubt on the firmness of the Soviet intention to protect the Castro regime and perhaps on their commitments elsewhere.'[14] However, it envisioned much more dramatic domino effects to the detriment of the United States should it acquiesce in the presence of the missiles:

> This course of action would provide strong encouragement to Communists, pro-Communists, and the more anti-American sectors of opinion in Latin America. We believe that, especially in the long run, there would be loss of confidence in US power and determination and a serious decline of US influence, particularly in Latin America.

> Should any additional Latin American government fall to the Communists the Soviets would feel free to establish bases in the country in question if they chose. A major immediate consequence would be that the Soviets would probably estimate lower risks in pressing the US hard in other confrontations, such as Berlin.[15]

US decision-makers were conscious that the Congressional elections were only one month away. They were not hoping for a victory in order to help them in the elections: they were much more concerned with loss avoidance (Kennedy 1971: 3; Hampson 1984–85; Paterson, Brophy 1986; Lebow, Stein 1994: 106–07, 335–6). Robert Kennedy claimed that, as the blockade went into effect on 24 October, he said to the President 'if you hadn't acted, you would have been impeached', and that the President concurred (Kennedy 1971: 45). It is absurd to imagine there was any prospect of impeachment because there would have been no legal foundation for it; nevertheless, the implicit point about the domestic political vulnerability of the administration is sound.

A possible compromise solution – the public, reciprocal withdrawal of US MRBMs from Turkey and Soviet MRBMs from Cuba – was opposed by the United States. Raymond Garthoff, Special Assistant for Soviet Bloc Political-Military Affairs in the State Department during the crisis, argued in a memo on 25 October that such a deal could possibly result in 'the unhinging of our whole overseas base and alliance structure'. He continued: 'I can think of nothing that would more encourage the Soviets to create new Cubas and new distant military bases and local conflicts than would a net gain from their Cuban venture'. He expressed concern that the Turks would feel that they were sold out and that once a deal on Turkey was agreed, the Soviet Union would demand more (quoted in Garthoff 1989: 197–8). Jervis reports, without conscious irony, that the United States did not want to trade the missiles in Turkey explicitly for those in Cuba because acting 'under duress' and 'accepting unequal bargains' would make domino effects more likely (1991: 34). The idea that the Soviet Union felt itself to be acting under duress and that an open missile swap was unfavourable when compared to keeping its missiles on Cuba does not seem to have been appreciated. The other main reason given by US decision-makers for resisting a trade for the missiles in Turkey was summed up in a memo on 27 October

1962 written by Garthoff, who argued that the Turks did not want to be 'used as a pawn' and valued their ability to strike back, and that in NATO the missiles symbolised 'our commitment to stand by the interests of each of its members'.[16] No mention was made of the interests of Cuba in not being used as a pawn or in having a capability to retaliate, or of the Soviet interests in standing by an ally. Two things are striking here: the double standards and the failure to perceive them. In a paper to Bundy, the Policy Planning Council led by Walt Rostow made an attempt to refute the Turkish analogy by arguing that 'the Cuban development is not parallel to what we have done in Turkey, Western Europe or elsewhere, but to what would be represented by our establishing a base in Finland or even Hungary'.[17] The premise of this argument seems to be that Finland and Hungary were in the Soviet sphere of influence and Cuba was in the US sphere of influence. This conveniently ignores the central fact that Cuba was an ally of the Soviet Union whereas Finland and Hungary were not allies of the United States.

A problem for Kennedy was that the trade would seem so reasonable to many outside observers, especially from non-aligned countries, some of whom had called for such a trade.[18] Before the crisis, Eisenhower said putting missiles in Turkey would be like the Soviet Union putting them in Mexico and Cuba. Eisenhower and Kennedy both wanted to withdraw them but did not do so due to Turkish opposition and, in Kennedy's case, fear that it would be seen by the Soviet Union as a sign of weakness (Lebow, Stein 1994: 43–5, 48). The analogy with the US missiles in Turkey was resisted by Kennedy for most of the crisis. The following comments, captured in Kennedy's secret recordings of the Ex Comm deliberations, illustrate the point:

> President Kennedy: 'It's just as if we suddenly began to put a major number of MRBMs in Turkey. Now that'd be goddam dangerous, I would think.'
>
> McGeorge Bundy: 'Well, we *did*, Mr. President.'

Kennedy's lame response was: 'Yeah, but that was five years ago . . . that was during a different period then.'[19] On the one hand it is astonishing that Kennedy had ignored a basic fact, even if only for an instant. Looked upon charitably, the key word in Kennedy's initial statement is 'suddenly'. It was the mode of the Soviet attempted deployment that was so outrageous to Kennedy.

Some things were different about the US deployment of missiles in Turkey – it was part of a programme of deploying missiles in a number of West European countries, the Soviet Union had not made a public commitment that it would not tolerate such a deployment, the United States had not declared that it would not deploy such missiles and had not then tried to sneak them in despite assurances to the contrary. The falsity of Soviet assurances that no such weapons would be deployed in Cuba produced a great deal of US moral outrage about the illegitimacy of the Soviet action. The breaking of promises by Khrushchev made him look to the United States not simply like a liar but a reckless liar (Lebow, Stein 1994: 79–80). This perception magnified the US assessment of the extent of the interests it had at stake. In contrast, Khrushchev's motivated bias, crucial to explaining the mode of the initial deployment, was gradually dispelled so that he came to understand Kennedy's perception of the extent of the interests the United States had at stake.

KHRUSHCHEV'S MOTIVATED BIAS, GRADUALLY DISPELLED

Khrushchev made the deployment decision in May 1961. Although he consulted a number of his colleagues, he made it clear from the start that he was determined to deploy the missiles and effectively stifled any serious disagreement or opposition (Lebow, Stein 1994: 72–7, 86–9, 112). It was obvious that the deployment could not be kept secret, as Cuba was monitored extremely closely by the United States. Khrushchev was told this but ignored the advice (Lebow, Stein 1994: 81, 82–6). Khrushchev also engaged in wishful thinking in denying that there were trade-offs between his objectives; in particular, his attempt to redress the strategic balance made an invasion of Cuba more rather than less likely (Lebow, Stein 1994: 88–91, 336–7). The alternative approach of asserting openly the right to deploy nuclear weapons on the soil of an ally – which was Castro's preference – was not explored seriously. In discussions years later, various US decision-makers said that they would have found it very much more difficult to prevent the deployment of Soviet missiles if it was announced in advance and done openly (Garthoff 1989: 24–5).

Khrushchev's reason for choosing secret deployment instead of an openly declared prior assertion of a right and intention to deploy appears to have been based on the belief that the United States would exploit its conventional military superiority to prevent the deployment, or even invade Cuba as a preventive measure. Khrushchev believed inaccurately that the United States was already on the verge of invading Cuba. This fear explains why the Soviet Union calls this crisis the 'Caribbean crisis' rather than the Cuban missile crisis (Garthoff 1989: 1–6, 14, 170, 181–6). As Lebow and Stein argue, Khrushchev acted the way he did not because he saw Kennedy as weak but because he believed him to be resolute (1994: 5, 69–72, 76–7, 80; see also Lebow 1983; Garthoff 1989: 24–5; Sergei Khrushchev 1990: 50–1). He also thought that once the missiles were operational, Kennedy would be too afraid of escalation to attack them (Lebow, Stein 1994: 78–9, 336). Khrushchev seriously underestimated US interests. In spite of his own anger at the deployment of the Turkish missiles, he did not consider the depth of US anger and emotion that would result from his actions (Lebow, Stein 1994: 80, 82, 90–1; see also Garthoff 1989: 27). He thought that if the presence of the missiles was announced after the November Congressional elections, Kennedy would not have excessively severe domestic political problems (Lebow, Stein 1994: 78).

The balance of interests was not fixed at the outset of the crisis but redefined during it. Both sides were able to clarify the interests they had at stake. At the outset, both sides believed they had more at stake, saw themselves as defensively motivated and saw the other side as offensively motivated: they concluded that the other side would back down first (Schlesinger, Jr. 1992: 5; Lebow, Stein 1994: 310–14). During the crisis, mutual fear of war encouraged both sides to put much effort into explaining their interests and to spend time listening to the other side's explanations (Lebow, Stein 1994: 312–13, 331). However, their correspondence shows that they made little progress in coming to an agreed perspective (Kennedy-Khrushchev correspondence 1992). Nor did they come to an equal compromise, as Lebow and Stein claim: instead, while Kennedy learned that Khrushchev had some reasonable concerns and would not see his limited concessions as weakness, Khrushchev had his false assumptions dispelled. Khrushchev learned that Kennedy did have more at stake. The blockade and the US military alert made Khrushchev realise just how much the US believed was at stake, and he learned that Kennedy was very angry and that he felt betrayed (Lebow, Stein 1994: 313–14).

CONCLUSION: CUBA, BERLIN AND THE BALANCE OF INTERESTS

The balance of interests favoured the United States over remaining in West Berlin because of the dramatic threat to its intrinsic and strategic interests, and because the Soviet Union's stabilisation of East Germany through the building of the Wall meant that much of the motivation for forcing the West out of West Berlin or securing recognition of East Germany had dissipated. The threat perceived by the United States to its interests from failure to compel the Soviet Union to remove its missile bases from Cuba was much greater than the threat perceived by the Soviet Union to its interests from failure to make the West recognise East Germany or withdraw from West Berlin. In both crises, nuclear and conventional superiority for either was neutralised by mutual fear of war. Although US nuclear superiority was not responsible for the outcome of the Cuban missile crisis, the existence of that superiority helped to provoke the Soviet Union into deploying missiles in the first place (Kahan, Long 1972: 585; Garthoff 1989: 188). The balance of interests still favoured the United States, even though it was faced with the burden of the first use of force; and the favourable balance of interests for the United States was reinforced by psychological factors. This is illustrated in Table 8.2. US decision-makers feared serious domino consequences: in particular they feared that the Soviet Union would move against West Berlin. The secret deployment in spite of Soviet assurances was also a powerful motivating factor for the United States. After an initial underestimation of US interests due to motivated bias, Khrushchev came to learn during the crisis just how much the United States perceived to be at stake. While the forced withdrawal was embarrassing, Khrushchev had embarked on an ambitious programme designed to catch up with the United States in the strategic nuclear arms competition. He could also take comfort from their perception that they had been given a guarantee that Cuba would not be invaded. The end result was not total victory for the United States,

Table 8.2 *'Balance of interests decisive' matrix*

	Berlin	*Cuba*
	Favourable to	
Nuclear balance	US	US
Fear of war	Strong and mutual	
Conventional balance	USSR	US
Burden of the first use of force	US	USSR
Balance of interests (reinforced by psychological biases)	US	US
Crisis outcome	US	US

but an outcome which favoured it, even if it had to make limited concessions.

NOTES

[1] Transcript, Presidential Recordings, 'Off-the-record [sic] meeting on Cuba', 16 October 1962, 6.30–7.55pm: 26, declassified, 'sanitised', in National Security Archive, Washington, DC. Kennedy secretly audiotaped the meetings of the Ex Comm (Executive Committee) of the National Security Council (NSC), which he convened to manage the crisis. For an edited version of the 27 October transcript at the peak of the crisis, see Bundy, Blight, 1987–88 and for a commentary on the transcript, see Welch, Blight 1987–88. The proceedings of a number of important conferences involving former participants and knowledgeable observers and analysts have also been published or are about to be published. These include the Hawk's Cay conference in March 1987 (Welch 1989), the Cambridge conference in October 1987 (Welch 1988), the Moscow conference in January 1989 (Allyn, Blight, Welch 1992), the Antigua conference

January 1991 (Blight, Lewis, Welch forthcoming) and the Havana Conference in January 1992 (Blight, Allyn, Welch forthcoming). For further documentation and reminiscences, see Pope 1982, Larson 1986, Blight, Welch 1989, Nikita Khrushchev 1990, Sergei Khrushchev 1990 and Kennedy-Khrushchev correspondence 1992.

[2] On the details of the deal and how it came about, and on Kennedy's secret fall-back position, see Welch, Blight 1987–88: 12–18; Allyn, Blight, Welch 1989–90: 163–5; Garthoff 1988: 24, 75–6, 87, 95; Nash 1991; Lebow, Stein 1994: 10–11, 120–43, 532–6.

[3] Among a number of subsequent incidents, the Soviet Union was pressured into not building a submarine base on Cuba in September 1970, and received a sharp rebuke for a visit by a nuclear missile submarine to Cuba in May 1972 (Garthoff 1989: 140–53). Although conservative US columnists Rowland Evans and Robert Novack alleged in May 1991 that US spy satellites had spotted a Soviet SS-20 IRBM in Cuba, this was never confirmed (*The Guardian*, 21 May 1991).

[4] On the DefCon system, see Sagan 1993, especially pp. 64–5. During the Vietnam War, Nixon set a deadline of 1 November 1969, in a letter of 15 July of that year to North Vietnamese leader Ho Chi Minh, for some 'serious breakthrough' in the Paris peace talks. Nixon claims that he wrote that if no progress was made, he would find himself 'obliged to have recourse to "measures of great consequence and force"' (Nixon 1978: 394). This threat was reiterated on a number of occasions. Ho died on 3 September 1969 and was replaced by Pham Van Dong, and there was no sign of any Vietnamese concessions. Seymour Hersh claims that SAC's B-52 bombers were put on DefCon *One* alert and that it was sustained for twenty-nine days between October and November 1969 (1983: 125–7). While it is likely that some bombers were alerted, if the whole bomber force had been alerted, or if the alert level was DefCon One, it is hard to believe that it would not have been noticed by many observers. Nevertheless, this is an episode which needs further research.

[5] Correspondence, Allison to Herring.

[6] Blair 1985: 129–30. On 2 November – fortunately after the peak of the crisis – the CIA received a pre-arranged telephone signal which was meant to indicate an imminent Soviet nuclear attack. This signal was meant to be given by Colonel Oleg Penkovsky, a Soviet military intelligence officer who was spying for the West. John McCone, the CIA Director, advised Kennedy that Penkovsky had probably been arrested by the KGB and had revealed the signal in the hope of saving himself (Sagan 1993: 148). The guess was correct: he had been arrested by the KGB

(Committee for State Security) on 22 October. He was shot for treason by the Soviet authorities early in 1963. Jerrold Schecter and Peter Deriabin suggest that the KGB knew the meaning of the signal but did not see it as dangerous as the missile crisis had peaked, and that they used it to gather more information. Alternatively, Scott Sagan suggests that Penkovsky may have told the KGB the signal but not its meaning and hoped that they would use it and bring about a nuclear attack which would destroy the Soviet Union (Garthoff 1989: 63–5; Schecter, Deriabin 1992: 262–3, 337–49; Sagan 1993: 146–50).

[7] Sagan 1993: 143–4, Garthoff 1989: 114–15, and US National Indications Center, 'The Soviet Bloc Armed Forces and the Cuban Crisis, a Chronology: July–November 1962', 18 June 1963, declassified, 'sanitised', in National Security Archive, Washington, DC.

[8] Garthoff 1989: 114–15, and US National Indications Center, 'The Soviet Bloc Armed Forces and the Cuban Crisis, a Chronology: July–November 1962', 18 June 1963, declassified, 'sanitised', in National Security Archive, Washington, DC.

[9] Garthoff 1989: 6, 9, 50–2, 53, 65–9, 73–4; and Office of the Secretary of Defence, 'Department of Defense operations during the Cuban crisis', February 1963, declassified, 'sanitised', in National Security Archive, Washington, DC.

[10] Transcript, Presidential Recordings, 'Off-the-record [sic] meeting on Cuba', 16 October 1962, 6.30–7.55pm: 6–7, declassified, 'sanitised', in National Security Archive, Washington, DC.

[11] Transcript, Presidential Recordings, 'Off-the-record [sic] meeting on Cuba', 16 October 1962, 11.50am–12.57pm: 22 (see also 23), declassified, 'sanitised', in National Security Archive, Washington, DC.

[12] Transcript, Presidential Recordings, 'Off-the-record [sic] meeting on Cuba', 16 October 1962, 6.30–7.55pm: 25, declassified, 'sanitised', in National Security Archive, Washington, DC.

[13] Transcript, Presidential Recordings, 'Off-the-record [sic] meeting on Cuba', 16 October 1962, 6.30–7.55pm: 46, declassified, 'sanitised', in National Security Archive, Washington, DC.

[14] SNIE 11–19–62, 'Major consequences of certain US courses of action on Cuba', 4, declassified, 'sanitised', in National Security Archive, Washington, DC.

[15] SNIE 11–19–62, 'Major consequences of certain US courses of action on Cuba', 5, declassified, 'sanitised', in National Security Archive, Washington, DC. An undated paper early in the crisis from the Policy Planning Council (PPC) – led by Walt W. Rostow – to Bundy emphasised

the potential domino consequences of Soviet missile bases in Cuba. Policy Planning Council, 'The Cuban base problem in perspective', undated [approx. 16 October 1962], 11, declassified, in the National Security Archive, Washington, DC.

[16] Raymond L. Garthoff, 'The Khrushchev proposal for a Turkey-Cuba trade-off', 27 October 1962: 2, declassified, in National Security Archive, Washington, DC.

[17] Policy Planning Council, 'The Cuban base problem in perspective', undated [approx. 16 October 1962], 12–13, declassified, in National Security Archive, Washington, DC.

[18] Transcript, Presidential Recordings, 'Off-the-record [sic] meeting on Cuba', 27 October 1962: 2–3, declassified, 'sanitised', in National Security Archive, Washington, DC.

[19] Transcript, Presidential Recordings, 'Off-the-record [sic] meeting on Cuba', 16 October 1962, 6.30–7.55pm: 26, declassified, 'sanitised', in National Security Archive, Washington, DC.

Chapter Nine

THE SINO-SOVIET BORDER CRISIS, 1969

> Due appreciation of Chinese moves to press the border issue and of Soviet steps to defuse the crisis is an important corrective to facile dramatic accounts that overemphasize Soviet military pressure and threats.
>
> Richard Wich (1980: 276)

From the late 1950s, the Soviet Union conducted an intense rivalry not only with the United States but also with China, which resented Soviet claims to ideological leadership of the Communist world and asserted its own ideological supremacy. It also resented the fact that Khrushchev had reneged on his promise to assist on nuclear matters. In 1959 the Soviets withdrew their technical advisers and halted their economic aid. Personal attacks flew back and forth, the Chinese renewed their territorial claims in Siberia, and from this time on both sides initiated border clashes sporadically. In March 1963, China stated its belief that the border treaties between pre-revolutionary China and Russia were unequal treaties from which the Soviet Union had acquired an enormous amount of Chinese territory. The Soviet Union rejected this position, but agreed to talks regarding the border (Gurtov, Hwang 1980: 208–09; Cohen 1991: 270–2). At the talks which began in February 1964, China claimed approximately 20,000 square kilometres in the Pamirs in the south-western border area, which the Soviets had inherited from tsarist times. In addition, while both sides accepted that their border ran along the Amur and Ussuri Rivers, the Soviet Union claimed that the border ran along the Chinese banks, whereas China claimed that the general principle of riverine borders being defined as the centre of the main channel (the Thalweg principle) should be applied. On this basis, China asserted its right to some 600 of the 700 islands on the rivers, including the Ussuri River island Zhenbao, which the Soviets called Damansky island, 180 miles south-west of the Soviet city Khabarovsk. There was some flexibility on the Soviet side regarding the Thalweg principle, but the talks broke down as Mao made the dispute much more public (*Keesing's* 1969: 23313–14; Gurtov, Hwang 1980: 208–11; Cohen 1991: 272).

After Khrushchev's removal from power in October 1964, his successor Leonid Brezhnev began to strengthen further the Soviet military presence on the border and to strengthen its deterrent threats against further border incidents. Beijing became particularly anxious at the conclusion in January 1966 of the twenty-year Treaty of Friendship, Co-operation and Mutual Aid between the Soviet Union and its suzerain neighbour Mongolia, which permitted the Soviet Union to deploy large military formations on Mongolian territory. In spite of substantial internal opposition, Mao's line simply hardened in response: his border patrols were told to fight if necessary rather than avoid fighting, although he kept a careful rein on the geographical scope of their patrolling and used a mix of soldiers, Red Guards (militant Communist Party activists) and civilians in order to avoid escalation (Cohen 1991: 273–6). Mao severed inter-party relations with the Communist Party of the Soviet Union (CPSU) and in 1967 initiated the Cultural Revolution in order to reinvigorate the revolutionary spirit of Chinese Communism by purging and repressing pragmatists. The result was chaos throughout China: as late as 1969 China had only one ambassador abroad (in Cairo), although Mao had begun to rebuild the state and party machinery (Kissinger 1979: 167). Had a Sino-Soviet war broken out, China would have been in no position to fight it. In late April 1968, the Soviet Union proposed technical talks on navigation on the Amur and Ussuri River sections of the border, but China rejected these in mid-August (Gurtov, Hwang 1980: 206). Chinese fears were heightened further in this period by a number of developments (Gurtov, Hwang 1980: ch. 6). The Soviet intervention in Czechoslovakia in 1968 and the Brezhnev doctrine (in which the Soviet Union reserved the right to intervene in any socialist country which it deemed to be deviating from its view of socialism) seemed particularly ominous. The Soviet Union also appeared to be arming large-scale revolts against

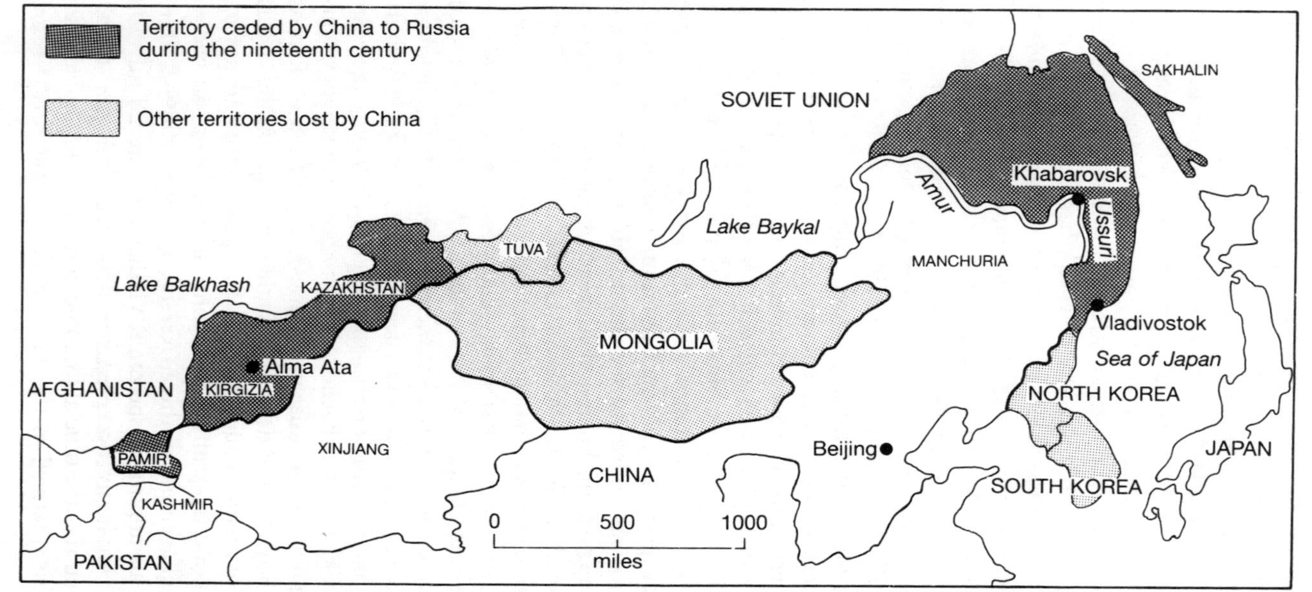

9.1 The Sino-Soviet border crisis, 1969

Beijing's rule in Xinjiang province, and stood to benefit from the spread of fighting such as that which took place between Chinese local and central army units in Shanxi. Improving Soviet relations with Japan and the United States, Soviet support for India in the Sino-Indian border dispute, US bombing of North Vietnam right up to the Sino-Vietnamese border and US violations of Chinese airspace led to Chinese fears of strategic encirclement by a hostile coalition. To show resolve, Mao ordered that the mixed groups of soldiers, Red Guards and civilians be replaced by armed, uniformed border guards who were to fight if necessary (Cohen 1991: 276–7). As clashes on the border became more frequent and as Soviet manoeuvres and incursions became more extensive, China claimed that Soviet forces were seeking to prevent Chinese troops from patrolling Zhenbao island (Gurtov, Hwang 1980: 233). On 2 March, around 300 Chinese troops ambushed Soviet military patrols as they headed for Zhenbao island. The ambush left many Soviet soldiers dead. The Soviets initiated large-scale retaliation on 15 March using tanks, heavy artillery and around 3,000 troops (*Keesing's* 1969: 23313–4; Maxwell 1973; Cohen 1991: 277–80). These were the only substantial military engagements ever between two nuclear powers. The confrontation continued through the summer and was ended by the discussion between Chinese and Soviet Premiers Zhou Enlai and Alexei Kosygin at Beijing airport on 11 September (Wich 1980: 275; Garthoff 1985: 210–11).

The border issue continued to be an irritant and an outlet for feelings of rivalry in Sino-Soviet relations. Minor clashes were reported as late as 12 July 1987, when Soviet troops killed one Chinese soldier and injured another (*Keesing's* 1987: 35065). In the late 1980s, the Soviet Union began to settle the riverine border issue on China's terms due to the determination of then Soviet President Mikhail S. Gorbachev to normalise relations with China. China demanded the withdrawal of Soviet forces from Afghanistan, the end of Soviet support for the Vietnamese occupation of Cambodia and dramatic reductions in the Soviet military presence on their border and especially in Mongolia, and has been satisfied with Soviet compliance on all three (*Keesing's* 1989: 35064–7, 36448, 36588). In his important speech in Vladivostock on 28 July 1986, Gorbachev implicitly accepted the Thalweg principle when he indicated that the 'the official [Sino-Soviet] border might pass along the main ship channel' of the Amur and Ussuri Rivers (*Keesing's*

1987: 35065; *Keesing's* 1988: 35840). In early August of that year, Mikhail Kapitsa, a Soviet Deputy Foreign Minister, confirmed that various border islands, including Zhenbao island, 'would in the future be transferred to China' (*Keesing's* 1987: 35065–6). The border talks restarted on 9 February 1987, and on 3 November 1990, the Chinese Foreign Ministry was able to announce 'unanimity' on the delineation of most of the border (*Keesing's* 1990: 37374). In the wake of the collapse of the Soviet Union, Russia, under the leadership of President Boris Yeltsin, has not changed this approach. Thus the question is on the verge of being resolved, with the Soviets keeping the disputed territory in the Pamirs and the other tsarist territories held through the 'unequal treaties', but accepting the Chinese position on their riverine border.

In this chapter, I argue that the Soviet attempt at compellence produced a mixed outcome, in spite of threats which sought to exploit clear Soviet conventional and nuclear superiority. I explain Chinese assertiveness in terms of the threat to Chinese interests posed by Soviet power in the context of Sino-Soviet rivalry.

SOVIET COMPELLENCE AND A MIXED OUTCOME

The Soviet Union was seeking to make China cease its border challenges, which falls into the overlap between deterrence and compellence. However, the main Soviet objective was one of compellence in trying to force China to resume technical border talks and come to an agreement acceptable to the Soviet Union. Moscow was quite happy to have talks, but only wanted them on its own terms. The conventional wisdom is that the outcome of this crisis favoured the Soviet Union because China ceased its aggressive border challenges, tolerated Soviet control of most of the islands and agreed to talks (Garver 1980: 224; Segal 1985b: 180, 197; see also Betts 1987: 81; Cohen 1991: 288). However, the outcome for the Soviet Union should be described as mixed at best. In efforts to defuse the crisis, the Soviet Union sought direct telephone contact with China on 21 March 1969, and requested on 29 March and 11 April immediate negotiations. To keep the pressure up, China rebuffed all three approaches (Cohen 1991: 281–2). The Soviets shifted position in agreeing to higher level talks than they had originally sought (Garthoff 1985:

211; Betts 1987: 81). This was a significant concession. The Soviets wanted talks only at the level of border guards to avoid implying any flexibility in their position. In agreeing to more, they were conceding the possibility of negotiation rather than just consultation (Wich 1980: 120–2, 205–12, 275–6). Although China dropped its demands for the return of territory, Soviet troop withdrawals, Soviet acceptance that the old treaties were unequal and illegitimate, and borders based on river courses, it soon renewed them all (Gelman 1982: 44–6). Furthermore, the Soviet Union tacitly ceded Zhenbao island and a few others to China and the talks soon deadlocked (Wich 1980; 207–14: Garver 1981: 225–6; Cohen 1991: 288). Finally, China had the broader political objective of showing that, in spite of its internal weakness, it was strong enough to stand up to the Soviet Union. It achieved this to a substantial degree, but the vigorous Soviet military threats provoked by its assertiveness ensured that the impression of Chinese weakness was not eliminated.

CLEAR SOVIET MILITARY SUPERIORITY

The Soviet Far Eastern conventional and nuclear build-up was a response to the new possibility of a two-front world war after the split with China, and to China's challenges on the border (Gelman 1982; MccGwire 1987). The result was that the local and short-term conventional balance and the nuclear balance all favoured the Soviet Union (Robinson 1981: 278; Segal 1985b: 192–3). The Chinese conventional forces had poor logistics, old equipment, limited mobility and few bombers. Soviet logistical superiority meant that it generally had local superiority, and any particular instances of local inferiority could quickly be remedied by drawing on its short-term superiority. The Chinese capital, Beijing, and China's primary industrial area, Manchuria, were both highly vulnerable to the Soviet conventional forces deployed in the region, and the Soviet Union conducted military manoeuvres to press these points home (Gelman 1982: 19–23). The Soviet campaign of conventional military intimidation had a number of facets. First, the Soviet leadership showed a willingness to out-escalate China, as exemplified by their use of force on 15 March at Zhenbao island (Gelman 1982: 34–5). Second, they took measures to advertise their military build-up, including the suspension of their normal rules of secrecy by inviting foreign correspondents to observe and report the build-up (Gelman 1982: 35–6). Third, they stressed many times that they had previously used large-scale conventional force in the Far East against Chinese forces in 1929 and against Japan in 1939 and 1945 (Gelman 1982: 36–7). In spite of its conventional superiority, the Soviet Union did not contemplate the prospect of war with equanimity (Wich 1980: 190). Arkady Shevchenko, as a UN Under-Secretary-General the highest-ranking Soviet defector ever, claims that the Soviet Politburo were deeply fearful that China might move with millions of troops to seize the disputed border territory, and that the Politburo believed that a massive invasion would be difficult to deal with (Shevchenko 1985: 217–18). China consistently maintained that the Soviet Union would get bogged down in a protracted conflict if it tried to fight a conventional war on Chinese territory, although the Soviet campaign of threats may have undermined Chinese confidence in this position (Gelman 1982: 42; see also Segal 1985b: 183–4). Mao's confidence that the Soviet Union was keen to avoid war and that therefore he had a relatively free hand to press the border issue only declined in July in the face of the concerted Soviet campaign of Soviet conventional and nuclear threats (Cohen 1991: 285–7).

China had tested its first atomic weapon in October 1964 and its first thermo-nuclear weapon in June 1967, but lacked a long-range missile or bomber delivery capability (Gurtov, Hwang 1980: 201). It said little about its nuclear capability other than declaring that it would not be the first to use nuclear weapons (Gurtov, Hwang 1980: 201–02). The Soviet Union had substantial nuclear superiority, but it existed in the context of the possession of an even larger arsenal by the United States. A nuclear attack on China's nuclear facilities would have reduced Soviet capabilities relative to those of the United States. This gap would have widened further if general war had ensued between China and the Soviet Union (Robinson 1981: 291–2), and the possibility that the United States would become embroiled could not be ruled out. The Soviet Union threatened China with the possibility of escalation to nuclear use, but mostly contented itself with pointing out that nuclear rockets were available for use if war should break out. These threats were much less blatant than the conventional threats, and at times Soviet organs even denied heatedly that the Soviet Union was making nuclear threats (Gelman 1982: 37–8). Even as the Soviet Union issued its own threats, it was not entirely dismissive of the Chinese nuclear capability (Wich 1980: 105–06, 110, 165–77, 190–1, 204–05, 208–09). Gelman suggests that the Soviet Union was trying to balance intimidating China with avoiding alienating world public opinion or embittering the Chinese elite to the point where there would be no hope for reconciliation with any future leaders (1982: 38; see also Wich 1980: 212).

Probably hoping that word would get back to China, the Soviet Union asked the United States in late summer 1969 what its reaction would be to a Soviet preventive attack on the nuclear capabilities of China. This option had been proposed by the United States twice before. In the summer of 1963 Kennedy proposed to Khrushchev that the Soviet Union or the United States or the two countries together should take military action to destroy China's nuclear weapon development facilities. Khrushchev decided not to co-operate. One month before the first Chinese nuclear test on 16 October 1964, President Lyndon B. Johnson made a similar approach to the Soviet Union, with the same negative result (Chang 1988b). The United States made the Soviet approach public on 27 August 1969 and indicated its opposition to such action (Kissinger 1979: 182–6, 764; Gelman 1982: 38–9; Shevchenko 1985: 164–6; Betts 1987: 80–1). Soviet bombers sent to the Far East practised bombing runs on mock-ups of Chinese nuclear facilities and the Soviet Union conducted secret war games which included nuclear attacks (Garthoff 1985: 209; Cohen 1991: 286–7). The Zhou-Kosygin meeting of 11 September brought the crisis to an end, but on 16 September, Victor Louis, a journalist well-known at the time as a Soviet agent, claimed that the Soviet Union was planning to use nuclear weapons to destroy the Chinese nuclear capability (Robinson 1981: 280–1; Gelman 1982: 39–40; Cohen 1991: 288), perhaps to keep the pressure on China for the planned border talks.

It is difficult to know whether China took seriously the possibility that the Soviet Union might at some point use nuclear weapons, but it is plausible. Repeated Chinese denunciations of Soviet nuclear 'blackmail' during the summer of 1969 and for years afterwards may not only have represented a Chinese effort to discredit the Soviet Union, but also have showed that the Chinese leadership was seriously worried by the Soviet nuclear threats, especially as their own nuclear forces were still very vulnerable (Gelman 1982: 42–4; Robinson 1981: 290–2; Garthoff 1985: 211). Chinese assertions of its ability to resist nuclear blackmail were made less often and more equivocally at the peak of the Soviet campaign of nuclear threats, and, for the first time in the face of nuclear threats it began to make preparations for war, such as the construction of air-raid shelters (Segal 1985b: 181, 185). China also began to stress that it was defensively motivated and did not want war (Cohen 1991: 285). Even if China was worried by Soviet conventional and nuclear capabilities, it continued to engage in military skirmishes as late as 13 August 1969. Indeed, its assertiveness was related to its fear of Soviet power.

CHINESE ASSERTIVENESS AND FEAR OF SOVIET POWER

According to Paul Robinson, it is 'difficult to imagine that it was the Chinese who took the military initiative' in general during the border clashes because of the disruption involved in the Cultural Revolution, Soviet military superiority and Soviet threats of escalation (1981: 279–80). Yet that is what happened. Although China kept its use of force limited to try to avoid provoking the Soviet Union, it combined aggressive border patrolling with a vast anti-Soviet propaganda campaign, even though the Soviet Union made it clear that it did not want trouble on the border and wanted to defuse the crisis (Wich 1980: 72–3, 103, 119–22, 274–5; Gelman 1982: 25–6, 28–9). In accepting the risks involved in a confrontation with the Soviet Union, the Chinese leadership was motivated by a powerful fear of loss. As Kissinger put it:

> They saw no possibility of compromise with the Soviet Union that was not debilitating . . . China sought safety in a reputation of ferocious intractability, in creating an impression, probably accurate, that it would defend its honor and integrity at any cost. It acted as if the smallest concession would start it down a slippery slope and hence had to be resisted as fiercely as an overt challenge to the national survival.
>
> (1982: 49)

China was under great threat from Soviet-sponsored rebellion in Xinjiang province and the Soviet military build-up in Mongolia, and was being pressed on its other borders by India and by the United States in Vietnam. While China was concerned about the Soviet military threat, it was prepared to behave provocatively on the border in the wake of the Soviet invasion of Czechoslovakia in order to show that China was not vulnerable in spite of the Cultural Revolution; that the Soviet Union and United States could not dominate the international system between them; that it was willing to challenge the Soviet Union's 'social imperialism', as China put it; that further action in Eastern Europe would incur costs in the Far East; and that Romania, Yugoslavia and Albania could resist Soviet pressure. Discouraging Soviet interference in Chinese affairs would provide Mao with a breathing space to continue consolidating his power (Gurtov, Hwang: 234, 238–41; Wich 1980: 55–73, 99–100, 114–15, 270–4, 276). The territory at stake along the border amounted to hundreds of islands of no particular value, if one leaves aside the Chinese claim on territory in the Pamirs, which it had no chance of acquiring, although both sides attached some value to the rivers along the border as substitutes for the roads which the region lacked. China stated that it wanted the status quo to be respected, but its demand that the Thalweg principle be applied required a change in Soviet behaviour (Wich 1980: 39–40). Neither side gained any great advantage from defence of the territorial status quo because it was unclear.

Although China did not look to be particularly threatening in the short term, the Soviet leadership was worried about the long-term challenge from China for leadership of the Communist world. In trying to compel China to settle the border issue on Soviet terms, it was trying to take advantage of the opportunity provided by its military superiority. However, it was China rather than the Soviet Union which provoked the border clashes initially, so the Soviets were forced to act to deal with them. The lack of any significant attempt by the Soviet Union to reassure China during this crisis is notable; it relied almost exclusively on military coercive means. Both sides were concerned about their strategic interests, but the balance of interests favoured China because the threat to China was so much more intense. The Soviet Union assumed that, because of China's military inferiority, its challenge was irrational. It was also concerned that China thought that its threats were bluffs (Gelman 1982: 33–4). The Soviet decision-makers showed no sign of understanding that the very credibility of the Soviet threat made China feel the need to demonstrate its resolve. The Soviet Union perceived China to be irrational not only because of the Chinese willingness to escalate the border conflict in the face of Soviet military superiority, but also because of the apparent self-destructiveness of the Cultural Revolution (Gelman 1982: 25–9, 33). In spite of the fact that both had Communist systems, the Soviet Union did not comprehend the implications of the Cultural Revolution for Chinese foreign policy. It produced militant rhetoric rather than external military adventurism because it was primarily an internal process which Mao understood would weaken China initially. Joseph Rothschild suggests that the Chinese aim of teaching the Soviet Union a lesson was very much in the Confucian tradition of teaching lessons to inferiors, and that this view of the opponent encourages a 'willful ignorance about the arms, organisation and capabilities of a foe definitionally deemed to be morally, culturally, and civilisationally their rebellious inferior' (1987: 57). China did try to teach the Soviet Union a lesson and to bolster its resolve with faith in its cultural and ideological superiority. However, China was not ignorant about its opponent in this case due to previous Sino-Soviet links, teaching lessons to other states is a common enough phenomenon in international politics, and the overtones of patronising arrogance in the phrase is characteristic of great power politics.

CONCLUSION: A SHOW OF RESOLVE AND A VIGOROUS RESPONSE

The Sino-Soviet border conflict was rooted in the ideological rivalry and military fears of the two states, while the unresolved territorial issues provided an outlet for their hostility. In this crisis, the main objectives of the Soviet Union were to make China cease its border provocations and settle the issue in technical talks. Especially in the light of events in Czechoslovakia, China was intent on showing that, in spite of Soviet strength and Chinese weakness, it could not be intimidated. In the face of Soviet military superiority, the Chinese took action which they hoped would be sufficiently escalatory to demonstrate their resolve and punish the Soviets and yet sufficiently limited and clearly delineated to make escalation to war unlikely. Mao calculated correctly at the outset that the Soviet Union did not want war, but under-estimated the vigour of the Soviet response to border provocations and, as the crisis progressed, appears to have worried that the Soviet Union was thinking seriously about going to war. On the Soviet side, the dominant feeling was one of consternation at the apparent recklessness of the behaviour of the Chinese. The outcome of the crisis was mixed in that both sides made concessions on the border issue and China made substantial headway in demonstrating its resolve. The mixed outcome was possible because the balance of interests favoured China to such an extent that Soviet superiority in the nuclear and conventional military balances was greatly, although not wholly, cancelled out. The Soviet Union misperceived China's actions as being based on an irrational hope of gain, while China actually appeared to be motivated primarily by fear of loss, combined with Mao's perception that he could control the risks involved in provoking a crisis. Like the Chinese, the Soviets did not seem to place a great deal of importance on the concrete intrinsic interests at stake: the crisis was dominated by the fears of both sides about threats to their long-term strategic interests.

Chapter Ten

ARGENTINA'S INVASION OF THE FALKLAND ISLANDS, 1982

> The truth is that the invasion could not have been foreseen or prevented.
>
> Margaret Thatcher (1993: 177)

In the 1700s Spain controlled a group of islands in the South Atlantic which it named *Las Islas Malvinas*. Its French settlers knew them as *Les Iles Malouines* and its British settlers knew them as the Falkland Islands.[1] They are located about 500 miles east of Argentina and nearly 7,000 miles from Britain. In November 1820, Argentina took the islands as the Spanish empire broke up, only to lose them to Britain in January 1833. Ever since, Argentina has pressed its claim of sovereignty over the islands, while in more recent years it has also proposed that the population, of mainly British descent, retain full autonomy over the islands' internal affairs. This option became known as 'leaseback'. The 1980 Falkland Islands census showed a population of 1,849, which was falling. In December 1981 one Argentine military government was replaced by another – a three-man junta led by General Leopoldo Galtieri (Commander-in-Chief of the Army), Admiral Jorge Anaya (Commander-in-Chief of the Fleet) as Galtieri's main backer and General Basilio Lami Dozo (Commander-in-Chief of the Air Force). The junta committed itself in December 1981 to regaining sovereignty over the islands by January 1983, the 150th anniversary of the British invasion. In an atmosphere of increasing tension, Argentina invaded the Falkland Islands on 2 April 1982, with the death of no islanders and one Argentine soldier. On 3 April, UN Security Council Resolution 502 called for an immediate end to hostilities, the withdrawal of Argentine forces and the resumption of talks between the two sides. In response to the invasion, the British government sent a naval task force. British forces landed on the Falkland Islands on 21 May and Argentine forces surrendered on 14 June. 712 Argentines and 255 Britons died. The junta collapsed in the face of public opposition and military defeat. In contrast, the British Prime Minister Margaret Thatcher called and won an early general election. The dispute over sovereignty has still not been resolved.

My objective in this chapter is to explain why Argentina invaded the Falkland Islands. Thatcher argues in her memoirs that 'The truth is that the invasion could not have been foreseen or prevented' (1993: 177). She quotes the conclusion of the Committee of Inquiry chaired by Lord Franks that 'we would not be justified in attaching any criticism or blame to the present Government for the Argentine Junta's decision to commit its act of unprovoked aggression in the invasion of the Falkland Islands on 2 April 1982' (quoted in Thatcher 1993: 177; see Franks 1983: para. 339). As will be explained, the Franks Report lets the British government off too lightly. I show that, while Argentina's threats were ambiguous, Britain became insensitive to the need for resolution of the Falklands dispute due to its unwillingness to either agree to the transfer of sovereignty through leaseback or to deploy an adequate deterrent capability. Although the particular occasion which resulted in invasion could not have been anticipated, the potential for an invasion was there and ought to have been defused through leaseback. If leaseback was to be ruled out, a proper deterrent capability, especially in the form of regular stationing of nuclear-powered submarines, was required. The invasion could not have been deterred if deterrence was to be left to the last minute: indeed, last-minute, half-hearted British military deployments helped prompt the invasion. For its part, the junta was strongly motivated to act and consequently underestimated the extent to which an invasion would be opposed and underestimated Britain's determination to retake the islands.

AMBIGUOUS ARGENTINE THREATS

The consistent British intelligence assessment from the mid-1960s onwards was that an invasion would be unlikely as long as

10.1 Argentina's invasion of the Falkland Islands, 1982

Argentina perceived that progress was being made towards a transfer of sovereignty (Franks 1983: paras. 32, 36, 59, 63, 75, 77, 87, 91, 94–6, 149–51). In the 26–27 February 1982 round of talks in New York, the British delegation agreed that a negotiating commission would be set up, the remit of which would include sovereignty. The underlying intention was to stall, as there was no plan to make any concessions of substance. The British delegation would not agree to the Argentine demand for a timetable for the transfer of sovereignty and left New York thinking mistakenly that it had bought more time. In order to make it clear that the outcome of the New York talks was unacceptable, the Argentine Foreign Ministry put out a unilateral communiqué taking a much harder line than that taken in New York (*Sunday Times* Insight Team 1982: 23–5, 75; Franks 1983: paras. 133–41, 297–303; Charlton 1989: 112, 182–3; Freedman, Gamba-Stonehouse 1990: 23–9). When Argentina publicly took a threatening line, Foreign Secretary Lord Carrington and the rest of the Foreign Office saw the situation as much more serious, but not as a radical departure from the past (Franks 1983: 299–302; Freedman, Gamba-Stonehouse 1990: 29–31, 35). From the British point of view, the talks had not collapsed and so an invasion was still seen as unlikely.

The junta tried to emphasise that matters were coming to a head in the hope of extracting concessions. In his Army Day speech on 29 May 1981 Galtieri said: 'Nobody can or will be able to say that we have not been extremely calm and patient in our handling of international problems, which in no way stem from any appetite for territory on our part. However, after a century and a half they are becoming more and more unbearable' (quoted in Franks 1983: para. 88). This was reinforced by a diplomatic note to the British Ambassador in Buenos Aires, Anthony Williams, on 27 July 1981, which mentioned the lack of progress in the negotiations and stated that 'The next round of negotiations cannot be another mere exploratory exercise, but must mark the beginning of a decisive stage towards the definitive termination of the dispute'. At the same time the Argentine Ministry of Foreign Affairs referred to that diplomatic note in a communiqué which stated that resolution was 'an unpostponable priority' and that 'national awareness' of the problem meant that 'it is not possible to defer this question' (quoted in Franks 1983: 97).

In December 1981, Galtieri and Anaya agreed that force would be used if necessary to regain the islands before the end of 1982. Their decision was supported by Lami Dozo and (when the latter was informed in February 1982) Foreign Minister Nicanor Costa Méndez. The junta began to brief the press to mobilise support (*Sunday Times* Insight Team 1982: 27; Freedman, Gamba-Stonehouse 1990: 23–4). An article in the leading Argentine newspaper *La Prensa* published on 24 January, which openly discussed invasion, was almost certainly sent to the Foreign Office accompanied by other similar articles (*Sunday Times* Insight Team 1982: 74; see also Lebow 1985a: 91–3). British intelligence tended to underestimate the seriousness of the threat because planning for the invasion was still very secretive, even if rumours did abound. In addition, Argentina was concerned that very overt threats might result in the deployment of a British deterrent force. While making threats, Argentina was engaged in diplomacy to gain concessions: Britain interpreted the threats as bluffs, and the fact that Argentina was still talking was taken as proof that diplomacy had not broken down (Freedman, Gamba-Stonehouse 1990: 23, 28n, 33–4, 90–4). The signals from Argentina were mixed, with reassuring noises coming in particular from Costa Méndez and yet with strong protests about British intransigence over sovereignty.

THE FALKLANDS LOBBY, IMPERIAL SENTIMENT AND INTRANSIGENCE ON SOVEREIGNTY

Britain was unwilling to put pressure on the islanders regarding leaseback, whereby sovereignty would pass to Argentina but the islands would retain internal autonomy: the only possible solution other than a collapse of the Argentine position was vetoed (Barnett 1982: 74–5). The leaseback idea had been pursued by the Labour government in 1977 and revived under Thatcher by Under-Secretary of State at the Foreign Office Nicholas Ridley (Barnett 1982: 24–5). Between 1965 and 1968, the British government negotiated on the basis that it would take into account the 'interests' – as opposed to the 'wishes' – of the islanders. The Falkland Islands lobby which opposed the transfer of sovereignty was well organised and vocal. Traditionalist Conservative Members of Parliament (MPs), who opposed any loss of dependent territories, combined with left-wing Labour MPs, who opposed giving anything to what they saw as a neo-fascist military dictatorship (Lebow 1985a: 105–06; Charlton 1989: 76–98; Dillon 1989: 55–89). Due to this lobby, the Government shifted after 1968 to referring to the wishes of the islanders as paramount (Charlton 1989: 22–8, 131–2; Freedman, Gamba-Stonehouse 1990: 8).

The Falkland Islands lobby was powerful in part because of Thatcher's nostalgia for empire and her perception that the islands (if not most of the islanders) were British (Barnett 1982: 81–2). Although she did tolerate the exploration of the leaseback proposal by the Foreign Office for a while (Franks 1983: para. 80), she was hostile to it and did not intend to let what she referred to as appeasement come to fruition (Freedman, Gamba-Stonehouse 1990: 15). When Ridley presented leaseback to Parliament on 2 December 1980, it met with great hostility and in September 1981 Thatcher replaced Ridley with Richard Luce, who was more in line with her perspective (Lebow 1985a: 96–7, 105). Her government was deeply unpopular at the time, and she had no wish to antagonise traditional Conservative supporters by pressing for the resolution of an issue which seemed minor, yet capable of generating much political controversy. In September 1981 a paper from the Defence Committee stressed that the need for resolution was becoming urgent, but Carrington felt unable to do much due to domestic political constraints (*Sunday Times* Insight Team 1982: 55; Franks 1983: 28). Those domestic political constraints were made more problematic by the position taken by Thatcher. If she had been behind leaseback she would have been handicapped rather than shackled by the Falklands lobby. She was not one for shying away from action that she believed to be appropriate simply because there was a lobby group opposing her. Indeed, she relished political battle. Hardly anyone in Britain had heard of the islands, somewhere between one-third and half of the islanders seemed to be prepared to accept leaseback, and islanders opposed to leaseback could have had the pill sugared with very generous compensation from the two governments (Barnett 1982: 25–6), but this would have been seen as the sacrifice of principle to expediency.[2] In the absence of a willingness to concede sovereignty, Britain should have maintained an adequate deterrent capability. In fact, deterrence was weak and getting weaker.

THE GRADUAL WEAKENING OF DETERRENCE

The South Atlantic had never been central to British naval policy. In 1976, the position of South Atlantic Commander-in-Chief was abolished and the frigate normally deployed in the region was withdrawn (Franks 1983: para. 278). Nevertheless, Callaghan made, or made preparations for, a number of naval deployments due to the prospect of a possible invasion of the Falklands. He ordered the despatch of a frigate and a support vessel to the vicinity in February 1976, prior to the reopening of negotiations. As it turned out, Argentina was mollified by the fact that the talks were to include the issue of sovereignty (Franks 1983: paras. 45, 49, 58). At the time of the talks, British negotiators had planned to be able to respond to any threat of force should the talks deadlock by pointing to the fact that a Royal Navy task group, comprising six warships, three support ships and a submarine, was in the Atlantic *en route* from Gibraltar to the Caribbean (Franks 1983: para. 59). The precautionary deployment which has become most well-known is the government's decision on 21 November 1977 to send a nuclear-powered submarine covertly, with two frigates and a supporting tanker, to the Falklands. The two sides had broken off diplomatic relations and Argentina had cut support services to the islands, fired on a British ship and occupied the British dependency of Southern Thule, 1,100 miles east of the Falkland Islands. The submarine was deployed close to the islands, while the frigates were kept about 1,000 miles away. The deployment was intended to remain secret and the Argentine government appears not to have known about its presence.[3] The intention was to reveal its presence if necessary to show that aggression would meet with resistance, even if the force could not cope with a full-scale attack (Charlton 1989: 65). The crucial point is that the lack of an invasion seems more to have been a result of the talks going well between the two governments: in particular, the British government was willing to discuss sovereignty (Franks 1983: paras. 59–6). The British naval force was withdrawn after one month and the government decided not to deploy it again in the run-up to the Lima stage of the negotiations in February 1978 (Franks 1983: para. 66). As it turned out, little progress was made at those talks and progress made at the next round, in December 1978 in Geneva, was vetoed due to the objections of the Falkland Islands' councillors (Franks 1983: para. 68–9). Nevertheless, the Argentine government still believed that Britain was serious about transferring sovereignty. Invasion had always been averted by political means, not by deterrence. Thatcher drew precisely the wrong lesson from 1977. Instead of seeing it as underscoring the need to discuss sovereignty, she saw it as indicating that precautionary military deployments were unnecessary and potentially provocative.

Thatcher's policies further weakened general deterrence and made it more difficult to attempt immediate deterrence. The Defence White Paper of June 1981 proposed that Britain cease to have naval forces in the South Atlantic or Antarctica, and HMS *Endurance* was to be retired by April 1982 (Franks 1983: para. 114; Freedman, Gamba-Stonehouse 1990: 10). Thatcher denied that HMS *Endurance* had any deterrent value because the lightly-armed vessel was a 'military irrelevance' (1993: 177). This ignored its symbolic importance, which was recognised by the Foreign Office, which argued that the withdrawal would be seen as a reduction of the British commitment to the islands (Charlton 1989: 66, 153; Freedman, Gamba-Stonehouse 1990: 20). Carrington wrote to Defence Secretary John Nott three times to say that the wrong signal was being sent.[4] The withdrawal of Britain's naval forces encouraged the Argentine belief that Britain would not and could not respond militarily to an invasion of the islands; this view was expressed in the Argentine press and was communicated to the British government in an intelligence report in September 1981 (Franks 1983: paras. 116, 287; Costa Méndez 1987). As part of a major Foreign Office policy review on the Falkland Islands, it was concluded on 30 June 1981 that, among other things, the Defence Committee of the Cabinet should prepare military contingency plans (Franks 1983: para. 93; see also paras. 100, 108), and on 3 March 1982 Thatcher noted in the margin of a telegram that 'we must make contingency plans' (1993: 177). Little was done (*Sunday Times* Insight Team 1982: 76; Franks 1983: paras. 152–3, 324–32, 295; Lebow 1985a: 93; 101–02). Contingency planning and deterrence were hobbled by an obsession to avoid spending more money, and a strong desire to avoid reversing the course of naval policy; rather than accept certain short-term costs, Britain opted for risking only possible, but much higher, long-term costs (Lebow 1985a: 93, 101–03, 111, 122–4; Hopple 1984: 347; Freedman, Gamba-Stonehouse 1990: 35–6).

British government policy was characterised, as Lebow has argued, by 'defensive avoidance' (1985a: 103–07). This occurs when decision-makers assess their options in a risky situation, find no good alternative, lose hope that one can be found and stop trying to find one. To defend themselves from the negative feelings which result from facing this situation, they procrastinate, transfer the responsibility to others and 'bolster', that is, overestimate the chances of success for the policy they feel forced to pursue, and twist or ignore evidence to the contrary. While bolstering may be useful in letting a decision-maker press on in a difficult situation, it can also make them insensitive to warnings that their policy is about to fail (Lebow 1981; 1985a: 103–04; Janis, Mann 1977: 57–8, 74, 197–233). The Falklands lobby and Thatcher's own preferences made transfer of sovereignty a politically difficult option, but a 'Fortress Falklands' approach clashed with the desire to save money and orientate the Royal Navy more closely with NATO. Thatcher did not face up to the probability that the taking of the islands by force would jeopardise her position as Prime Minister. The British government procrastinated and hoped to pass responsibility onto a future government by dragging its feet in the negotiations with Argentina.

While it is difficult to distinguish serious threats from bluffs, Lebow argues that 'it was incumbent upon the British to develop indicators to help distinguish bluff from the real thing' (Lebow 1985a: 93; see also 107, Hopple 1984: 350–1, and Freedman, Gamba-Stonehouse 1990: 86–7). Actually, in various British intelligence assessments between July 1981 and March 1982, the indicators used to measure the Argentine threat to the islands were the state of the Argentine-Chilean dispute over control of the Beagle Channel, Argentine political and economic conditions, Argentine inter-service rivalry, and especially Argentine satisfaction with progress on the issue of sovereignty. Those assessments concluded that invasion was unlikely (Franks 1983: paras. 307–08). Yet all these measures showed unfavourable trends. In 1977 an International Court of Arbitration, and in December 1980 a Papal mediator, found in favour of Chile. Argentina rejected the first judgement, prevaricated on the second and early in 1982, Argentina tried to prevent the dispute from going to the International Court of Justice. It was also worried about Chile supporting Britain over the Falklands (Franks 1983: para. 275; Freedman, Gamba-Stonehouse 1990:

6–7, 11–12). In addition, the junta was tottering politically and economically, Anaya – an exceptionally militant figure regarding the Falklands – was a key player in the junta, and dissatisfaction with the negotiations was particularly high once leaseback had stalled. The intelligence assessments that an invasion was not an immediate prospect were correct. However, the signs also suggested that the situation was unusually explosive.

THE JUNTA'S BALANCE OF INTERESTS IN FAVOUR OF INVASION

Opportunity is rarely enough to prompt an invasion. The junta was also strongly motivated to act, which helped to tip its balance of interests in favour of the use of force. It had made itself highly unpopular, mainly due to the desperate state of the economy and the dirty war of kidnapping and murder (the 'disappearances') against its political opponents, which claimed perhaps 20,000 lives (Lebow 1985a: 97–9). A wave of strikes began on 30 March, which put the junta under further pressure (Franks 1983: para. 227). It desperately needed a victory of some kind and it hoped to cash in on popular nationalist sentiment about the islands (*Sunday Times* Insight Team 1982: 29–30; Paul 1994: 155, 159–62). Geopolitical factors were also of some importance. In the run-up to the 1991 review of the 1959 Antarctic Treaty, which suspended competing territorial claims and provided for demilitarisation, Argentina had in mind the economic potential of possible future exploration in the Antarctic (Freedman, Gamba-Stonehouse 1990: 6–7). Argentina also sought to assert itself as a regional power in its rivalry with Chile (Barnett 1982: 110). In contrast, Britain was gradually withdrawing from the South Atlantic and shifting its strategic emphasis towards NATO.

Argentina was convinced that its claim was legitimate, and that deep down Britain accepted its legitimacy. This could be seen in Britain's occasional willingness to negotiate on sovereignty. One internal British government paper in 1946 even described the seizure of the islands in 1833 as 'an act of unjustified aggression' (quoted in Barnett 1982: 24). Successive British governments had shown little interest in the Falkland islanders and had hinted at a desire to hand sovereignty to Argentina. Only about 10 per cent of the population had UK citizenship. The rest had Commonwealth passports and Thatcher had refused to grant them British citizenship in the British Nationality Bill in 1981. They were awarded British citizenship six months after the invasion (Barnett 1982: 28; Hoffmann, Hoffmann 1984: 175; Freedman, Gamba-Stonehouse 1990: 21). As former Argentine diplomat Roberto Guyer, who had negotiated with Britain in the 1960s over the Falklands, put it: 'we thought our claim was legitimate. It was so legitimate that *you continued discussing it*' (quoted in Charlton 1989: 104–05). The UN Committee on Decolonisation designated the islands in 1964 as territory to be decolonised, referred to them officially as the Falkands-Malvinas and requested a negotiated settlement. Non-binding UN General Assembly Resolution 2065 of 16 December 1965 requested negotiations which took into account the interests, rather than wishes, of the islanders (Freedman, Gamba-Stonehouse 1990: 7–8). Whereas the story of the islands and the looming anniversary were common knowledge to all Argentines, only a few government and academic specialists in Britain were aware of the background (Barnett 1982: 126; Hopple 1984: 349; Charlton 1989: 102; Freedman, Gamba-Stonehouse 1980: *xxxiii*).

When the danger signals came, the British Government interpreted them as not being serious and argued that, even if they were serious, responding to them would only make matters worse. The modest military precautions it took did indeed make matters worse because they were misperceived by the junta, which quickly decided to invade before its window of opportunity closed.

A WINDOW OF OPPORTUNITY PERCEIVED TO BE CLOSING

Simply in terms of hardware, Argentina's maximum military opportunity would have come in 1983. The aircraft carriers HMS *Invincible* and *Hermes* would have been sold to Australia, and a number of frigates and the amphibious assault ships *Intrepid* and *Fearless* scrapped (Hopple 1984: 3512–2; Lebow 1985a: 122; Paul 1994: 153). Argentina would have doubled its number of French Super Etendard jets, had many more Exocet missiles, more German submarines, and extra fuel tanks for its Skyhawk jets, which would have given them much more time in the air over the islands

(Barnett 1982: 113). Even a few more weeks would have made sending a task force much more difficult, as British naval forces would have been dispersed after their exercises and winter would have been that much closer.

The specific trigger for the invasion was the mistaken belief that Britain had sent a substantial deterrent force. As British intelligence had suspected, the junta had not – until that point – generally envisioned an invasion until the second half of 1982. A dispute arose over the legality of the operations of an Argentine scrap-metal merchant on the British-controlled island of South Georgia, 700 miles east of the Falklands. Work began on December 1981 and on March 23 Britain informed Argentina that it was sending HMS *Endurance* to remove the workers, by force if necessary, if Argentina did not remove them immediately. Argentina sent a naval auxiliary vessel on March 24, which arrived on March 25. Rather than remove the workers in the context of a threat of force publicised by the press, the junta decided on March 26 to deploy troops from that vessel on South Georgia. Argentina saw the tough stand taken by Britain over the South Georgia incident as proof that hard-liners controlled British policy, and that they were using the incident as a pretext to reverse Britain's military withdrawal from the South Atlantic, to put an end to any real negotiations and to support the islands via Chile (Moro 1989: 15; Freedman, Gamba-Stonehouse 1990: 68–77). The junta calculated that a large deterrent force could arrive by 4 April and felt impelled to act. The junta knew about the sending of the supply ships RRS *John Biscoe* (with forty marines on board to relieve the Falklands garrison) and RRS *Bransfield* to the Falkands from Uruguay on 23 March and Chile on 25 March respectively. It also knew about the decision taken on 26 March to keep HMS *Endurance* on station and double the number of marines on the Falklands by not removing those about to go on leave. The junta took at face value much exaggerated speculation that a British task force, possibly drawing on HMS *Exeter* off Belize, seven destroyers and frigates off Gibraltar and nuclear-powered submarines, may have been sent as early as 25 March. This would rule out their use of force should diplomatic pressure fail. From 23 March, the junta had convened daily meetings on the escalating South Georgia crisis, and on the evening of 26 March it decided to invade the Falklands (Moro 1989: 2, 7–8, 14–16; Charlton 1989: 110–15; Freedman, Gamba-Stonehouse

1990: 67). The junta wanted Britain to have some awareness of their military preparations in the hope of wringing concessions at the last minute and thus making an invasion unnecessary. However, they did not want the full extent of their preparations to be known; as Anaya put it in an interview some years later: 'If the British found out in sufficient time they could do two things which would be impossible for us to deal with. One was a major reinforcement of the garrison on the Malvinas. The other was the appearance in the South Atlantic of a large naval force, especially if it included submarines which we could not fight.'[5] The British news media mistakenly reported that the nuclear-powered submarine HMS *Superb* had left Gibraltar for the Falklands on 25 March, when it actually left some days later and anyway was headed for Faslane, where it arrived on 16 April (Freedman, Gamba-Stonehouse 1990: 77). When the junta was given this inaccurate information on 31 March, it saw its window of opportunity beginning to close and decided to carry out immediately the invasion it had concluded on 26 March would be necessary (Franks 1983: para. 263; Charlton 1989: 116–18; Moro 1989: 15; Freedman, Gamba-Stonehouse 1990: 77; Paul 1994: 154).

Argentina's window of opportunity was closing much more slowly than it believed. British decision-makers had been constantly aware of the need to avoid being provocative in any attempt to reinforce deterrence (Thatcher 1993: 175, 177). To some extent this had been a rationalisation of, rather than the reason for, inaction, as it fitted with the gradual military withdrawal from the South Atlantic. However, it was also a legitimate concern. In the end, the junta perceived a much greater attempt to deter than actually existed. The Foreign Office told Carrington on 5 March 1982 of the covert deployment of forces in November 1977, but did not recommend a similar course of action. Carrington's only response was to ask whether Argentina knew of the deployment: he was told it had not known (Franks 1983: paras. 148, 300). On their way to Brussels on 29 March, Thatcher and Carrington decided to send a nuclear-powered submarine to support HMS *Endurance*.[6] The submarine HMS *Splendid* left Faslane in Scotland on 1 April, while another – HMS *Superb* – left Gibraltar the same day for Faslane to be made ready. In addition, the RFA *Fort Austin* auxiliary vessel left Gibraltar and headed south to replenish HMS *Endurance*. The Navy was also ordered to prepare a group of ships from among those on exercises off Gibraltar for possible despatch to the South Atlantic (Franks 1983: para. 213). Although intelligence reports suggested that the action on South Georgia was a probe of British intentions, and that a full invasion was unlikely, Thatcher claims that 'we knew that they were unpredictable and unstable, and that a dictatorship might not behave in ways that we would consider rational' (1993: 179). However, there is no evidence that discussions about such questions took place at the time or, if they were simply unspoken assumptions, that these assumptions influenced policy.

Thatcher was 'not too displeased' when the news of the sending of the submarine leaked to the news media, which reported it on 31 March:[7] 'The submarine would take two weeks to get to the South Atlantic, but it could begin to influence events straight away. My instinct was that the time had come to show the Argentines that we meant business' (1993: 178). She was not attempting to deter Argentina but hoped that the leaked news would have a deterrent effect nevertheless. If she thought it could have a deterrent effect, why not try to achieve that effect deliberately? Furthermore, the sudden reversal of her past concern with avoiding provocation is an important issue left unexplained, especially as the leak helped prompt the invasion. Whereas Thatcher and the Ministry of Defence thought the leak would have a deterrent effect, the Foreign Office worried that it would be provocative (Freedman, Gamba-Stonehouse 1990: 77). On 30 March the Government decided to send a third submarine and have a fourth made ready. The sending of a surface force was rejected as provocative and as inadequate in military terms unless it was very large (Franks 1983: paras. 224–5). However, on 1 April, with invasion looking almost certain, Thatcher, Carrington and Nott agreed to send troops as part of a full-scale task force as soon as possible (Franks 1983: para. 71). It was too late for deterrence: the job of the task force would be to try to reverse a successful invasion.

UNDERESTIMATION OF OPPOSITION TO AN INVASION

The junta did not expect its actions to be seen by most states as blatant aggression, although Costa Méndez reported on 26 March that there would probably be a majority against Argentina in the UN Security Council if it invaded (Hoffman, Hoffmann 1984: 173). As the world had paid very little attention to the dispute, the invasion came like a bolt from the blue as unprovoked aggression, rather than the result of a storm which had been building for years. The balance of legitimacy was suddenly reversed for the crucial reason that, while its sovereignty claim could be construed as legitimate, the way in which it pursued it was seen as unacceptable. Its poor image, as prone to coups and human rights abuses, made it even easier for much of international opinion to be against it, even though the islanders were to be allowed to retain all their political, legal and other structures and were not mistreated during the occupation (Barnett 1982: 24–7; Hoffman, Hoffmann 1984: 173). The invasion was seen by the junta less as an act of aggression or war than an occupation to force Britain to negotiate seriously on sovereignty, and to propel the issue onto the international agenda. The invasion was intentionally virtually bloodless in the hope of minimising international, and especially British, reactions (Freedman, Gamba-Stonehouse 1990: 82, 90, 105–06, 142; Paul 1994: 153; cf. *Sunday Times* Insight Team 1982: 15). The main invasion force was to withdraw and leave behind a police force about 500 strong. However, the strength of Argentine public reaction and the strength of the British reaction made it very hard for the junta to be willing to negotiate at all (Freedman, Gamba-Stonehouse 1990: 68, 79, 90, 148–9, 415). The United States was expected by the junta at least to stay neutral, as Argentina had supported the Reagan agenda in Central America (*Sunday Times* Insight Team 1982: 28; Hoffman, Hoffmann 1984: 173; Lebow 1985a: 112–14; Charlton 1989: 167–8; Paul 1994: 157–9). Argentina had a prominent advocate in the Reagan administration of a neutral line – UN Ambassador Jeane Kirkpatrick. In the end Secretary of State Alexander Haig's preference for lining up with the British won the day with Reagan (*Sunday Times* Insight Team 1982: 123–40; Charlton 1989: 158–81). No doubt this outcome was aided by the close personal relations between Reagan and Thatcher.

A key miscalculation which favoured invasion over diplomacy was the belief that Britain would not use force to recapture the islands. The junta did not think that the islands were very important to Britain in comparison with the potentially very high costs of such an operation (Lebow 1985a: 110–11; Costa Méndez 1987; Dillon 1989: 104–08; Freedman, Gamba-Stonehouse 1990: 79). The junta was so confident of this that it did not make serious contingency plans for major fighting, even after the task force was despatched (*Sunday Times* Insight Team 1982: 28; Hoffman, Hoffmann 1984: 173; Hopple 1984: 352; Paul 1994: 153, 157). It also gave Britain's nuclear monopoly hardly a moment's thought.[8] Although the United States told the junta that Britain would fight and win, Galtieri did not think that Britain could retake the islands due to logistical problems and Argentine air superiority (Charlton 1989: 173). This view was shared by many US analysts (Lebow 1985a: 111–12). On the British side, because there was so little faith in the view that the islands could be retaken without air cover, there were, according to Rear-Admiral Sir John Woodward, commander of the task force, no contingency plans for trying to retake them. Only the Chief of the Naval Staff, Sir Henry Leach, believed that the islands could be recovered by force (Thatcher 1993: 179). It was a gamble necessary to save Thatcher's government from inevitable collapse due to what was perceived as a great national humiliation. The junta failed to consider this and it totally underestimated the drive and determination of Margaret Thatcher as an individual, who was proud to be known as the 'Iron Lady' and who had a confrontational personal style (Lebow 1985a: 118; Charlton 1989: 173).

Ethnocentrism, in terms of incuriosity about the opponent, ensured that Argentina did not understand that Britain would see the crisis in terms of the Munich analogy and the need to avoid appeasement. The British press and politicians returned to this theme again and again (Lebow 1985a: 115–16; Dillon 1989: 114–16, 135, 136, 178, 233; Thatcher 1993: 173, 187, 192, 231). Britain feared that inaction would put its interests at risk by encouraging other states to press their claims against territories held or supported by Britain, including Spain regarding Gibraltar, China regarding Hong Kong, Mauritius regarding Diego Garcia,[9] Guatemala regarding Belize, and Venezuela regarding Guyana (Hopple 1984: 348n; Lebow 1985a: 117–18; Thatcher 1993: 192, 231). The analogies which preoccupied the junta were rather different. One was Goa: the junta even called one of its invasion scenarios Operation Goa, after the incident in 1961 when India invaded and declared its sovereignty over this Portuguese colony without serious

Portuguese opposition.[10] The other analogy was Suez: when Britain, France and Israel invaded Egypt in 1956 in response to its nationalisation of the Suez Canal, US economic sanctions (especially on Britain) forced a rapid withdrawal and the collapse of the British government (Paul 1994: 151–2, 159; Charlton 1989: 115, 119, 120, 167). An important rule in using analogies is to consider the ways in which the situation is different as well as similar. Suez was a poor fit. First, as Sir Nicholas Henderson, British Ambassador to the United States in 1982, pointed out, in 1956 Britain was the invader, whereas in 1982 Argentina was the invader (quoted in Charlton 1989: 194–6; see also 191–3). Hence the Munich analogy overrode US antipathy to British imperial ventures. Second, as US Secretary of State Alexander Haig and General Vernon Walters explained to the Argentines, in 1982 the British Parliament was united in its call for action, whereas in 1956 the Labour Party was opposed to military action and the Conservative Party was divided (Charlton 1989: 168, 191; Barnett 1982). Although Britain was worried that the United States would act on the basis of the Suez analogy anyway (Charlton 1989: 157, 193, 195, 203), the junta's analogies were self-serving ones. This suggests a substantial element of wishful thinking.

CONCLUSION: MOTIVATED BIAS AND MUTUAL MISPERCEPTION

At no point did Argentina present Britain with an implicit or explicit ultimatum to concede sovereignty. Instead it used less vigorous threats to try to achieve the same objective, without pushing Britain into reversing its steady military withdrawal from the South Atlantic. It did successfully communicate an increased sense of urgency to Britain but this did not yield any results in the negotiations. British policy was paralysed by Thatcher's imperial sentiment and the Falklands lobby, which combined to stymie leaseback, and by strategic and budgetary priorities which left the islands virtually undefended. As a result, Britain stalled in the talks and just hoped for the best. It was insensitive to the junta's strengthening motivation to act due to the junta's domestic unpopularity, geopolitical interests and conviction that Britain was frustrating the achievement of a legitimate and important objective.

Once strongly motivated to act, Argentina's policy was also affected by motivated bias in its underestimation of international opposition to an invasion, its expectation that the United States would at least stay neutral, its conviction that Britain would not try to retake the islands and its resort to the dubious Goa and Suez analogies. Motivated bias can be seen to be operating because all of these miscalculations systematically served to support the view that invasion was the best policy, and because no alternative perspective was considered seriously. Its belief in its military superiority encouraged the junta's lack of curiosity about its opponent, and its exaggerated concern that this superiority was about to be undermined was the catalyst for the decision to invade. It is true, as the Franks Report argues, that 'the Government had no reason to believe before March 31 that an invasion would take place at the beginning of April' (Franks 1983: paras. 261, 265–6). The junta's decision that it would definitely invade was taken only at the last minute, and its threats had been kept ambiguous. Nevertheless, even if the specific timing of the invasion could not be anticipated, the increased general likelihood should have been recognised and action taken accordingly, either to increase deterrence by covert deployment of submarines to make invasion impractical or, better, by grasping the political nettle and agreeing to leaseback.

NOTES

[1] Although I refer to the Falkland Islands rather than *Las Islas Malvinas*, this should not be interpreted as favouring the British over the Argentine view of the dispute.

[2] Charlton 1989: 57, 59. The contrast with the policy of those same British governments towards the 1,800 people of the Chagos Islands is stark (Madeley 1985). As part of the British empire they were a dependency of Mauritius. In order to turn Diego Garcia – the main Chagan island – into a military base to be leased to the United States, the islands were separated from Mauritius in 1965 and renamed the British Indian Ocean Territory before Mauritian independence in 1968. Between 1965 and 1971, 1,000 of the islanders were pressured into leaving by the nationalisation and closing down of their small industries, or were not allowed to return after going on holiday to Mauritius. The rest of the people were removed against their will to two of the smaller Chagan islands in 1971,

and then to Mauritius in 1973 with no compensation. Their fate was successfully kept secret until 1975. In March 1982, the British government was offering small sums of compensation in return for written promises never to return. In July 1982 it increased the amount to a total of £4.7 million, but the Mauritian government has claimed sovereignty over the islands and the Chagans have claimed the right to return. British governments would probably have acted this way towards groups of any race if it felt it strategically useful and politically feasible. Still, the fact that they were not white but a mix of Africans, Malagasys and Indians will not have helped their case with the government, and will have made it less likely that any lobby group on their behalf would be well connected.

[3] The deployment is sometimes presented as successful deterrence (see, for example, Barnett 1982: 29–32, 37–9). One version is that the deterrent threat was communicated via a businessman who had good Latin American government contacts (*Sunday Times* Insight Team 1982: 51). Another claims that Sir Maurice Oldfield, head of the British overseas intelligence organisation MI6, quietly let Argentina know of the presence of the submarine in the South Atlantic and the invasion was called off (UK Channel Four television, *The Falklands War* 1993). Oldfield is now dead, but it is known that Callaghan informed Oldfield of the deployment (Hastings, Jenkins 1983: 36–7). US Admiral Harry Train, who interviewed Anaya for a classified US study after the Falklands War, claims that Anaya told him that Argentina knew about the submarine deployment in 1977 and was deterred from invading by it. However, Rear-Admiral Carlos Busser, who was closely involved in planning the invasion and who commanded the landing, denied that Argentina knew of the deployment (quoted in Charlton 1989: 117).

[4] UK Channel Four television *The Falklands War* 1993.

[5] UK Channel Four television *The Falklands War* 1993.

[6] Franks 1983: para. 213. Thatcher's memoirs have the date as 28 March (1993: 178). *The Observer* newspaper claimed that Carrington had asked for the despatch of a submarine to the Falklands two weeks before the invasion, but that the Cabinet Defence Committee chaired by Thatcher refused (11 June 1982, cited in Barnett 1982: 75). However, this was not true, and the Defence Committee did not meet at that time (Franks 1983: 91).

[7] Franks 1983: para. 229. Thatcher's memoirs have the date of the leak as 29 March (1993: 178).

[8] Paul 1994: 152. Mention of Britain's nuclear weapons is absent from virtually all accounts of the crisis. However, there is a fair probability that

British nuclear weapons were in the South Atlantic. There were some reports that the HMS *Sheffield* had nuclear depth charges on board when it was sunk on 4 May (Barnett 1982: 145; *The Guardian* 23 September 1991). This has been denied by an officer who was serving on the ship at the time (Interview, May 1993). However, British ships routinely carry tactical nuclear weapons, and the *Sheffield* was one of the ships detached hurriedly from the NATO naval exercise Spring Train and sent to the South Atlantic. There is some evidence to suggest that tactical nuclear weapons were on a British vessel which was kept away from the immediate battle zone, and that a *Resolution*-class SSBN with sixteen *Polaris* missiles (each of which carries three nuclear warheads) was despatched to the area. These and other nuclear aspects of the crisis are currently being investigated by Paul Rogers.

[9] See note 2.

[10] Lebow 1985a: 115; Paul 1994: 161. Other limited amounts of territory had been captured using naval forces in the 1970s, and then retained successfully in spite of protests: Iran took islands in the Persian Gulf, China took the Paracels, Vietnam took the Spratleys and Turkey took part of Cyprus (Hopple 1984: 352).

Chapter Eleven

IRAQ'S REFUSAL TO WITHDRAW FROM KUWAIT, 1990–91

There can be no face-saving.
US President George Bush (quoted in Smith 1992: 222)

Yours is a society that cannot accept ten thousand dead in one battle.
Saddam Hussein to US Ambassador April Glaspie
(quoted in Stein 1992: 175)

Iraq invaded and occupied neighbouring Kuwait on 2 August 1990. That same day, the United Nations passed Security Council Resolution 660, which demanded the immediate and unconditional withdrawal of Iraqi forces from Kuwait. The initial concern of the United States was that Saddam Hussein might head straight for Riyadh after success against Kuwait. The United States secured Saudi Arabia and built up a coalition of some twenty-eight states under the UN flag. The economic sanctions imposed were comprehensive, and the coalition deployed enormous military capabilities, including symbolic forces from many Arab states, under the name Operation Desert Shield. The aim was to make it clear that, in the event of a military conflict, Iraq was certain to be expelled from Kuwait. The coalition, by demonstrating a capability to operate in a chemical environment, tried to convince Iraq that the Iraqi chemical weapon arsenal would not deter it from attacking. The United Nations also passed Resolution 678 of 29 November 1990, which authorised UN members to use 'all means necessary to uphold and implement Resolution 660 and all subsequent relevant resolutions'. The resolution required that Iraq withdraw 'on or before 15 January 1991'. When Iraq did not comply, air and naval attacks began from close to midnight on 16 January (Operation

Desert Storm), and, when Iraq still failed to withdraw, the land offensive was launched on the evening of 24 February. On 27 February, Iraq announced its unconditional acceptance of the UN resolutions and the coalition military operations were suspended as a result. Coalition dead numbered around 250. Approximately 3,000 Iraqi civilians and 3,000 Iraqi military personnel died: initial estimates were much higher. Between 10,000 and 100,000 Iraqis died in the wake of the war as a result of the repression of the Kurdish and Shiite uprisings, the collapse of sanitation and health services due to the bombing, and continuing economic sanctions (Mueller 1994: 156–8).

COMPELLENCE AND SELF-ENTRAPMENT

This crisis is generally seen in terms of either failed compellence or successful entrapment. The compellence perspective is that Bush issued military threats, reinforced by punishment inflicted through air attacks and economic sanctions, in an attempt to make Saddam Hussein withdraw from Kuwait (Stein 1992; George 1993; Herrmann 1994). The threats did not work, various opportunities for a face-saving withdrawal were spurned by Saddam Hussein and his forces were expelled from Kuwait by the offensive use of conventional force. Although 'the orchestration of coercive diplomacy by the United States after the invasion of Kuwait met textbook requirements' (Stein 1992: 170), compellence failed due to Saddam Hussein's miscalculations. The entrapment perspective is that the United States did not want Iraq to withdraw because it would retain its armed forces intact, would possibly require the long-term deployment of substantial forces in the region, similar to the US commitment in South Korea, and would not constitute sufficient punishment for aggression. President Bush therefore set terms calculated to be impossible for Saddam Hussein to accept (Ridgeway 1991: 222; Heikal 1992; Smith 1992). If he wanted war then he did not want compellence to work.

Although the available evidence does not yet permit firm judgement, my interim conclusion is that this was a case of self-entrapment by both leaders. Bush showed strong signs of ambivalence. On the one hand, he never seemed to believe that compellence would work, he was confident that Iraq would lose

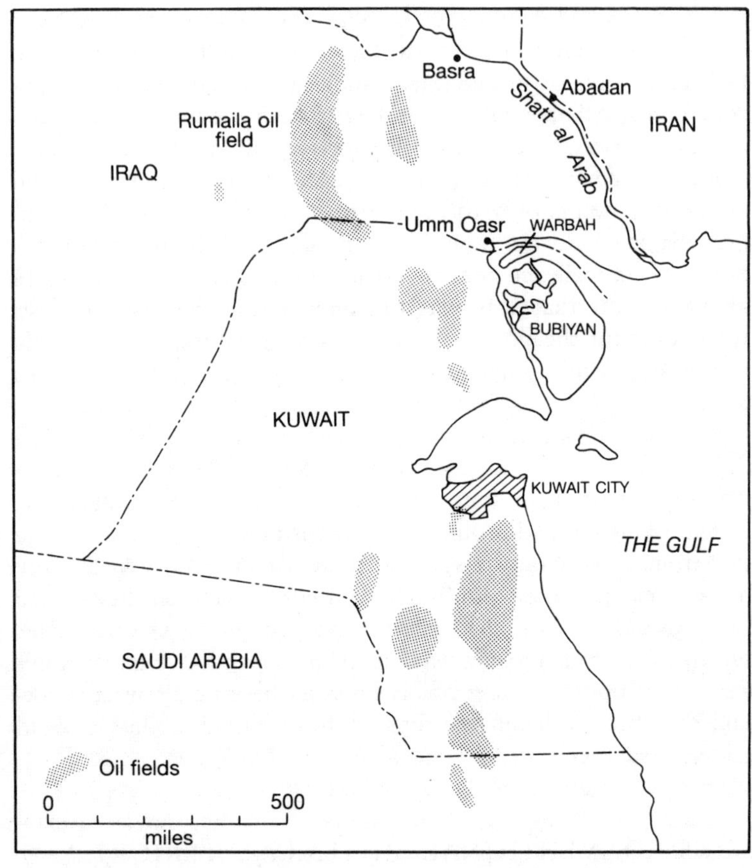

11.1 Iraq's refusal to withdraw from Kuwait, 1990–91

the war, he had objectives (such as the overthrow of Saddam Hussein, the reduction of Iraq's conventional military strength and the elimination of its nuclear, biological and chemical weapons programmes) that would be difficult to achieve without war and he did his best to eliminate the sort of face-saving deal which would allow for a peaceful outcome. He offered reassurances and face-saving points only to the extent necessary to hold the coalition together. On the other hand, he did in many ways adopt a policy of compellence because he needed to show those who were averse to war that war was the only option, he was (at first) worried about the potential level of US casualties, and he could accept successful compellence if the terms were humiliating for Saddam Hussein. Bush wanted compliance without negotiation or face-saving. He never believed compellence would work and he did not mind if it did not work: neither is the same thing as wanting it to fail. In spite of – not because of – US diplomacy, Saddam Hussein had a number of opportunities for a face-saving exit from Kuwait but he spurned them. At first this was because he believed that force would not be used. Then, when he realised force would be used, he believed that his interests were better served by fighting a losing war rather than withdrawing in humiliation. He took this view of his interests because he was a risk-taker and because he underestimated the coalition's ability to avoid taking casualties.

US CONVENTIONAL MILITARY SUPERIORITY UNDERESTIMATED

The US-led coalition had in its favour overwhelming local and short-term superiority in conventional forces. This was demonstrated by the effectiveness of the allied air offensive, which began on 16 January 1991. It so demoralised the Iraqi forces, who were already war-weary after a decade of war with Iran, that the ground offensive took only three days (24 to 27 February) and met with minimal resistance. In retrospect, the allied forces had total superiority, but at the time many commentators took much of Saddam's bluster to be true and overestimated the quantity and quality of his armed forces, and worried about Iraq's chemical weapons, static defences (which proved to be an Iraqi weakness) and other elements of their arsenal (Mueller 1994: 55, 154–5; Simpson 1991: *xiv-xv*, 319, 322, 324). The Iraqis expected to be able to fight a long war of attrition in similar fashion to their war against Iran and did not believe that the coalition's total dominance in the air would be very important (Salinger, Laurent 1991: 159, 187; Heikal 1992: 343–4). Iraq was not alone in this miscalculation, in that unofficial US predictions of US casualties (that is, wounded as well as killed) were in the thousands and the official US worst-case figure was between 10,000 and 20,000 (Mueller 1994: 124).

Shortly before the invasion of Kuwait, Saddam Hussein said to US Ambassador April Glaspie 'Yours is a society that cannot accept ten thousand dead in one battle' (quoted in Stein 1992: 175; see also Heikal 1992: 399). His ethnocentric contempt for Western squeamishness was accurate in that US public opinion showed itself to be highly sensitive to the possibility of US casualties (Mueller 1994: 76–7). However, his belief that Western sensibilities about Iraqi casualties, especially civilian ones, would force an end to the air war very quickly before a ground offensive could be launched was unfounded (Karsh, Rautsi 1991b: 257–9; Simpson 1991: 273, 274, 281–2; Taylor 1992: 222; Mueller 1994: *xiii*, 122–3). He underestimated the accuracy of most of the attacks on Baghdad, and the ability of the coalition to convey to the watching Western public an exaggerated sense of the accuracy of the allied bombing in general. Both the White House and Saddam Hussein overestimated US public sensitivity to Iraqi casualties. In the event, support for the war was not eroded heavily even when the real damage being done by the bombing started to become obvious.

Iraq was reputed to have the fourth biggest army in the world, with 540,000 troops estimated to be available for combat in Kuwait. In reality, the Iraqis at full strength in January had 260,000 troops, and with desertions estimated at 30 per cent or more by the allied Commander General Norman Schwarzkopf, the Iraqi forces were probably below 200,000 when the coalition launched the ground offensive. US troops numbered 350,000 and the total coalition forces numbered 525,000 (La Rocque, Carroll, Jr. 1991: 45; Simpson 1991: 332–5). In addition to outnumbering the Iraqis at least two-to-one, the coalition had better and more plentiful equipment, excellent logistics, high morale, total control of the air, and a reasonable amount of time, so it won easily (Mason 1991; Simpson 1991: 334–7, 343; Taylor, Jr., Blackwell 1991). The US military and political establishment had become convinced that it had failed in Vietnam because it had used gradual increases of force, limited both in scale and in geographical scope. It was determined not to repeat what it saw as the mistakes of Vietnam and so adopted a doctrine of the immediate application of invincible force (La Rocque, Carroll, Jr. 1991: 55, 57–8; Simpson 1991: 196; Smith 1992: 224–6; Mueller 1994: 21, 45).

THE ROLE OF WEAPONS OF MASS DESTRUCTION

Fear of Iraqi nuclear and biological weapons potential and its large stockpile of chemical weapons helped reinforce support for the coalition. Although it was generally accepted that Iraq had no nuclear weapons, Saddam Hussein occasionally pretended that he had, in the hope of deterring an attack on his forces in Kuwait. Israel had destroyed the Iraqi Osiraq nuclear facilities by air attack on 7 June 1981, in an effort to inhibit Iraq's attempt to acquire nuclear weapons. In 1988, Israel concluded that Iraq was going flat-out to develop its own nuclear weapons, and its apprehension increased as Iraq announced in December 1989 that it had developed and tested ballistic missiles with a range of 1,200 miles (Miller, Mylroie 1990: 154–61, 167–76; Simpson 1991: 52, 67, 72, 121). Iraq's nuclear ambitions were not in doubt, as indicated by Saddam's statement as early as 1979 that 'if you ask any person in the world whether he would like to possess a nuclear bomb, he will tell you that he would' (quoted in Simpson 1991: 68), and by his attempts to smuggle electrical triggers for nuclear weapons to Iraq (Karsh, Rautsi 1991a: 23).

Saddam Hussein said on 2 April 1990 that 'We do not need an atomic bomb, because we have sophisticated binary chemical weapons' (quoted in Simpson 1991: 68). Binary chemical weapons have two chemicals which are relatively safe when separate. When the weapon is fired, the different chemicals in its two compartments mix to form a lethal gas. Saddam Hussein's statement was made in the context of his implicit threat to retaliate with chemical weapons for an Israeli attempt, which he believed to be imminent, to destroy his nuclear weapons research facilities (euphemistically termed 'some metal industry factory'): 'The West is deluding itself if it imagines it can protect Israel if Israel comes and strikes at some metal industry factory of ours. By God, we will devour half of Israel by fire if it tries to do anything against Iraq' (quoted in Simpson 1991: 68). Saddam Hussein sought to make it clear that he was trying to deter an Israeli attack.[1] Nevertheless, the United States concentrated on condemning Saddam Hussein for his threat, while Israel implied that a chemical attack would meet with nuclear retaliation (Cockburn, Cohen 1991: 11; Ridgeway 1991: 26; Hersh 1991). In addition to its chemical weapons, Iraq was developing biological weapons (Miller, Mylroie 1990: 161–7). There were fears that Iraq would either launch SCUD missile attacks with chemical warheads against cities such as Tel Aviv or against troop concentrations, or that chemical artillery shells would be used against a ground offensive. There was much debate about whether or not Iraq had the technical capability to fit chemical warheads to its SCUD missiles, although it did possess such warheads.[2] It is possible (but it has not been confirmed) that Iraq may have used a few chemical weapons against allied bases in Saudi Arabia; this is one of the explanations given for an illness known as Desert Storm Syndrome afflicting many allied personnel who served in the Gulf (*The Guardian*, 11 February 1994). Even if a few were used, the question remains as to why Saddam Hussein did not use a substantial number of chemical weapons. He may have been afraid that the United States or Israel might respond with nuclear weapons, or the coalition might respond by an offensive on Baghdad to remove him from power (Heikal 1992: 369–70). He may have wanted to use them but the winds may have been blowing towards his forces, the allied attack may have been too swift or his officers may have ignored orders to use them.[3]

There was no serious prospect of the United States using nuclear weapons as long as there was no large-scale chemical weapon use by Iraq, although Yasser Arafat, the leader of the dominant faction of the Palestine Liberation Organisation (PLO), claims that Saddam Hussein was worried in August about a US nuclear attack on Baghdad in retaliation for the invasion of Kuwait (Simpson 1991: 158). In January 1991, *Newsweek* reported that Schwarzkopf had proposed exploding a nuclear weapon high above Iraq at the beginning of a war in order to generate an electro-magnetic pulse (EMP), which would disrupt Iraqi communications and burn out every other electronic device (*Newsweek*, 14 January 1991: 12–13). If the report is true, it is hard to believe that he ever thought the proposal would be accepted for political reasons, and as a military tactic it made no sense, as the EMP would have disrupted the communications of the allies as well as Iraq. The allies were able to almost eliminate Iraqi communications with conventional weapons, and to exercise their advantage in communications and surveillance technology to great effect. In public Bush ruled out the nuclear option, but the Department of Defence still ordered a study into the use of tactical nuclear weapons to destroy airfields, missile bases, roads, bridges and infantry positions (*Newsweek*, 14 January 1991: 12–13), and a Swedish liaison officer who was based in Saudi Arabia claimed that detailed guidelines were issued for possible nuclear use in response to chemical attack (*The Guardian*, 28 September 1991). There was little support for the nuclear option; according to *Newsweek*, unspecified 'key allies' made it a condition of joining the coalition that nuclear weapons would not be 'brandished'. An opinion poll in the United States indicated 72 per cent opposition to, and 24 per cent support for, the use of tactical nuclear weapons against Iraq 'to quickly end any hostilities and save the lives of US forces' (*Newsweek*, 14 January 1991: 12–13). One member of Congress voiced this preference on television (Cumings 1992: 108). Thus a substantial minority of those polled did support conditionally nuclear use. However, this result may have been influenced by a clear echo of the widely accepted justification of US nuclear use against Japan in 1945. As it turned out, the US armed forces used fuel-air bombs which have the explosive power of small atomic bombs without the political and radiological fallout (Cumings 1992: 125).

US INTERESTS AND OBJECTIVES

Saddam Hussein's miscalculation of the conventional military balance was an important factor in his refusal to withdraw from Kuwait. He did not think that he could defeat the allies in full-scale combat, but he underestimated just how dramatic his military defeat would turn out to be. His main strategy was to try to deter the United States from attacking, partly by trying to convince it that it would lose, but mainly by trying to make it appear that the cost of a military victory in Kuwait would be excessively high. In other words, he tried to manipulate the US assessment of the interests at stake. In a key public statement in November 1990, Bush gave three reasons why he had sent troops to the Gulf (*Newsweek*, 26 November 1990: 30–1). First, aggression had to be shown to be unproductive because 'The history of this century shows clearly that rewarding aggression encourages more aggression', and the precedents for the post-Cold War era had to be the right ones. Second, Saddam must not be allowed to have a 'stranglehold' on the oil of the Middle East. Third, the hostages taken by Saddam must be set free. He then listed the goals he had been reiterating since August: 'First, the immediate and unconditional withdrawal of all Iraqi forces from Kuwait. Second, the restoration of Kuwait's legitimate government. Third, security and stability for the Gulf . . . And fourth, the protection of American citizens abroad'. The first, second and fourth of these goals could have been achieved by a peaceful withdrawal and the release of the hostages. However, there was plenty of oil, Iraq was being punished severely through economic sanctions for the invasion, and by that time Saudi Arabia was secure (Mueller 1994: 53). The issue of protecting access to Middle East oil was very important to Bush, but his fears – at least those expressed publicly – were greatly exaggerated: the world was faced with an oil glut and dropping oil prices before the invasion, and other countries were keen to sell oil to replace that which Iraq was not allowed to sell due to UN sanctions. Iraq did not have a stranglehold on oil or anything like it: at the time, Iraq and Kuwait combined accounted for only 20 per cent of world proven oil reserves and 8 per cent of world oil production (Mueller 1994: 145–6). One might argue that Bush's third goal could only have been achieved through war. A peaceful withdrawal would have left Iraq's conventional military power and its NBC (nuclear, biological and chemical) and ballistic missile programmes intact. Bush's statement referred to Iraq's NBC capabilities as 'ominous'. At this point he did not include their elimination in his list of objectives, and he could still have been hoping to neutralise them through deterrence and limits on technology transfer. In contrast, US public opinion attached primary importance to overthrowing Saddam Hussein (who was perceived as utterly monstrous), preventing Iraq from acquiring nuclear weapons and freeing US hostages; secondary importance to reversing aggression and preventing atrocities in Kuwait by Iraq; and little importance to protecting access to oil supplies or reinstating the Kuwaiti government (Mueller 1994: 20, 23, 39–42, 118, 142). The crisis represented a domestic political threat to, and opportunity for, Bush. He had been dogged by the 'wimp' factor, that is, the perception that he was weak and indecisive, and now he had a chance to lay that assertion to rest (Simpson 1991: 119). Some references have been made to 'macho' Arab culture (Matthews 1993: 221; Mueller 1994: 21), but Bush also sought to look macho. His wimp factor was writ large in the nation as a whole in the 'Vietnam syndrome', that is, US fears of the consequences of large-scale military intervention. Action in the Gulf would let him deal with both at once. It also provided him with an opportunity to show that the 'new world order' meant that the United States and Soviet Union would co-operate under US leadership and operate through the United Nations to deal with aggressive regional powers, instead of competing for their diplomatic allegiance.

GOING THE EXTRA MILE FOR PEACE – BUT NOT GIVING AN INCH

The basic view held by Bush was that if Saddam Hussein was to have peace it could only be peace with dishonour. The exhortation printed on top of a picture of Saddam Hussein on *The Economist*'s front page summed it up: 'Don't Save This Face'. Alexander George maintains that the United States 'did convey several assurances that Saddam could have used for face-saving purposes' if he withdrew, specifically that Iraq would not be attacked, that the United States would not maintain forces in the region and that the Middle East peace conference requested by Iraq would be possible. On this basis, he concludes that, however reluctantly, 'the door was left open' for a withdrawal which would not threaten Saddam's hold on power (1993: 83–5; see also George 1991b: 574). This gives far too much weight to these assurances, which were very vague, were not to be linked formally to an Iraqi withdrawal and were totally overwhelmed by highly hostile and inflammatory rhetoric, insults and calls for the overthrow of Saddam Hussein. Bush gave no serious consideration to a Middle East peace conference after withdrawal and in December 1990 in the UN General Assembly the United States and Israel were the only countries to vote against such a conference, with 144 votes in favour (Chomsky 1992: 423; Smith 1992: 169–71; Mueller 1994: 36). Bush's position is summarised more accurately by Robert W. Tucker and David C. Hendrickson as 'No negotiations, no compromises, no attempts at face-saving, and no rewards for aggression' (1992: 91). Bush only explored compromise to the extent necessary to persuade public opinion that there was no alternative to war, due to Saddam Hussein's – not his own – intransigence. This was epitomised by Bush's declaration on 30 November of his desire to 'go the extra mile for peace' by sending Baker to see Saddam Hussein and asking for the Iraqi Foreign Minister Tariq Aziz to come to Washington (Karsh, Rautsi 1991b: 236–68; Simpson 1991: 248–52, 263–4; Freedman, Karsh 1991: 234–7, 241–5; Smith 1992: 218–20). No sooner had he done so than he made it clear that 'There can be no face-saving' and 'There will be no give' (quoted in Smith 1992: 222–3). Bush claimed to be going the extra mile for peace: in fact he would not give an inch. At first the Iraqis misinterpreted Bush's declaration as proof that Bush was not serious about Resolution 678, passed the previous day by the UN Security Council, which authorised the use of force to retake Kuwait if Iraq did not withdraw. Simpson sums up Saddam Hussein's view of what appeared to be a US offer of talks as follows: 'It confirmed everything he believed about the United States – that it had no stomach for war, that democracies could not accept casualties for long and that they had no fixity of purpose' (1991: 251, also 259). In the end Baker met Aziz, rather than Saddam Hussein, on 9 January 1991. At that meeting it became clear that Baker was there to deliver an ultimatum, not to negotiate or make a deal.

SPURNED OPPORTUNITIES FOR PEACE WITH HONOUR

Opportunities for peace with honour for Iraq did exist, but they did not come from the United States and they were not pursued by Saddam Hussein, who was just as intransigent as Bush. He responded only vaguely to proposals put forward jointly by Jordan, Algeria and Morocco on 22 September, by the Soviet Union on 5 October, by France on 10 October and by former British

Prime Minister Edward Heath on 21 October (Heikal 1992: 332–6, 339–41; Stein 1992: 171; Herrmann 1994: 237–8, 250–2). The same response was given to the Soviet proposal of 19 February (Herrmann 1994: 252–4). Indeed, the United States was sufficiently worried about a partial or conditional withdrawal – an option which former British Prime Minister Edward Heath proposed to Saddam Hussein on 21 October – to call it the 'nightmare scenario' (Heikal 1992: 339; Stein 1992: 172; George 1993: 82; Herrmann 1994: 246). On 5 and 6 August, Saddam Hussein signalled his conditional willingness to withdraw from all except the disputed territories (one border oilfield and some islands) once the strength of the US reaction became clear (Heikal 1992: 308–20). However, on 9 August he announced the annexation of Kuwait and the following day linked the dispute to the overall Arab-Israeli dispute and the Syrian occupation of most of Lebanon (Heikal 1992: 317–18). His interest in negotiations only ever appeared to be a tactic designed to forestall military action so that he could retain control of Kuwait. When the United States announced the 'extra mile for peace' move, both sides began to quibble about dates for the proposed meetings.[4]

Why did Saddam Hussein spurn these opportunities? Basically, he claimed that withdrawal would be disastrous in two ways. First, he maintained that Bush's hands could not be tied: the United States would see withdrawal – even partial withdrawal – as weakness, that it would not stop a US attack, or that the United States would impose conditions such as the dismantling of his NBC capabilities. He demanded security guarantees against a US attack (Heikal 1992: 332–6, 339–41, 348), but did not pursue them with any vigour. He also suspected that the United States would not remove its sanctions until he fell from power even if he did pull out (Tucker, Hendrickson 1992: 89–90; Heikal 1992: 325–6; Record 1993: 51–5; Mueller 1994: 21). Saddam Hussein perceived the United States as dedicated to bringing down his political system along the lines of the collapse of Communism in Eastern Europe (Stein 1992: 161–5). Certainly, the United States had gradually increased its public objectives, from securing Saudi Arabia to liberating Kuwait to also eliminating Iraq's NBC capabilities, demanding compensation for Kuwait and calling for Saddam Hussein's overthrow (Heikal 1992: 365). Second, he argued that he would be overthrown by domestic opponents if he withdrew.

He was acutely aware of the fate of Romanian leader Nicolae Ceauşescu, who was executed during the revolution of 1989–90, and he distributed pictures of Ceauşescu to his colleagues on the ruling Revolutionary Command Council (RCC) of Iraq to drive the point home (Simpson 1991: 17). He said 'The Iraqi people will not forgive me for unconditional withdrawal from Kuwait.'[5] He also said to the PLO on 26 August 1990 that he did not want to withdraw in exchange for the islands and oilfield which Iraq claimed from Kuwait, because 'the people will never accept it. It will be bigger than losing the war' (quoted in Cooley 1991: 135; see also Salinger, Laurent 1991: 187). This was also the view he expressed to Yevgeny Primakov, Gorbachev's special envoy, in October 1990 (Simpson 1991: 227–31).

If he could concede to Iran equal access to the Shatt-al-Arab waterway, even though it was a key feature of their eight-year war, could he not also cope with another about-turn? This was the view of the Bush administration (Post 1991; Heikal 1992: 341–2; Herrmann 1994: 244). When Heath put the point to him, he replied only that it would be 'difficult', not impossible (quoted in Heikal 1992: 342). Saddam was a risk-taker, who had reversed in the past if he saw it as necessary for his survival (Post 1991; George 1993: 83–5; Herrmann 1994: 244). The public debate which took place in the United States helped Saddam Hussein to believe he could avoid war. Although Bush was utterly opposed to negotiation and required the humiliation of Saddam Hussein, US public opinion showed a majority in favour of compromise, concessions (including territorial concessions) and negotiation to avert war (Mueller 1994: 20, 36–37). There was also elite opposition to war across the political spectrum (Cumings 1992: 105–06). When it came to the vote in the US Congress on 12 January, the House of Representatives effectively voted for war 250 to 183; the figure for the Senate was 52 to 47 (Freedman, Karsh 1993: 294). Note that Saddam Hussein was not mirror-imaging: he understood that the US political system also operated differently. Nor was this caricature, as he did not exaggerate this aspect of democracy. For a man who thought that Bush's hands could not be tied, he put a great deal of effort into doing just that by trying to break up the coalition. Overall, while in the end Saddam Hussein may have come to believe these arguments, he seemed to be trying to reinforce his resolve and the resolve of those around him. If all other options are portrayed as unacceptable, if there is no alternative, then it is easier to press on. This framing of the situation also suited his willingness to take risks. Opportunities for peace with honour were rejected because he was a risk-taker who thought that there was a good chance he could avert war and that, if war did occur, he could ensure that it was a glorious defeat.

This interpretation makes unnecessary recourse to cultural arguments about Saddam Hussein being entrapped by Arab notions of honour. Raymond Cohen describes Arab cultures as group cultures and shame cultures in which honour is of the highest importance and in which humiliation demands vengeance, even from a position of military weakness. He contrasts this with the Israeli decision-makers in the days before the Middle East War of 1967, whose Western individualist rationality led them to believe that obvious Arab military weakness would result in inaction (until Arab rhetoric changed their minds) (1988: 5–8). This is the kind of cultural issue which Karsh and Rautsi say prevented Saddam from publicly accepting the US ultimatum of complete and unconditional surrender, even as his armed forces were being routed (1991b: 261). Similarly, Jerrold Post – who wrote a personality profile of Saddam Hussein which was circulated widely in Washington during the crisis, and which portrayed him as a risk-taking opportunist who knows when to back down – says that 'In the Arab world . . . having courage to fight a superior foe can bring political victory, even through a military defeat' (cited in George 1993: 85). This is not peculiar to Arab culture. For example, in the Tet offensive of 1968, the Vietminh achieved a great political victory even though they were defeated heavily by US and South Vietnamese Government forces. In fact, Saddam Hussein thought he could hang onto his gains and his honour until very late in the crisis. If war did occur, Saddam Hussein expected it to produce an outcome along the lines of the military defeat but political victory of Egyptian President Gamal Abdel Nasser in 1956, when he faced the combined forces of Israel, France and Britain: recall his comment that even partial withdrawal 'will be bigger than losing the war' (quoted in Cooley 1991: 135). Indeed, after being driven out of Kuwait, Baghdad Radio broadcast songs with words which tried to create the impression that the Kuwait fiasco was a glorious episode: 'By standing alone, O Iraq/The whole world will regard you/With pride and dignity/Until the end of time' (quoted in

Simpson 1991: 368). Still, better glorious victory than glorious defeat, an outcome which Saddam Hussein sought to secure by breaking up the coalition. Iraqi hopes of avoiding war without having to withdraw varied in two phases. Between August and October, when the coalition relied on economic sanctions, war looked avoidable. From 8 November onwards, when Bush indicated that he was preparing an offensive option and would be building up US troop numbers in Saudi Arabia by an additional 150,000 rather than rotating units, the potential for war was much higher. However, even in this second phase Saddam Hussein and his generals still hoped to avoid war (Train 1991: 24; Simpson 1991: 273). The Iraqis were particularly heartened by the news that Margaret Thatcher had resigned as British Prime Minister on 22 November, to be replaced by John Major (Simpson 1991: 246–8, 120–1). Simpson claims that the Iraqis perceived Thatcher's fall as the product of her policy on the Gulf issue, but their statements to that effect can be interpreted as rhetoric. They perceived Thatcher as the strongest advocate of war in the coalition but, because they overestimated her importance, they incorrectly expected the coalition to disintegrate quickly.

MANIPULATING PERCEPTIONS OF INTERESTS

In deciding not to withdraw from Kuwait in the face of the superior military capabilities of the coalition, Saddam Hussein was motivated primarily by potential loss but also by potential gain. He wriggled as hard as he could to turn the possibility that the allies would not use force into a reality. As for economic sanctions, he probably believed that he could survive them if they stayed in place, and that some states would cease to co-operate with them. Saddam Hussein tried to create an opportunity for his forces to remain in Kuwait and then to negotiate a withdrawal on less than humiliating terms by manipulating the coalition states' perceptions of their interests. He tried to make the allies believe that, while they might win, they would only do so at excessive cost. He tried to maximise assessments of the likely costs of a war by references to 'the mother of all battles', by creating images of fanaticism and willing martyrdom and contrasting them to the weak materialism of Westerners, by threatening to use chemical weapons and showing aircraft being armed with chemical bombs, by mobilising the reserves, by making civil defence preparations, and by keeping foreign citizens as hostages at key military installations, especially those linked to NBC weapons (Karsh, Rautsi 1991b: 221–2, 233). In the Western media Saddam Hussein was often portrayed as having a great deal of popular support, but most ordinary Iraqis (that is, excluding the Kurds, who had been in more or less open rebellion for many generations against a series of rulers) expected to lose the war and many of them welcomed the prospect of defeat as a way of getting rid of him. Although the people were too afraid to show their opposition openly before the war, they were more bold after it – at least for a short while (Simpson 1991: 4–5, 9–10, 159–60, 182–8, 210, 267–70, 280, 328–9, 336).

Saddam Hussein tried to play on the differing interests within the coalition in order to break it up. He emphasised the costs of war, as discussed above, and he tried to get member states to break ranks by indicating that the release of hostages would be linked to the behaviour of their individual governments (Karsh, Rautsi 1991b: 232–6). On 6 December 1990 he announced the release of the hostages. This might have been a switch of tactics to split the alliance by improving his image (Stein 1992: 174; Herrmann 1994: 247–8). Alternatively, or additionally, he might have believed that the allies would begin air raids regardless, and the killing of hostages would mean that the allies would settle for nothing less than his downfall. He tried to appeal to the Arab states by linking an Iraqi withdrawal from Kuwait to the *prior* settlement of the Arab-Israeli conflict, among others (Karsh, Rautsi 1991b: 228–31, 242–3). He offered money to Third World states, the Soviet Union and China, and he tried to convince West European states and Japan that they were being manipulated by the United States (Karsh, Rautsi 1991b: 231–2). He tried unsuccessfully to provoke Israeli retaliation to attacks with SCUD missiles (armed with conventional warheads but which implied the possibility of chemical attacks) in the hope that Arab states would find it impossible to be part of a coalition of which Israel was a *de facto* member (Salinger, Laurent 1991: 158–9; Welch 1993). His line that the dispute had to be linked to the resolution of wider issues struck a real chord amongst many Arabs, and in particular revived a sense of Arabs being a unified and proud nation. He also believed strongly that he could use this sentiment to undermine the Arab members of the coalition (Schlesinger, Laurent 1991: 159; Heikal 1992: 323–5; Stein 1992: 175–6; Herrmann 1994: 248, 250, 256–7). It also meant that the political costs of withdrawal would be much higher unless he also secured some progress on those wider issues (Heikal 1992: 323–5), which served the purpose of reinforcing his resolve.

DOMINANT LEADERS AND FLAWED DECISION-MAKING

The decision-making on both sides was flawed because of the impact of dominant leaders. Saddam Hussein has, and has exercised, the power of life or death over his colleagues, and has ruled through Stalinesque terror (al-Khalil 1990). Throughout the crisis many emissaries from many countries – Arab and non-Arab – told him very bluntly things which he did not want to hear (Heikal 1993). However, there does not appear to have been any strong articulation from within his government of the value of, or potential for, the kind of negotiated withdrawal which might have been secured. Saddam Hussein simply denied that such a possibility existed: this psychological bias made it easier for him to go for complete political victory over the United States. In many other respects – such as the attacks on Israel to split the coalition – he miscalculated, although it was reasonable for him to hope that his tactics would work. US decision-making was also flawed in that no alternative policies were taken seriously. Bush dominated the decision-making process through his National Security Adviser Brent Scowcroft, and to a lesser extent through his Secretary of Defence Richard Cheney. Their approach was influenced heavily by the Munich analogy, from which they concluded that appeasement would only result in further aggression, and by the Vietnam analogy, which inclined them towards the immediate rather than gradual application of massive use of force so that victory would be swift. Preoccupation with these analogies created the need to dismiss alternative conceptions of the situation (Hybel 1993: 8–10, 75–7).

Although the offensive option was not put in place until November, Bush decided that force would be used if necessary to expel Iraq from Kuwait in the days immediately following the invasion at the beginning of August (Hybel 1993: 69–70). Those in favour of giving sanctions more time included James Baker (Secretary of State), General Colin Powell (Chairman of the Joint Chiefs of Staff), General Norman Schwarzkopf (Commander of Central Command), Lt. General George Lee Butler (Head of Plans and Policy at the Department of Defence), Paul Wolfowitz (Under-Secretary of Defence for Policy), Admiral William J. Crowe, Jr. and General David C. Jones (both former chairmen of the Joint Chiefs of Staff). However, as they knew the preference of the President, they were very reluctant to tell him that they disagreed. Before formal meetings, Bush and Scowcroft would meet to decide their approach, and meetings would begin with Scowcroft laying out his perspective, with it being clear that he spoke for the President (Simpson 1991: 245–56; Woodward 1991: 225; Smith 1992: 174–87; Hybel 1993: 72–5). Although various rational steps were taken, such as an analysis in early October of the possible role of an ultimatum by the Interagency Deputies Committee of the NSC, and Post's personality profile of Saddam Hussein (cited in George 1993: 80–2, 84–5), the NSC functioned within a highly constrained framing of the situation.[6]

CONCLUSION: TWO LEADERS ENTRAPPED IN WAR THROUGH INTRANSIGENCE

In choosing not to withdraw from Kuwait, Saddam convinced himself that he had no choice if he wanted to avoid being overthrown by domestic opposition, or if he wanted to avoid increased US demands. The gains to be made from facing off the UN coalition would have been very substantial, and he worked hard to create an opportunity to secure those gains. He seemed to feel that he could survive the economic sanctions imposed and, although the allies used force in the end, it was reasonable of him to believe that he had an opportunity to avoid war. When war looked likely, he believed that he could impose high casualties on coalition forces and the United States did not dispel that illusion because it was worried that it might be true. George argues that 'Bush did not succeed, despite considerable efforts, to convince Saddam that getting Iraqi forces out of Kuwait was more important to the United States than refusing to remove them under threat of war was to Iraq' (1993: 88). However, this is less important than the balance of interests between war and peace: neither side was averse to war. Bush might have been able to get an Iraqi withdrawal if he had not been so unbending on the terms, and Saddam Hussein might have been able to withdraw and obtain very substantial concessions against US wishes. But, in a curious symmetry, both leaders entrapped themselves into war through their unbending approach to the crisis.

NOTES

[1] Karsh, Rautsi 1991a: 24; 1991b: 210. See also 110, 111; Heikal 1993: 314, 371. Hybel sees this as an attempt to ensure that Israel would not attack Iraq if he invaded Kuwait (1993: 34–5, 54). It is more plausible that Saddam Hussein was concerned with preventing a repeat of Israel's 1981 attack on his nuclear weapon development facilities at Osiraq, independently of the dispute with Kuwait. On the attack on Osiraq, see Feldman 1982.

[2] UN inspectors, who were in Iraq after the war in order to carry out the various UN resolutions, soon found twenty chemical warheads for SCUDs (*The Independent*, 3 August 1991), and the Iraqi government reported having a total of 134 (Heikal 1992: 413). Stein puts the number at thirty (1992: 179n).

[3] Taylor 1992: 236–7. Simpson claims that although Iraq had vast chemical weapon stockpiles, none were distributed to the forces in Kuwait (1991: 336; see also Watson *et al.* 1991: 154). However, some chemical weapons, including chemical landmines, were found in Kuwait by coalition forces (Interviews with British armed forces personnel, May and September 1993).

[4] For two differing interpretations of Iraqi behaviour, see Simpson 1991: 252 and Karsh, Rautsi 1991b: 239. On US backtracking regarding dates see Smith 1992: 222.

[5] Quoted in Freedman, Karsh 1993, 431. For similar statements see Mueller 1994: 147; Karsh, Rautsi 1991b, 240–1; Freedman, Karsh 1991: 9n; Simpson 1991: 17, 228, 231, 274; Heikal 1992: 338, 341–2, 371.

[6] Smith 1992: 218, 223–4. In addition, very little advice was taken from Middle East experts (Hybel 1993: 8, 68). US university specialists on Iraq of Arab origin may even have played a part in making war more likely. According to Heikal, one of them advised Bush that he could offend and humiliate Saddam Hussein by calling him 'Saddam' and referring

to him as a 'thug' and so on (Heikal 1992: 337–8). Smith reports a similar claim in the April 1991 *Washingtonian* magazine that the CIA advised Bush to stress the first syllable of 'Saddam', so that the meaning of the name would be 'a little boy who cleans the shoes of old men' rather than 'one who confronts' (1992: 232). However, neither story has been confirmed. Some Middle East specialists who might have been consulted would have provided unhelpful observations. For example, Edward Peck characterised Americans as 'New Testament' types who 'turn the other cheek', unlike Iraqis who are 'an Old Testament People' (quoted in Cumings 1992: 107; see also 121). Apart from the problem of seeing a direct causal link between culture and behaviour (a problem I discussed in Chapter Three), the US response to the invasion can hardly be seen as turning the other cheek.

Part III

CONCLUSION

EXPLAINING INTERNATIONAL CRISIS OUTCOMES

In this final chapter, I provide an overview of the factors which are most important in explaining the crisis outcomes I have identified. I argue that the differences between deterrence and compellence played a part in the conduct of the crises examined, but that those differences were not important in explaining the crisis outcomes. Much more significant is strength of motivation to act in spite of deterrence, or to resist compellence. This strength of motivation helps explain the narrow middle range in which threats can work, as opposed to those occasions where the opponent's weak motivation makes threats unnecessary or strong motivation makes threats doomed to failure. Then I discuss the relationship between threats, ambiguity and difficulties of nuanced crisis signalling. Whether or not those difficulties result in war is strongly influenced by the extent to which the decision-makers involved are averse to war. I relate the military balance and perceptions of the costs of war to the question of war aversion. From this discussion emerges the possibility that aversion to nuclear war has generated a taboo on the use of nuclear weapons, although one which is not universal. Crisis behaviour, I suggest, is different in some important ways when the value of peace is low. In the next section I discuss various tactics used to manipulate the balance of interests and I assess the problems of perceiving interests and resolve accurately. I argue that the end of the Cold War does not require a radical change in explanations of international crisis outcomes, and I discuss the relationship between academic research and policy-making.

Of the eight case-study outcomes, five were unfavourable in that the Soviet Union's attempts at compellence failed in both Berlin crises, Chinese immediate extended deterrence failed to deter the US invasion of North Korea, British general deterrence failed to deter an Argentine invasion of the Falkland Islands, and the United States failed to compel an Iraqi withdrawal from Kuwait. Some decision-makers were not particularly worried if the policy they were pursuing failed. Truman was encouraged by General MacArthur to believe that Chinese intervention could be defeated easily. Especially once Bush was reassured that US casualties would be low, he believed that it would be no bad thing if the policy of trying to compel Iraq to withdraw from Kuwait failed, so that Iraq's conventional and NBC capabilities could be destroyed through the use of force. A mixed outcome was produced by the Soviet Union's attempt to compel China to settle their border dispute on Soviet terms. The two successes were the use of immediate extended deterrence by the United States in preventing a Chinese attack on the offshore islands, and the use of compellence by the United States to make the Soviet Union withdraw its missiles from Cuba. I do not agree with the conventional wisdom which sees the outcome of the Sino-Soviet border dispute as a Soviet success. Nor do I agree with the revisionist claims that China was not seriously considering an invasion of the offshore islands in 1954–55, or that the concessions made by the United States during the Cuban missile crisis were substantial enough to classify the outcome as mixed. Short-term outcomes were usually not the end of the matter because the underlying issues were usually not resolved. This explains repeated crises, tensions and incidents over Berlin, the islands off the Chinese mainland, the Falkland Islands and Kuwaiti-Iraqi relations. Decision-makers sometimes conclude that, even if pressure by them or their predecessors failed in the past, they would have more success due to changed circumstances. In the 1954–55 Taiwan Straits crisis, Mao sought to find out whether the United States would be less willing to get involved in another crisis over the offshore islands as the Korean War was over, and Khrushchev thought he could succeed where Stalin had failed due to his perception of a shift in the correlation of forces. Although the longer term is important, it is also important to understand what brings about initial, short-term crisis outcomes; this focus also has methodological merit, in preventing the connections between causes and effects from being too distant.

STRENGTH OF MOTIVATION AND THE NARROW MIDDLE RANGE

If deterrence is left until late in a crisis it can shade into compellence. China did attempt to deter the United States from invading North Korea before Truman had made up his mind that he would invade, which is why it can be classified as a case of immediate extended deterrence. However, the clearest Chinese threats were not made until after Truman had made up his mind to invade. China was still engaged in deterrence in that the invasion had not taken place, but by this stage was engaged in compellence in terms of having to change Truman's mind. Once US forces entered North Korea, the Chinese abandoned deterrence in favour of luring US forces to their destruction. In the eight crises, there was one compellence success (for the United States in the Cuban missile crisis), one mixed outcome (for the Soviet Union in the Sino-Soviet border crisis), and three failures (for the Soviet Union in both Berlin crises and for the United States in the Gulf crisis). There was one immediate extended deterrence success (for the United States in the Taiwan Straits crisis), one immediate extended deterrence failure (the US invasion of Korea) and one general extended deterrence failure (the Argentine invasion of the Falklands). Conclusions about success and failure rates should be drawn from this only tentatively, because the methodology used in this study lends itself to discovering causal patterns rather than success rates; the latter requires the use of statistical methods. Schelling's proposition that deterrence is easier than compellence is widely assumed to be true, but the difficulties of demonstrating this have not been fully appreciated. All other things being equal, deterrence may be easier than compellence. My case studies suggest that decision-makers were sufficiently aware of the distinction to try to make the opponent's task one of compellence through the use of crisis tactics such as blockade. However, none of the crisis outcomes were influenced decisively by the differences between them. What counts most is whether decision-makers are highly motivated to refuse to do the thing which the opponent is trying to make them do (such as withdraw from Kuwait), or are highly motivated to do the thing which the opponent is trying to deter them from doing (such as invade North Korea or the Falkland Islands).

The importance of strength of motivation brings to mind the

point made by Gray that 'the practice of deterrence has an all but missing middle range. Specifically, deterrence is either not needed at all or is needed to a degree that is close to impossible to satisfy' (1993: 665n). He attributes this to a failure to attend to the size of a country's over-all military capabilities and hence to the military opportunity which a potential attacker might perceive:

> Day by day, a country will maintain a military posture that even in a slim peacetime mode looks to be excessive to current demonstrated need. That excessive posture, however, is likely to be much too slim to inspire the deterrence of some clear and present danger in future. It is the lot of military establishments typically to be too large for peace and too small for crisis-time diplomacy and war.
>
> (1993: 665–6n)

An inadequate overall military capability can be part of the explanation of the failure of deterrence. If Britain had maintained much larger forces, then it would not have had to choose between South Atlantic and NATO deployments. However, the Falkland Islands were militarily vulnerable to Argentina for many years (as was Kuwait to Iraq), so the state of the military balance is an insufficient explanation of the invasion. China did not enter the Korean war at the time of maximum military opportunity, when South Korean and US forces had been pushed back to the Pusan perimeter. Similarly, Argentina did not wait until the arrival of the new weapons it had on order and until important British naval vessels had been scrapped or sold, and Iraq did not wait until it had nuclear weapons so that a military response to an invasion of Kuwait would be less likely. To the extent that there is a narrow middle range, it is more about strength of motivation: when decision-makers are very weakly motivated, the use of threats to influence them will be easy, but when they are very strongly motivated, threats will not be very effective. This applies to threats in general and not just deterrence.

A further limitation of the value of military superiority is that the opponent may not believe that you will use it. This is especially true in cases of extended deterrence: it is easy to believe that an attacked country will defend itself, whereas it is much harder to believe a state not under attack will choose to come to the aid of another state, even if only to protect its own interests. This was partly what underlay the Iraqi declaration in 1990 that Kuwait was the nineteenth province of Iraq: it was trying to reinforce its deterrence of an attack by the US-led coalition. Direct and extended deterrence can be distinguished in theory, but the difference can blur in practice if the protégé shares a border with the state seeking to extend deterrence. Although China was trying to extend deterrence to North Korea, it saw that attempt as intimately related to its own security. In defending North Korea, China was sure that it was defending itself. In contrast, US decision-makers felt able to separate the two states and thus underestimate China's resolve. Although the Falkland Islands were separated from Britain by thousands of miles of ocean, the British government still saw them as British. In that sense, British decision-makers were engaging in direct rather than extended deterrence. Like the US decision-makers regarding Korea, Argentine decision-makers saw it differently and thus underestimated British resolve.

THREATS, AMBIGUITY AND NUANCED CRISIS SIGNALLING

Despite suggestions to the contrary in the literature on strategic culture, attempts at nuanced crisis management were not the monopoly of the West. Decision-makers showed an understanding of the difference between military clashes or limited uses of force (such as the Chinese shelling of the offshore islands, the shooting down of a U-2 aircraft over Cuba and the Sino-Soviet border clashes) and acts of war. In the Taiwan Straits crisis, Mao made his challenges cautiously by going for the smallest, least strongly defended islands first, and by avoiding attacking US forces. In trying to prevent the United States from invading North Korea, Mao used threats which were deliberately calibrated in their degree of explicitness. In the Sino-Soviet border crisis, Mao chose carefully the composition of the units and amount and location of force to be used. The management of the Berlin crisis by Stalin and Khrushchev was marked by very fine distinctions between different actions regarding the ways in which access to West Berlin could be restricted or harassed. Brezhnev understood Mao's signal of limited use of force and responded by deliberately escalating beyond that level in order to intimidate him. Argentina and Britain both tried to manage the details of crisis signalling during the mini-crisis over South Georgia, which preceded Argentina's invasion of the Falklands.

Decision-makers often underestimate the strength of reaction which their behaviour will cause. Mao did not expect the United States to react so strongly to his bombardment of the offshore islands, or the Soviet Union to escalate so much in response to his border provocations. Khrushchev did not expect the United States to respond so strongly to his secret deployment of missiles in Cuba; and Truman, the Argentine junta and Saddam Hussein expected the reactions to the invasions they launched against North Korea, the Falkland Islands and Kuwait respectively to be much less severe. Failure of an opponent to engage in immediate deterrence and reliance on general deterrence should not be interpreted as proof that a strong response will not be forthcoming from that opponent if the prohibited action is taken. General extended deterrence was relied on by Britain to deter Argentina and by the United States to deter Iraq. Those who issue ambiguous threats or who rely on general deterrence may be bluffing, but they may be trying to retain some freedom of action or to avoid being provocative. Similarly, ambiguous threats by a potential attacker – such as Argentina and Iraq – should not be interpreted as proof that an attack will not occur. Ambiguity allows motivated bias to cause threats to be ignored or dismissed. Unmotivated bias can work in the opposite direction in that actions not intended as signals are perceived as credible threats, because the actions of the opponent are all presumed to be coherent, centrally co-ordinated efforts to signal. In the Cuban missile crisis, the United States perceived unconnected incidents, such as the shooting down of a U-2 spy aircraft, as evidence of a new hard line in Moscow, and inaccurate intelligence reports persuaded the Politburo that the United States was about to invade Cuba and perhaps even launch a nuclear first strike against the Soviet Union itself. In March 1982, Britain was trying to increase its military capabilities in the vicinity of the Falkland Islands in a non-provocative way, and did not think that anything more than general deterrence was necessary. However, Argentina combined accurate and inaccurate information to conclude that Britain was engaging in immediate deterrence, and believed that it had to act immediately before the local balance of conventional forces shifted. From their analysis of the Cuban missile crisis and the Middle East War of 1973, Lebow and Stein concluded that 'judgements of adversarial resolve bore little relationship to the deliberate attempts to make . . . threats credible' (1994: 319). Although I did not find this to be the case consistently in my case studies – for example, Chinese perceptions of Soviet resolve were reasonably accurately related to the threats made by the Soviet Union in the 1969 border crisis – signals are often misread, and signals are often perceived where no signals were actually sent. Indeed, decision-makers manipulate the possibility of loss of control, such as the misreading of signals, in order to increase the credibility of their threats.

MILITARY BALANCES AND AVERSION TO WAR

Superiority in the local balance of conventional forces may be better than inferiority, but that superiority can encourage irrationality, as decision-makers become insensitive to the possibility that the opponent may be highly motivated and can therefore still be resolute. It encourages them to ignore or at least not take seriously the interests of their opponents. They often simply presume that the opponent will back down solely because of the military balance, and that military action by the opponent is or would be irrational. This perspective was an important part of US perceptions of the potential for Chinese intervention in the Korean War, of Soviet perceptions of China's border provocations, of US perceptions of Iraq's refusal to withdraw from Kuwait, and of Argentine perceptions of the potential for a military reaction from Britain in response to its invasion of the Falklands. A combination of perceived political vulnerability and military superiority is particularly likely to produce irrationality: the former creates danger of motivated bias underlying the need to avoid thinking rationally, and the latter creates the opportunity for the associated miscalculations to appear plausible. Those who rely on military superiority should recall that fighting and losing is often considered to be preferable to capitulation. From this it can be seen that the role of military balances in crises can only be understood in relation to the extent to which those involved in the crisis are averse to war. The United States had the double advantage of local and short-term conventional superiority in trying to compel Iraq to withdraw from Kuwait. However, this advantage was undermined by the fact that Iraq was not averse to war, even a losing war. The Soviet Union in the Berlin and Sino-Soviet border crises and the United States in the Cuban missile crisis also had the double advantage of local and short-term conventional superiority, but their ability to exploit it successfully was restricted by the fact that they were highly averse to war. This aversion to war also explains China's restraint in the Taiwan Straits crisis and in the border crisis with the Soviet Union. An important aspect of war aversion is a focus by decision-makers on the absolute costs of war. Strategic culture will influence the weight attributed to particular costs. A significant shift in US strategic culture since the Vietnam War is that US presidents have been fearful of the domestic political costs of even very small numbers of US casualties. Saddam Hussein showed himself to be much less politically vulnerable to the costs of war and sought to exploit Bush's aversion to casualties. War aversion is also linked to fear that military conflict could escalate out of all proportion to the original stakes. This can be true of general conventional war but is most obviously true of nuclear war.

Decision-makers who possessed a nuclear monopoly in the cases I examined were not able to use it to impose their will. One might think that such an advantage would result in a very one-sided fear of war, but it did not work out that way. Stalin did not use more forceful means once it was clear that his blockade of West Berlin was not working because he did not think that West Berlin was worth risking general war, whether or not nuclear weapons would be used. The West was also averse to war, even though it had a nuclear monopoly. In other words, nuclear weapons played a part in conjunction with an assessment by both sides of their interests. It is noteworthy that Mao felt able to fight a war against US forces in Korea in spite of US nuclear weapons. He did think that there was a possibility of a US nuclear and conventional attack, but felt that he had to risk it. In contrast, he did not see the offshore islands as worth such a risk and sought only to find out whether or not the United States was committed to their defence. Although China drew some comfort from the fact that the Soviet Union had broken the US nuclear monopoly in 1949, this was not an important factor in its crisis behaviour. The British nuclear monopoly *vis-à-vis* Argentina was irrelevant to Argentine calculations about whether or not to invade the Falklands, just as the US nuclear monopoly *vis-à-vis* Iraq was irrelevant to Iraq's refusal to withdraw from Kuwait. Nuclear use was highly implausible because it would have been so disproportionate to the interests at stake. As far as we know, it was simply assumed by Argentina and Iraq that nuclear weapons would not be used, although there was some speculation about possible nuclear use by Israel, Britain or the United States in response to large-scale Iraqi use of chemical weapons. A nuclear factor could have become relevant – if Iraq had managed to deploy a nuclear force, the coalition may have felt it would have been too risky to attack Iraqi forces which were occupying Kuwait. It is possible that decision-makers without nuclear weapons feel *more* able to resist nuclear pressure than those who do possess them. When both sides have nuclear weapons, the possibility exists of escalation to nuclear use through mutual fear of surprise attack. When only one side has nuclear weapons, the burden of choosing nuclear escalation lies clearly with one side only.

What of those cases in which both sides had nuclear weapons? Decision-makers did derive some comfort from a favourable nuclear balance and sought to exploit it. However, this increased confidence was not responsible for favourable crisis outcomes. Perceptions of nuclear superiority were important to Khrushchev and Kennedy in the Berlin and Cuban missile crises. Khrushchev sought to exploit a false perception of Soviet nuclear superiority to extract concessions on the German question from Eisenhower and then Kennedy. Kennedy's announcement to the world in the autumn of 1961 that the United States was actually far ahead of the Soviet Union in nuclear arms undermined Khrushchev's rocket-rattling diplomacy, and spurred him to try to reduce the gap by deploying missiles in Cuba. During the Cuban missile crisis, Kennedy was comforted by nuclear superiority only a little: in that crisis, nuclear vulnerability, regardless of the details of the nuclear balance, was uppermost in the minds of both Kennedy and Khrushchev. Betts (1987) argues that the outcomes of both crises were determined by the nuclear superiority of the United States. In coming to this conclusion he makes the assumption that the balance of interests was against the side which was faced with the burden of the first use of force. Looking at the balance of interests more broadly, Khrushchev was able to protect his most important interests in terms of the stabilisation of East Germany, and was able to accept failure on the lesser objectives of securing formal recognition of East Germany or Western withdrawal from West Berlin. In the Cuban missile crisis, Khrushchev gradually learned that the stakes for the United States were higher and that Kennedy was therefore willing to run a greater risk of war than he was. Nevertheless, aversion to war made Kennedy believe from the start that he would have to make some kind of concession (Lebow, Stein 1994: 300–01), and he very nearly made the major concession of a public trade of the missiles in Turkey for the missiles in Cuba. Betts also sees the outcome of the Sino-Soviet crisis of 1969 as favourable to the Soviet Union and determined by Soviet nuclear superiority. However, I have argued that the outcome was roughly equal rather than clearly favourable to the Soviet Union.

While fear of nuclear escalation was often present in the minds of decision-makers during crises and increased their caution, especially in crises between nuclear states, Bundy (1988) overstates the cautiousness – and rationality – of decision-makers. In addition, in stressing how unlikely deliberate nuclear war has been, he pays insufficient attention to the possibility of inadvertent nuclear war, which could have come about through unauthorised use of nuclear weapons by subordinates, or by launching of nuclear missiles in the mistaken belief that the opponent had already launched first (Blair 1993; Sagan 1993). In spite of the perceived potential for escalation to nuclear war with the Soviet Union, Eisenhower committed the United States to the nuclear defence of Jinmen and Mazu. This was extraordinary when one considers that these islands were not necessary for the defence of Taiwan. Furthermore, Eisenhower talked in terms of the desirability of widening a war if one developed from the Taiwan Straits crisis to include the Soviet Union. Jiang tried to provoke a war with China which would drag the United States in on his side. Although US decision-makers did not want this to happen and were concerned primarily with deterring a Chinese attack on the offshore islands, this task was made more difficult by the fact that they wanted Taiwan to use the islands to continue its harassing attacks on the mainland (*FRUS 1952–54* **14**: 423). Kennedy is supposed to have read Barbara Tuchman's book *The Guns of August* and to have concluded from it that World War I was caused unintentionally by the interaction of military mobilisations. Yet that did not stop him from ordering the highest-ever level of world-wide US nuclear alert, or mobilising a massive conventional force capable of invading Cuba. Lower-level decision-makers were also not restrained by nuclear risk during the Cuban missile crisis, including the officer who went ahead with a test launch of a US ballistic missile at the peak of the crisis, the naval officers who ordered the depth-charging of Soviet submarines to force them to surface and the SAM commander in Cuba who ordered the shooting down of a U-2 spy aircraft (Sagan 1993). Alliances involve actors with differing sets of priorities, and there is usually a process of bargaining and manipulation to reconcile the priorities or impose the priorities of one side. Smaller states may take a tougher stance for fear of having their interests sacrificed by their stronger ally. Castro wanted Soviet nuclear weapons to be used if Cuba was invaded and was opposed to the withdrawal of Soviet missiles in the face of US threats and limited concessions (Lebow, Stein 1994: 116, 139, 378n). Turkey was also opposed to trading publicly the missiles on its territory (Lebow, Stein 1994: 126–7). Alternatively, those smaller allies may try to use the crisis to advance their own agenda. East German leader Erich Honecker proposed that West Berlin be blockaded in response to the US blockade of Cuba (Lebow, Stein 1994: 61–2, 292–3). Decision-makers usually react to a crisis initially in a very aggressive and belligerent fashion, even if only privately. Given enough time, more information and an aversion to war, learning about the opponent's interests and a more moderate course of action are possible (Blight 1992; White 1992; Lebow, Stein 1994: 144–5; cf. Leng 1983). Serious risks of nuclear escalation were taken many times. Nevertheless, aversion to starting a nuclear war deliberately was generally strong.

A STRENGTHENING NUCLEAR TABOO?

Widespread (but not complete) aversion to starting a nuclear war led Schelling to perceive as early as 1960 a tradition of non-use of nuclear weapons. By this he meant 'a jointly recognized expectation that they may not be used in spite of declaration of readiness, even in spite of tactical advantages in their use' ([1960] 1980). More recently, Bundy claimed that 'the "tradition" of nonuse is the most important single legacy of the first half century of fission' and that:

> its power is visible in the behavior of superpowers, lesser nuclear powers, and nonnuclear nations. No government that has nuclear weapons is now unaware of the enormous political cost of using them for any but the gravest and most obviously defensive reasons. No government without such weapons needs to be easily coerced by nuclear threats from others, because both history and logic make it clear that no government will resort to nuclear weapons over a less than mortal question.
>
> (1988: 587–8)

Describing the use of nuclear weapons as breaking with tradition would be to use inappropriately pallid language. Much more penetrating and apposite is the idea of the nuclear taboo, which evokes a host of images of the most basic fears and the most fundamental values. By nuclear taboo I mean a strategic cultural prohibition against the use of nuclear weapons: it is an assumption that nuclear weapons should not be used rather than a conscious cost-benefit calculation. The minutes of a US National Security Council (NSC) meeting on 31 March 1953 record that 'the President and Secretary [of State John Foster] Dulles were in complete agreement that somehow or other the tabu which surrounds the use of atomic weapons would have to be destroyed', and summarised Dulles' view as being that 'in the present state of world opinion, we could not use an A-bomb, [and] we should make every effort to dissipate this feeling' [*FRUS 1952–54* **15**: 827). Dulles made a similar, lengthy statement at an NSC meeting on 10 March 1955 regarding the Taiwan Straits crisis (*FRUS 1955–57* **2**: 347). Although Eisenhower claimed in his memoirs that he had decided during the Korean War that he 'would not be limited by any world-wide gentleman's agreement' (Eisenhower 1963: 181), and whether US nuclear threats contributed to bringing the Korean War deadlock to an end, the point is that he perceived the existence of the nuclear taboo.

Thus far, references to the nuclear taboo have been few and far between in the academic literature, as have references to the tradition of non-use.[1] It is ironic that, although their importance has been asserted or implied, their content has not been analysed extensively. There is much scope for further research on these important concepts. An outright rejection of the idea that either the nuclear taboo or a tradition of non-use exists is offered by

Steven Lee, on the grounds that the United States and Soviet Union 'contemplated the use of nuclear weapons in certain situations and so were not deeply committed to the belief that their use is illegitimate' (1993: 407). Lee uses the ideas of nuclear taboo, tradition of non-use, (a high degree of) self-deterrence and delegitimisation of nuclear weapons as synonyms. He argues that 'The delegitimisation of nuclear weapons will have occurred when there is an objective basis in shared habits of mind for the mutual expectation that nuclear weapons would not be used by one's opponent, even in situations where their use might seem prudentially appropriate' (1993: 320). Lee's scepticism about the extent to which the leaders of nuclear states have that expectation is justified, but his tendency to see the nuclear taboo in absolute terms is unhelpful in a number of ways. First, as his own analysis suggests, the delegitimisation of nuclear weapons, if it happens, is unlikely to occur overnight: it more likely to take place as part of a gradual process. Second, Lee does not look for evidence of the nuclear taboo among ordinary people or among elites of non-nuclear countries, even though those who have referred to the nuclear taboo have generally been giving their assessments of popular attitudes and those of leaders of third-party states, rather than those of nuclear decision-makers. Third, among those who support nuclear deterrence are many who do so in the belief that nuclear weapons should under no circumstances be used first, and that, if nuclear deterrence fails, retaliation is pointless. Lee quite reasonably does not see bluff as a practical formal policy for states, but there can be little doubt that many who support nuclear deterrence hope that their leaders are bluffing, and there is a good chance that at least some leaders have been bluffing. Finally, Lee qualifies his own absolutism. He states that thoughts about using nuclear weapons are compatible with the delegitimisation of nuclear weapons if the option is instantly rejected rather than subjected to serious analysis. He also states that the unthinkability of nuclear use would rest on an expectation of the absence of 'major aggression' and of the serious possibility that 'a confrontation sparked by a lesser aggression could escalate out of control to nuclear war' through nuclear rearmament (Lee 1993: 320–1). Certainly, the nuclear taboo does not guarantee that nuclear weapons will not be used, whether deliberately or inadvertently: it serves the social – and strategic cultural – function of making nuclear use less likely by helping to control those who might violate it. It is not necessary for decision-makers to have the nuclear taboo as part of their strategic culture for them to be restrained by it; it can be enough that they do not want to incur the political costs of violating a taboo perceived by others. Eisenhower and Dulles wanted to use nuclear weapons but understood the political costs of doing so.

CRISIS BEHAVIOUR WHEN THE VALUE OF PEACE IS LOW

In the nuclear context, decision-makers usually see the value of peace as high. When the value of peace is low, crisis behaviour changes substantially. In particular, the crisis participants can afford to be intransigent much more often. This can be illustrated by the diplomacy relating to Argentina's invasion of the Falkland Islands and Iraq's invasion of Kuwait: there are very strong parallels between the two cases. Before the invasions, Thatcher and Bush misinterpreted ambiguous threats as bluffs. While the precise timing of the invasions could not have been predicted, the dangerous nature of the circumstances could and should have been perceived. The Argentine junta and Saddam Hussein were domestically very weak and, after campaigns of threats aimed at extracting concessions, decided at the last minute to launch their invasions. Once the invasions had occurred, Thatcher and Bush were obsessed with the Munich analogy and the view that aggression must be seen not to pay. They believed from the outset that compromise was unacceptable because it would reward aggression and that war was virtually inevitable. However, neither the Argentine junta nor Saddam Hussein were entrapped into war. Instead, they entrapped themselves into war by failing to exploit diplomatic opportunities presented to them by third parties. In the Falklands case, peace plans were promoted jointly by the United States and Peru and by the UN Secretary-General Javier Perez de Cuellar in the first few days of May 1982, the most important aspects of which were mutual military withdrawal, interim administration of the islands by a third party, and a timetable for a resolution of the issue of sovereignty. The Argentine junta, just like Saddam Hussein, was determined not to make any concessions and only showed an interest in talks to try to undermine the possibility of military counter-action. The sinking of the Argentine battleship *Belgrano* by a British submarine on 3 May was not, despite speculation to the contrary, designed to sink the peace plan, but the strength of feeling among the Argentine public about the sinking made it much harder for the junta to negotiate seriously. Thatcher and Bush had to show some willingness to talk so that they would not be seen as trying to prevent a diplomatic solution, but both were determined not to have their military timetables derailed: the fighting had to be over before winter arrived in the South Atlantic and before summer arrived in the Gulf. The Argentine junta and Saddam Hussein both believed for far too long that they would not have to fight. Then they believed war was preferable to withdrawal, in the Argentine case because they thought they could win and in the Iraqi case because they did not think they would lose badly.

TACTICS TO MANIPULATE THE BALANCE OF INTERESTS

Crisis outcomes are influenced more by the balance of interests than the military balance. A closely related set of tactics to influence the perceptions of the balance of interests involves placing the burden of the first use of force upon the opponent, manoeuvring to be in the position of the defender of the territorial status quo and imposing a blockade. The value of these tactics increases if the opponent is highly averse to war, but these tactical issues form only part of a much bigger picture; a tactical advantage is useful, but no more than that. In analysing crises, a situational assessment of the status quo is more useful than the characterisation of individual states as status quo-orientated or revisionist. Knowing whether a state has an outlook on politics which is status quo-orientated or revisionist is a poor predictor of its role in a crisis. The supposedly revisionist Soviet Union was seeking to consolidate the *de facto* status quo of a divided Germany, although legal recognition of East Germany by the West would have been a change in the status quo. The supposedly status quo-orientated Western states regularly pursued revisionist goals. The United States sought to reunify Korea by force in 1950, was tempted by the idea of supporting a Nationalist invasion of mainland China in the early 1950s, and sought a reunified Germany until the early

1960s. These desires made it unwilling to clarify and codify the status quo. Even the West's containment policy was predicated on the (accurate) belief that successful containment would lead to the overthrow of Communism from within eventually.

The balance of interests can also be manipulated through reassurance: basically, one tries to convince opponents that their losses will be limited if they accept an unfavourable outcome. This tactic has two important limitations. The first is the powerful tendency to assume that the opponent is motivated by potential gain from the exploitation of a good opportunity, and therefore actually needs to be threatened more rather than less. The second is that reassurance strategies in practice are frequently based on the assumption that the opponent's fears are not genuine. A state attempting reassurance may be ineffective not because it is deliberately trying to lull the opponent into a false sense of security (although this is possible), but because it does harbour threatening tendencies. The United States tried to reassure China in Korea in 1950 and in the Taiwan Straits crisis in 1954–55 that no attack on China was being prepared. While the messages were genuine in that they represented policy at the time, the reassurance signals were weak, and were contradicted by threatening behaviour, because US decision-makers foresaw a range of circumstances in which they would attack China. Successful reassurance usually requires that you really mean it, and even then it may not work.

PROBLEMS OF PERCEIVING INTERESTS AND RESOLVE

Perceptions of legitimacy are very important in estimates of interests and resolve. Khrushchev was infuriated by the presence of US missiles in Turkey, horrified when the United States revealed its nuclear superiority and worried about the possibility that the United States would invade Cuba: he saw the deployment of missiles to Cuba as a legitimate response. The Argentine junta was blinded by its deep conviction that its territorial claim was legitimate, and by its belief that occasional British acceptance of the need to discuss sovereignty showed that, deep down, Britain accepted its claim. Saddam Hussein argued that, in exceeding OPEC oil-production quotas and thus driving down the price of the oil, Kuwait was conducting economic warfare against Iraq at a time when the Iraqi economy was in a dire state as a result of the war with Iran. These decision-makers failed to appreciate that how they acted upon their concerns would be widely regarded as illegitimate. The secret deployment of missiles to Cuba, despite assurances to the contrary, helped give US decision-makers a deep sense of their own rectitude, and made the tough US response look reasonable. Similarly, perceptions that Argentina and Iraq had legitimate grievances were mostly overwhelmed by condemnation of the way they had acted to deal with those grievances.

Analogies communicate in short-hand arguments regarding legitimacy, the value attached to interests and expectations about the factors that will contribute to the crisis outcome (such as how third parties will react). Decision-makers often fail to anticipate that the opponent will see the crisis primarily in terms of a different analogy. Non-Western decision-makers frequently failed to appreciate the extent to which the Munich appeasement motivated Western decision-makers; this was true in the Berlin, Cuban missile, Falklands and Gulf crises. In the Cuban missile crisis, the principal analogy for Khrushchev was the US missile deployment in Turkey. The important difference lay in the mode of the deployment, but the analogy was so obvious that Kennedy could not avoid accepting its partial validity. In contrast, the Argentine junta was preoccupied with the Goa and Suez analogies. Its failure to appreciate the obvious analogy that would be evoked in Britain by an invasion helps to explain its surprise at the strength of the British reaction. The Munich analogy also encouraged the United States to come down on the side of Britain.

If decision-makers wish to understand their opponents (and their allies and other states), then knowledge of the analogies they tend to employ would provide a very direct and easily comprehensible way of understanding their strategic culture. However, behaviour cannot be predicted directly from an assessment of strategic culture for the simple reason that strategic culture influences behaviour only indirectly. It shapes priorities and the limits of available options: actions result from the interaction of culture and context. Predictions based on the assumption of a direct connection between culture and behaviour are likely to fail. Accepting that this is so can be difficult if the connection appears to be direct: in fact, the same cultural factor will have different effects in different contexts.

For example, Raymond Cohen argues that the hyperbolic, vivid rhetoric of the Arabic language means that diplomatic threats by Arab leaders can be taken too seriously (1988: 8–11). He maintains that a central factor in the origins of the Middle East War of 1967 was that the Israelis took at face value Egyptian rhetoric about launching a war to wipe Israel off the face of the earth and ignored the qualifications in official statements. In 1990, the problem was that Iraq's threats were not taken seriously enough and could be dismissed as rhetoric – even Arabs, including the Kuwaitis, got it wrong. Similarly, one of the reasons that the United States did not anticipate the Soviet missile deployment in Cuba was that the Soviet Union had never before deployed land-based nuclear weapons outside its own territory, never mind outside its own hemisphere (Garthoff 1989: 46). Thus, ironically, sensitivity to the strategic culture of the opponent made it more likely that the United States would fail to anticipate Soviet behaviour.

Even when decision-makers are aware of their opponent's interests, they will often be unsure of how much weight they attach to them, and will find out only during the crisis. The weight decision-makers attach to their interests changes in response to external events, shifts (or perceptions of shifts) in the military balance, coalition politics within governments, domestic politics and changes in strategic culture. Preventing the fall of South Korea and Taiwan to Communist forces were not even defined as US interests at all, yet Truman and then Eisenhower ended up risking a Third World War over both of them. The fact that interests are so open to redefinition emphasises the usefulness of analysing perceptions of them at the very point at which crises are resolved. The shifting weight attached to interests implies the importance of communicating them to the opponent and trying to understand accurately the opponent's efforts to communicate. As indicated above in my discussion of signalling, this is easier said than done. As interests become clarified, much misperception can be filtered out. In some cases this is never achieved to a sufficient degree to prevent miscalculated escalation; in others, even when interests are perceived clearly, both sides may prefer war. Crises are not only caused by misperception: decision-makers often choose to provoke them in order to clarify relative bargaining power.[2]

Uncertainty may often be so great that miscalculations are inevitable, even by the most able decision-maker. This may relate to lack of information or to the ambiguity of information even when it exists. Some crises involved probes: the probability of success was unclear and so pressure was used to see how the opponent would react. This was the case with China's bombardment of the offshore islands. In invading North Korea, US decision-makers tended to think of the advance towards the Yalu River as a constant process of probing the limits of Chinese tolerance. This was a misperception, as Mao had decided on large-scale intervention shortly after US forces crossed into North Korea. The ambiguity of available information was Thatcher's defence of her failure to anticipate Argentina's invasion of the Falkland Islands: Argentina's threats were ambiguous and it did not decide to invade until the last minute. A second cause of miscalculation is that decision-makers are victims of unmotivated bias. The problem here is that decision-makers would like to be able to calculate accurately, but employ faulty methods. Unmotivated bias often results in a failure to recognise ambiguity. For example, actions may or may not be intended as signals: decision-makers tend to assume that all actions by an opponent are intended as signals. A third cause of miscalculation is motivated bias. My case studies confirm the view that motivated bias is rooted much more deeply in danger than opportunity – in fear of loss than hope of gain – although the latter is also a factor. This was the case regarding the US invasion of North Korea, the Soviet deployment of missiles in Cuba, British policy towards Argentina over the Falkland Islands and Argentina's invasion of the Falkland Islands. If the problem is lack of information, then the solution suggests itself: develop greater information-gathering capabilities. If the problem is unmotivated bias, then the solution is adaptations in the methods used by decision-makers to calculate. If the problem is motivated bias, then the solution is to address the issues which explain why the decision-makers feel the need to misperceive the situation. Any of these problems may prove to be intractable, but motivated bias may be the most intractable, because the decision-maker has a strong incentive to deny that there is a problem.

The fact that interests are often misperceived has led Lebow and Stein to make a number of claims regarding the idea of a balance of interests. They concluded from their analysis of the Cuban missile crisis and the Middle East War of 1973 that 'The credibility of threats was not established because of leaders' recognition of their adversary's interests. Rather, threats succeeded in communicating interests' (1994: 320). It is certainly true that threats are used to communicate interests, but recognition of the interests of the adversary can influence the credibility of threats as well. This is most obvious in direct deterrence: it is easy to believe that, if attacked, an opponent will fight back due to the interests that would be jeopardised by failure to do so. For example, in 1950 the United States expected China to fight if China itself was invaded because the fate of the Communist Government would be at stake. Lebow and Stein state that 'Theorists of deterrence, like other bargaining theorists, assume that the side with more at stake can make more believable threats to use force. It is generally assumed that interests are obvious and easily comunicated' (1994: 320). Whether deterrence and bargaining theorists actually make these assumptions – especially the second one – is debatable. Either way, the two assumptions are separable: one can adopt one without assuming the other. They can also be treated as hypotheses to be tested rather than assumptions. My preference is to reformulate the first hypothesis so that the question is whether the side with more at stake is more likely to have a favourable crisis outcome. My cases suggest that the favourable balance of interests for the West in the Berlin crises was an important factor in their successful resistance to Soviet compellence. The favourable balance of interests for the United States helped it to compel the withdrawal of Soviet missiles from Cuba; it also helped China stand up to vast Soviet military superiority in the 1969 border crisis. Of course, in studying social phenomena, we will usually discern tendencies rather than iron laws. Having more at stake will not result in a favourable outcome if, for example, the opponent prefers war to accepting an unfavourable outcome. Regardless of whether their opponents had more at stake, Argentina decided to invade the Falklands and Iraq refused to withdraw from Kuwait.

Whether or not interests are obvious or easily communicated will vary dramatically. Lebow and Stein argue that 'For the balance of interests to be a useful analytical tool, two conditions must be met: leaders and scholars must be able to calculate the interests that both sides have at stake, *and* the resulting balance must be interpreted roughly the same way by the protagonists' (Lebow, Stein 1994: 309–10). This need not be so, for two reasons. The first is that the balance of interests can manifest itself in a greater willingness to risk war. Even if Khrushchev had not learned why Kennedy would not tolerate Soviet missiles being in Cuba, there was a point beyond which he was not prepared to risk war. As Lebow and Stein accept: 'It is possible, even likely, that Khrushchev would have withdrawn the missiles in the absence of clarification of interests and reassurance' (1994: 318). Although it was a close-run thing, Kennedy was prepared to risk war longer than Khrushchev in the Cuban missile crisis. The second point is that, to return to the distinction between holistic understanding and social scientific explanation developed by Hollis and Smith (1990), Lebow and Stein demand an account of crisis behaviour from the holistic perspective. Yet it is perfectly valid by the criteria of social science that one make no assumptions about the perceptions of the actors. Huth and Russett have used surrogate measures of interests: they have looked for statistical correlations between the extent of defender-protégé ties and the success or failure of immediate extended deterrence.[3] It is quite possible for the two approaches to diverge in their conclusions – a holistic approach relying on historical evidence tends to show decision-makers to be preoccupied with their own interests, while a social scientific approach tends to show that decision-makers are still influenced by the nature and extent of the opponent's interests. Deciding that the historians have proven the social scientists 'wrong', or vice versa, runs into the fundamental problem of choosing the criteria for deciding who is right or wrong. That approach leads to clashing methodological absolutism, which can only polarise and impoverish the study of politics. Rather than deciding that ne'er the twain shall meet, it is more fruitful and interesting to try to relate the two.

EXPLAINING CRISIS OUTCOMES AFTER THE COLD WAR: MORE CONTINUITY THAN CHANGE

The end of the Cold War has important implications for international crises. During the Cold War, two massive alliances faced each other with the intention of fighting global nuclear and conventional war if they deemed it necessary. The crises centred on Berlin, Cuba and the Taiwan Straits had the potential to cause that global war. The end of the Cold War and the subsequent collapse of the Soviet Union defused the potential for global war. Those events also created the potential for new crises and wars between the states of Eastern Europe and the former Soviet Union. There has been tension between a number of those states, including Russia and Ukraine, and war broke out over the secession of Nargorno-Karabakh from Azerbaijan and the attempted secession of South Ossetia from Georgia. War also broke out among and within the states of the former Yugoslavia. The end of the US-Soviet strategic rivalry changed the dynamics of the United Nations, in that the Soviet Union and then post-Soviet Russia have been less likely to veto US attempts to act through the United Nations; Saddam Hussein's failure to appreciate this was one of the many miscalculations surrounding his invasion of Kuwait. The end of US-Soviet strategic rivalry also ameliorated the United States' obsessive anti-Communism, which had led it to perceive important US interests in every local disturbance world-wide.

The receding prospect of global war and the US-led war against Iraq was interpreted for a short while as evidence that the United States would be more willing to use force to achieve its objectives. However, reduced fear of escalation has been cancelled out by the fact that, where US decision-makers do not see important interests at stake, they are very wary about risking the political costs of incurring casualties. The perception of low stakes and high political risks explains why there has never been a serious prospect of US troops – or troops from any other Western country – being sent in a combat role to support the government of Bosnia-Hercegovina against externally-supported Serbian and Croatian rebels. It also explains why US President Bill Clinton withdrew his forces from Somalia, and why he tried so hard to find a way of ousting the Haitian military dictatorship which would avoid the use of force. The Haitian regime knew that Clinton attached a very high value to peace. It played on this by threatening him with 'Another Somalia', which was a reference to the politically damaging images of dead US soldiers being dragged through the streets of the Somali capital Mogadishu. This vivid analogy helped ensure that, in spite of the vast military capability assembled by the United States off the Haitian coast, Clinton made important political concessions to the members of the military government. In the end, compellence combined with a hefty dose of reassurance worked and the military government stepped down, with some of its members going into comfortable exile. The characteristics of these episodes of crisis bargaining are familiar: the end of the Cold War was more about the contexts, issues and locations of crises rather than about what explains their outcomes. Decision-makers still have to deal with ambiguous threats, with the difficulties of balancing threats and reassurance, with the need to interpret ambiguous threats, with the problems of signals sent but not seen or seen but not sent, with tactics such as trying to put the burden of the first use of force on the opponent, and with communicating interests to opponents and third parties across strategic cultures and in spite of psychological biases. Overall, there is more continuity than change.

ACADEMIC RESEARCH AND POLICY-MAKING

I would like to end with a few points regarding the relationship between academic research and policy-making. First, those who seek to produce maxims to guide policy-makers are in danger of producing plausible but banal statements on how to relate politics and military power: many hands make light work but too many cooks spoil the broth, look before you leap but who hesitates is lost. Second, those who seek to produce maxims which are not trivial run the risk of representing politics as an exact science rather than what it is – an inexact art of judgement. There are no precise principles of crisis behaviour: recommendations such as 'Analyse the analogies which are important to your opponent' can make decision-making more effective but cannot guarantee success. Third, although there is increasing pressure on academics to engage in policy-relevant research, my case studies add to the great weight of evidence that decision-makers frequently ignore inconvenient advice and seek to ensure that they are not offered it in the first place.[4] I distinguish between what is policy relevant and what is policy acceptable. Those who are sought out by decision-makers are often those whose views the decision-makers expect to be congenial: policy-acceptable research is a much narrower category than policy-relevant research. Those academics who are keen to have their recommendations listened to by decision-makers may find themselves engaging, self-consciously or unconsciously, in self-censorship in order to become or remain part of the inner circle. It is difficult to speak truth to power or even perceive truth when power is providing money, status or influence. Fourth, for better or worse, research often has its greatest impact when it becomes part of the general intellectual climate. One of the most dangerous aspects of the Cold War was the US obsession with deterrence: it became excessively concerned with perceptions of its resolve and with the supposed delicacy of the balance of terror. Finally, the relationship between research and ethics is ambiguous. On the one hand, research is not neutral because ethical assumptions are inescapable. I have assumed that it is legitimate and worthwhile to examine interstate crisis behaviour and to focus on crisis outcomes rather than, say, crisis prevention. On the other hand, research is neutral, in that it may be used for a whole range of moral purposes. I would value further research on the nuclear taboo: my hope is that this can uncover ways of making it less likely that nuclear weapons will be used in the future. However, Eisenhower and Dulles explicitly sought to undermine the nuclear taboo: a better understanding of it would have helped them achieve their objective of making nuclear weapons more usable. Research, like crisis, creates dangers as well as opportunities.

NOTES

[1] On the nuclear taboo, see Aron 1958: 69, 1965: 59–60; von Weiszäcker 1980: 205; Waltz 1981: 90; Booth 1987a: 270; Jervis 1989b: 133; Dunn 1991: 52, 53, 54, 60, 66, 69; and Herring 1991. On the chemical weapons taboo see Price 1993, 1994. Richard Price, who wrote his PhD on the chemical weapons taboo, and Nina Tannenbaum, who wrote her PhD on the tradition of nuclear non-use, are bringing these two themes together in a chapter for the forthcoming volume *Norms and National Security*, edited by Peter Katzenstein. I am exploring the relevance of ideas about strategic culture, anthropological concepts of taboo and ideas on the power of metaphor in order to shed light on the nuclear taboo.

[2] On the clarification of interests during crises, see McCalla 1992. Geoffrey Blainey says something similar in his explanation of the causes of war and peace: 'Wars begin when two nations disagree on their relative strength, and wars usually cease when the fighting nations agree on their

relative strength' (1988: 293). However, wars can also begin even if both sides essentially agree on their relative strength. Saddam Hussein and Bush both believed that the United States would win, but Saddam Hussein believed that his interests were better served by war than by withdrawal from Kuwait. Saddam Hussein's miscalculation lay in his initial belief that the United States would not send large-scale forces in the first place. Lebow and Stein (1994: 321–3) distinguish usefully between two types of crisis. In crises of misunderstanding, decision-makers miscalculate the opponent's intentions and interests, often due to a strong fear of loss, domestic or foreign. They will ignore an unfavourable military balance, and threats are liable to provoke escalation. In crises of incompatibility, both sides understand each other's interests but seek relative advantage. Threats may work, but not if the target prefers war (for instance if the stakes are high) or if the presence of nuclear weapons undermines the credibility of threats.

[3] In their 1984 study, they conclude that success is much more likely when the protégé imports a high proportion of its major weapons from the defender, when the protégé accounts for a high share of the defender's foreign trade, when the military capability of the protégé relative to the defender is large, and when the defender and protégé possess a common border (1984: 512–18). However, their later studies found no link between extended immediate deterrence outcomes and these factors, or additional measures (Huth, Russett 1988; Huth 1988b: 44–7, 63–5, 83–4). Huth and Russett found in 1984 that the existence of an alliance between the defender and protégé tends to be associated with the *failure* of immediate extended deterrence, as a state will only seriously consider attacking a member of an alliance if the crisis is very severe and war is likely. It is possible that alliances strengthen general deterrence and ensure that there are fewer occasions which require immediate extended deterrence, but this is conjecture (Huth, Russett 1984: 511–12, 519). In contrast, Huth's later study found no link either way between alliances and immediate extended deterrence (1988b: 43–4, 62–3, 82–3). Huth explains his own results in two ways. First, he suggests that the more valuable the protégé, the greater the incentive for the potential attacker to attack it or put military pressure on it. Second, he found that the bargaining behaviour of the defender was a better predictor of outcomes (1988b: 83–4). In particular, he found that matching the military and diplomatic behaviour of the opponent is more conducive to the success of immediate extended deterrence than either out-escalating the opponent or being more conciliatory than the opponent (1988b: 47–55, 65–8). But see

Levy 1988, p. 505; 1989, p. 116 on the discrepancies between the two studies.

[4] For valuable discussions of the 'lessons' of history and the relationship between academics and policy-makers see Brodie 1948–49; Chomsky 1969, 1973: 86–103; Jervis 1976: 217–87; Gooch 1980; Kaplan 1984; Herken 1987; Neustadt, May 1986; George 1991a, 1993; Gray 1982a,b; and Hill, Beshoff 1994.

BIBLIOGRAPHY

Achen, Christopher H. and Duncan Snidal (1989), 'Rational deterrence theory and comparative case studies', *World Politics*, **41**:2, 143–69.

Acheson, Dean (1965), *Present at the Creation: My Years in the State Department*, New York, NY, W. W. Norton.

Adams, Sherman (1961), *Firsthand Report: The Story of the Eisenhower Administration*, New York, NY, Harper.

Adomeit, Hannes (1982), *Soviet Risk-Taking and Crisis Behaviour: A Theoretical and Empirical Analysis*, London, George Allen & Unwin.

Akopov, Pogos, Victor Kremenyuk, Georgi Mirsky, Oleg Peresypkin, Vladmimir Polyakov, Sergei Sinitsyn, Nikolai Spassky, Kim Tsagolov, Robert Turdiyev, Alexei Vasilyev (1988), 'The USSR and the Third World', *International Affairs*, Moscow, 12, 133–45.

al-Khalil, Samir (1990), *Republic of Fear: The Inside Story of Saddam's Iraq*, New York, NY, Pantheon.

Allison, Graham T. (1971), *Essence of Decision: Explaining the Cuban Missile Crisis*, Boston, MA, Little, Brown.

Allison, Roy (1985), *Finland's Relations With the Soviet Union, 1944–84*, London, Macmillan.

—— (1990), 'Use of the military instrument short of war' in Carl G. Jacobsen (ed.), *Strategic Power: USA/USSR*, London, Macmillan, 398–412.

Allyn, Bruce J., James G. Blight and David A. Welch (1989–90), 'Essence of revision: Moscow, Havana and the Cuban missile crisis', *International Security*, **14**:3, 136–72.

—— (eds.) (1992), *Back to the Brink: Proceedings of the Moscow Conference on the Cuban Missile Crisis, January 27–28, 1989*, Cambridge, MA, Center for Science and International Affairs (CSIA), Harvard University, CSIA Occasional Paper no. 9. Lanham, MD, University Press of America.

Bibliography

Andrew, Christopher and Oleg Gordievsky (1990), *KGB: The Inside Story*, New York, NY, HarperCollins.

Appleby, Joyce, Lynn Hunt and Margaret Jacob (1994), *Telling the Truth about History*, New York, NY, W. W. Norton.

Arnett, Robert L. (1979), 'Soviet attitudes towards nuclear war: do they really think they can win?', *Journal of Strategic Studies*, 2:2, 172–91.

Aron, Raymond (1958), *On War. Atomic Weapons and Global Diplomacy*, London, Secker & Warburg.

—— (1965), *The Great Debate. Theories of Nuclear Strategy*, Garden City, NY, Doubleday.

Aspaturian, Vernon (1980), 'Soviet global power and the correlation of forces', *Problems of Communism*, 20, 1–18.

Baldwin, David A. (1979), 'Power analysis and world politics: new trends versus old tendencies', *World Politics*, **21**:2, 161–94.

—— (1981), 'The power of positive sanctions', *World Politics*, **24**:1, 19–38.

—— (1985), *Economic Statecraft*, Princeton, NJ, Princeton University Press.

—— (ed.) (1993), *Neorealism and Neoliberalism: The Contemporary Debate*, New York, NY, Columbia University Press.

Ball, Desmond (1981), *Can Nuclear War Be Controlled?*, Adelphi paper 169, London, International Institute for Strategic Studies.

—— (1990), 'Revising the SIOP: taking war-fighting to dangerous extremes', *International Security*, **14**:4, 65–92.

Barnett, Anthony (1982) *Iron Britannia. Why Britain Waged its Falklands War*, London, Allison and Busby.

Baylis, John and Gerald Segal (eds.) (1981), *Soviet Strategy*, London, Croom Helm.

Beschloss, Michael C. (1991), *The Crisis Years: Kennedy and Khrushchev, 1960–1963*, New York, NY, HarperCollins.

Betts, Richard K. (1977a), *Soldiers, Statesmen and Cold War Crises*, Cambridge, MA, Harvard University Press.

—— (1977b), 'Paranoids, pygmies, pariahs and nonproliferation', *Foreign Policy*, 26, 157–83.

—— (1987), *Nuclear Blackmail and Nuclear Balance*, Washington, DC, The Brookings Institution.

—— (1988), 'Nuclear peace and conventional war', *Journal of Strategic Studies*, **11**:1, 79–95.

Biderman, Shlomo and Ben-Ami Scharfstein (1989), *Rationality in Question. On Eastern and Western Views of Rationality*, Leiden, E. J. Brill.

Bibliography

Blainey, Geoffrey (1988), *The Causes of War*, London, Macmillan, 3rd edn.

Blair, Bruce G. (1985), *Strategic Command and Control: Redefining the Nuclear Threat*, Washington, DC, The Brookings Institution.

—— (1987), 'Alerting in crisis and conventional war' in Ashton B. Carter, John D. Steinbruner and Charles A. Zraket (eds.), *Managing Nuclear Operations*, Washington, DC, The Brookings Institution, 75–120.

—— (1993), *The Logic of Accidental Nuclear War*, Washington, DC, The Brookings Institution.

Blechman, Barry M. and Douglas M. Hart (1982), 'The political utility of nuclear weapons: the 1973 Middle East crisis', *International Security*, 7:1, 132–56.

—— and Stephen S. Kaplan, *et al.* (1978), *Force Without War: U.S. Armed Forces as a Political Instrument*, Washington, DC, The Brookings Institution.

—— and Robert Powell (1982–83), 'What in the name of God is strategic superiority?', *Political Science Quarterly*, **97**:4, 589–602. Correspondence, *Political Science Quarterly* (1983) **98**:3, 571–2.

Blight, James G. (1992), *The Shattered Crystal Ball. Fear and Learning in the Cuban Missile Crisis*, Lanham, MD, Littlefield Adams.

——, Bruce J. Allyn and David A. Welch (eds.) (forthcoming), *Cuba on the Brink. Castro, the Missile Crisis and the Soviet Collapse*, New York, NY, Pantheon Books.

——, David Lewis and David A. Welch (eds.) (forthcoming), *Cuba Between the Superpowers: The Antigua Conference on the Cuban Missile Crisis*, Savage, MD, Rowman and Littlefield.

——, Joseph S. Nye (Jr.) and David A. Welch (1987), 'The Cuban missile crisis revisited', *Foreign Affairs*, **66**:1, 170–88.

—— and David A. Welch (eds.) (1989), *On the Brink: Americans and Soviets Re-examine the Cuban Missile Crisis*, New York, NY, Hill and Wang.

Booth, Ken (1978), 'American strategy: the myths revisited' in Ken Booth and Moorhead Wright (eds.), *American Thinking About Peace and War*, Sussex, Harvester, 1–36.

—— (1979), *Strategy and Ethnocentrism*, London, Croom Helm.

—— (1987a), 'Nuclear deterrence and "World War III": how will history judge?' in Roman Kolkowicz (ed.), *The Logic of Nuclear Terror*, Boston, MA, Allen & Unwin, 251–82.

—— (1987b), 'New challenges and old mindsets: ten rules for empirical realists' in Carl G. Jacobsen (ed.), *The Uncertain Course: New Weapons,*

Strategies and Mindsets, Oxford, Oxford University Press for the Stockholm International Peace Research Institute, 39–66.

—— (1990), 'The concept of strategic culture affirmed' in Carl G. Jacobsen (ed.), *Strategic Power: USA/USSR*, London, Macmillan, 121–8.

—— and Nicholas J. Wheeler (1992), 'Beyond Nuclearism' in Regina Cowen Karp (ed.), *Security Without Nuclear Weapons?*, Oxford, Oxford University Press for the Stockholm International Peace Research Institute, 1–36.

Bown, Colin and Peter J. Mooney (1981), *Cold War to Détente, 1945–80*, London, Heinemann, 2nd edn.

Bracken, Paul (1983), *The Command and Control of Nuclear Forces*, New Haven, CT, Yale University Press.

Bradley, Morris (1993), 'The psychology of risk compensation and its implications for accidental nuclear war' in Håkan Wiberg, Ib Damgaard Petersen and Paul Smoker (eds.), *Inadvertent Nuclear War. The Implications of the Changing Global Order*, Oxford, Pergamon Press, 157–67.

Brands Jr., H. W. (1988), 'Testing massive retaliation: credibility and crisis management in the Taiwan Strait', *International Security*, **12**:4, 124–51.

Brecher, Michael, Jonathan Wilkenfeld and Sheila Moser (1988), *Crises in the Twentieth Century:* Vol. 1, *Handbook of International Crises*, Oxford, Pergamon.

—— and Jonathan Wilkenfeld (1989a), *Crisis, Conflict and Instability*, Oxford, Pergamon, with contributions by Patrick James, Hemda Ben Yehuda, Mark A. Boyer and Stephen R. Hill.

—— and Jonathan Wilkenfeld (1989b), 'Framework' in Michael Brecher and Jonathan Wilkenfeld, *Crisis, Conflict and Instability*, Oxford, Pergamon, with contributions by Patrick James, Hemda Ben Yehuda, Mark A. Boyer and Stephen R. Hill.

Brenner, Philip (1992), 'Kennedy and Khrushchev on Cuba: two stages, three parties', *Problems of Communism*, **41**, 24–7, special edition.

Brittain, Victoria (ed.) (1991), *The Gulf Between Us. The Gulf War and Beyond*, London, Virago.

Brodie, Bernard (1948–49), 'Strategy as a science', *World Politics*, **1**:4, 467–88.

—— (1973), *War and Politics*, London, Macmillan.

Brook-Shepherd, Gordon (1988), *The Storm Birds: Soviet Postwar Defectors*, New York, NY, Weidenfeld Nicolson.

Brown, Archie H. (ed.) (1984), *Political Culture and Communist Studies*, London, Macmillan.

Brzezinski, Zbigniew (1984), 'The Soviet Union: her aims, problems and challenges to the West' in *The Conduct of East-West Relations in the 1980s*, Adelphi paper 189, London, Brassey's for the International Institute for Strategic Studies, 3–12.

Bulloch, John and Harvey Morris (1991), *Saddam's War. The Origins of the Kuwait Conflict and the International Response*, London, Faber & Faber.

Bundy, McGeorge (1969–70), 'To cap the volcano', *Foreign Affairs*, **48**:1, 1–20.

—— (1984), 'Existential deterrence and its consequences' in Douglas Maclean (ed.), *The Security Gamble: Deterrence Dilemmas in the Nuclear Age*, Totowa, NJ, Rowman and Allenheld, 3–13.

—— (1986), 'Risk and opportunity: can we tell them apart?' in Catherine McArdle Kelleher, Frank J. Kerr and George H. Quester (eds.), *Nuclear Deterrence: New Risks, New Opportunities*, New York, NY, Pergamon-Brassey's, 27–36.

—— (1988), *Danger and Survival: Choices about the Bomb in the First Fifty Years*, New York, NY, Random.

—— (transcriber) and James G. Blight (ed.) (1987–88), 'October 27, 1962: transcripts of the meetings of the ExComm', *International Security*, **12**:3, 30–92.

Burlatskiy, Fedor (1992), 'The lessons of personal diplomacy', *Problems of Communism*, **41**, 8–13, special edn.

Buzan, Barry (1987), *An Introduction to Strategic Studies. Military Technology and International Relations*, London, Macmillan.

—— (1991), *People, States and Fear. An Agenda for International Security Studies in the Post-Cold War Era*, London, Harvester Wheatsheaf, 2nd edn.

Calvert, Peter (1982), *The Falklands Crisis: The Rights and Wrongs*, London, Frances Pinter.

Carlton, David (1988), *Britain and the Suez Crisis*, Oxford, Blackwell.

Carnesale, Albert, Joseph S. Nye, Jr. and Graham T. Allison (1985), 'An agenda for action' in Graham T. Allison, Albert Carnesale and Joseph S. Nye, Jr. (eds.), *Hawks, Doves, and Owls: An Agenda for Avoiding Nuclear War*, New York, NY, Norton, 223–46.

Carr, E. H. (1946), *The Twenty Years' Crisis: 1919–1939*, New York, NY, Harper & Row.

Carroll, Lewis ([1872] 1988), *Through the Looking Glass*, London, Puffin.

Carter, Ashton B., John D. Steinbruner and Charles A. Zraket (eds.)

(1987), *Managing Nuclear Operations*, Washington, DC, The Brookings Institution.

Chan, Steve (1978), 'Chinese conflicts calculus and behavior: assessment from a perspective of conflict management', *World Politics*, **30**:3, 391–410.

Chang, Gordon H. (1988a), 'To the nuclear brink: Eisenhower, Dulles and the Quemoy-Matsu Crisis', *International Security*, **12**:4, 96–123.

—— (1988b), 'JFK, China and the bomb', *The Journal of American History*, **74**, 1287–1310.

Charlton, Michael (1989), *The Little Platoon. Diplomacy and the Falklands Dispute*, Oxford, Basil Blackwell.

Chomsky, Noam (1969), *American Power and the New Mandarins*, New York, NY, Pantheon.

—— (1973), *For Reasons of State*, London, Fontana.

—— (1989), *Necessary Illusions: Thought Control in Democratic Societies*, London, Pluto Press.

—— (1992), *Deterring Democracy*, London, Vintage.

Chow Ching-wen (1960), *Ten Years of Storm. The True Story of the Communist Regime in China*, New York, NY, Holt, Rinehart & Winston.

Christensen, Thomas J. (1992), 'Threats, assurances, and the last chance for peace: the lessons of Mao's Korean War telegrams', *International Security*, 17:1, 122–54.

Cleary, Thomas W. (1988), Translator's introduction, in Sun Tzu, *The Art of War*, Shaftesbury, Shambala, 1–38.

Cockburn, Alexander and Andrew Cohen (1991), 'The unnecessary war' in Victoria Brittain (ed.), *The Gulf Between Us. The Gulf War and Beyond*, London, Virago, 1–26.

Cohen, Arthur A. (1991), 'The Sino-Soviet border crisis' in Alexander L. George (ed.), *Avoiding War. Problems of Crisis Management*, Boulder, CO, Westview, 269–96.

Cohen, Raymond (1988), 'Intercultural communication between Israel and Egypt: deterrence failure before the Six-Day War', *Review of International Studies*, **14**:1, 1–16.

—— (1991), *Negotiating Across Cultures. Communication Obstacles in International Diplomacy*, Washington, DC, United States Institute of Peace Press.

Cooley, John K. (1991), 'Pre-war Gulf diplomacy', *Survival*, **33**:2, 125–39.

Costa Méndez, Nicanor (1987), 'Beyond deterrence: the Malvinas-Falklands case', *Journal of Social Issues*, **43**:4, 119–22.

Cumings, Bruce (1992), *War and Television*, London, Verso.

Dannreuther, Roland (1991–92), *The Gulf Conflict: A Political and Strategic Analysis*, Adelphi paper 264, London, Brassey's for the International Institute for Strategic Studies.

Darwish, Adel and Gregory Alexander (1991), *Unholy Babylon: The Secret History of Saddam's War*, London, Victor Gollancz.

Daugherty, William, Barbara Levi and Frank von Hippel (1985–86), 'The consequences of "limited" nuclear attacks on the United States', *International Security*, **10**:4, 3–45.

David, Steven R. (1991a), *Choosing Sides: Alignment and Realignment in the Third World*, Baltimore, MD, Johns Hopkins University Press.

—— (1991b), 'Explaining Third World alignment', *World Politics*, **43**:2, 233–56.

—— (1992–93), 'Why the Third World still matters', *International Security*, **17**:3, 127–59.

Davison, W. Phillips (1958), *The Berlin Blockade: A Study in Cold War Politics*, Princeton, NJ, Princeton University Press.

Deane, Michael J. (1976), 'The Soviet assessment of the "correlation of forces": implications for American foreign policy', *Orbis*, **20**:3, 625–36.

Dillon, G. M. (1989), *The Falklands, Politics and War*, London, Macmillan.

Dinerstein, Herbert S. (1959), *War and the Soviet Union*, New York, NY, Praeger.

Douglas, Mary and Aaron Wildavsky (1982), *Risk and Culture. An Essay on the Selection of Technical and Environmental Dangers*, Berkeley, CA, University of California Press.

Downs, George W. (1989), 'The rational deterrence debate', *World Politics*, **41**:2, 225–37.

Druckman, Daniel and P. Terrence Hopmann (1989), 'Behavioral aspects of negotiations on mutual security' in Philip E. Tetlock, Jo L. Husbands, Robert Jervis, Paul C. Stern and Charles Tilly (eds.), *Behavior, Society, and Nuclear War*, **2**, New York, NY, Oxford University Press, 85–173.

Dunn, Lewis A. (1991), *Containing Nuclear Proliferation*, Adelphi paper 263, London, Brassey's for the International Institute for Strategic Studies.

Dyson, Freeman (1984), *Weapons and Hope*, New York, NY, Harper & Row.

Eckstein, Harry (1988), 'A culturalist theory of political change', *American Political Science Review*, **82**:3, 789–804.

Eisenhower, Dwight D. (1963), *Mandate for Change*, London, Heinemann.

Elkins, David J. and Richard E. B. Simeon (1979), 'A cause in search of its effect, or what does political culture explain?', *Comparative Politics*, **11**:2, 127–45.

Erickson, John (1982), 'The Soviet view of deterrence: a general survey', *Survival*, **24**:6, 242–51.

Ermath, Fritz (1978), 'Contrasts in American and Soviet strategic thought', *International Security*, **3**:2, 138–55.

Etzold, Thomas H. and John Lewis Gaddis (eds.) (1978), *Containment: Documents on American Policy and Strategy, 1945–1950*, New York, NY, Columbia University Press.

Evangelista, Matthew A. (1982–83), 'Stalin's postwar army reappraised', *International Security*, **7**:3, 110–38.

Feaver, Peter Douglas (1992), *Guarding the Guardians: Civilian Control of Nuclear Weapons in the United States*, Ithaca, NY, Cornell University Press.

Feldman, Shai (1982), 'The bombing of Osiraq – revisited', *International Security*, **7**:2, 114–42.

Fish, M. Steven (1991), 'The Berlin blockade crisis of 1948–49' in Alexander L. George (ed.), *Avoiding War. Problems of Crisis Management*, Boulder, CO, Westview, 195–21.

Fisher, Glen (1988), *Mindsets*, Yarmouth, Intercultural Press.

Flynn, Gregory (ed.) (1989), *Soviet Military Doctrine and Western Policy*, London, Routledge.

Foot, Rosemary (1985), *The Wrong War. American Policy and the Dimensions of the Korean Conflict, 1950–53*, Ithaca, NY, Cornell University Press.

Franks, The Rt. Hon. Lord (1983), *Falkland Islands Review. Report of a Committee of Privy Counsellors. Chairman: The Rt Hon The Lord Franks, OM, GCMG, KCB, CBE*, London, HMSO, Cmnd. 8787.

Freedman, Lawrence (1988), 'I exist; therefore I deter', *International Security*, **13**:1, 177–95.

—— (1989a), *The Evolution of Nuclear Strategy*, New York, NY, St. Martin's, 2nd edn.

—— (1989b), 'General deterrence and the balance of power', *Review of International Studies*, **15**, 2, 199–210.

—— and Virginia Gamba-Stonehouse (1990), *Signals of War. The Falklands Conflict of 1982*, London, Faber & Faber.

—— and Efraim Karsh (1991), 'How Kuwait was won: strategy in the Gulf War', *International Security*, **16**:2, 5–41.

—— (1993), *The Gulf Conflict 1990–91. Diplomacy and War in the New World Order*, London, Faber & Faber.

Friedberg, Alan L. (1980), 'A history of U.S. strategic "doctrine" – 1945–1980', *Journal of Strategic Studies*, 3:3, 37–71.

Friedman, Edward (1971), 'Problems in dealing with an irrational power: America declares war on China' in Edward Friedman and Mark Selden (eds.), *America's Asia. Dissenting Essays on Asian-American Relations*, New York, NY, Pantheon Books, 207–52.

—— (1975), 'Nuclear blackmail and the end of the Korean War', *Modern China*, 1:1, 75–91.

—— and Mark Selden (eds.) (1971), *America's Asia. Dissenting Essays on Asian-American Relations*, New York, NY, Pantheon Books.

FRUS 1948 2 [Department of State, *Foreign Relations of the United States 1948* 2: *Germany and Austria*], Washington, DC, US Government Printing Office, 1973.

FRUS 1948 3 [Department of State, *Foreign Relations of the United States 1948* 3: *Western Europe*], Washington, DC, US Government Printing Office, 1974.

FRUS 1948 4 [Department of State, *Foreign Relations of the United States 1948* 4: *Eastern Europe: The Soviet Union*], Washington, DC, US Government Printing Office, 1974.

FRUS 1949 3 [Department of State, *Foreign Relations of the United States 1949* 3: *Council of Ministers: Germany and Austria*], Washington, DC, US Government Printing Office, 1974.

FRUS 1950 7 [Department of State, *Foreign Relations of the United States 1950* 7: *Korea*], Washington, DC, US Government Printing Office, 1976.

FRUS 1952–54 14 [Department of State, *Foreign Relations of the United States 1952–54* 14: *China and Japan*], Washington, DC, US Government Printing Office, 1985.

FRUS 1952–54 15 [Department of State, *Foreign Relations of the United States 1952–54* 15: *Korea*], Washington, DC, US Government Printing Office, 1984.

FRUS 1955–57 2 [Department of State, *Foreign Relations of the United States 1955–57* 2: *China*], Washington, DC, US Government Printing Office, 1986.

Futrell, Robert Frank (1980), *Ideas, Concepts, Doctrine: A History of Basic Thinking in the United States Air Force, 1907–1964*, New York, NY, Arno Press.

Gaddis, John Lewis (1986), 'The long peace: elements of stability in the postwar international system', *International Security*, **10**:4, 99–142.

—— (1987), *The Long Peace. Inquiries Into the History of the Cold War*, New York, NY, Oxford University Press.

Garnett, John (1975a), 'The role of military power' in John Baylis, Ken Booth, John Garnett and Phil Williams, *Contemporary Strategy. Theories and Policies*, London, Croom Helm, 50–64.

—— (1975b), 'Limited war' in John Baylis, Ken Booth, John Garnett and Phil Williams, *Contemporary Strategy. Theories and Policies*, London, Croom Helm, 187–208.

Garrett, Banning and Bonnie Glaser (1988), *Chinese Estimates of the US-Soviet Balance of Power*, occasional paper 33, Asia Program, The Wilson Center, Smithsonian Institution Building, Washington, DC.

Garthoff, Raymond L. (1958), *Soviet Strategy in the Nuclear Age*, New York, NY, Praeger.

—— (1966), *Soviet Military Policy. A Historical Analysis*, London, Faber & Faber.

—— (1978), 'Mutual deterrence and strategic arms limitation in Soviet policy', *International Security*, **3**:1, 112–47.

—— (1982), 'A rebuttal by Ambassador Garthoff', *Strategic Review*, **10**:4, 58–63.

—— (1985), *Détente and Confrontation: American-Soviet Relations From Nixon to Reagan*, Washington, DC, The Brookings Institution.

—— (1988), 'The Cuban missile crisis – the Soviet story', *Foreign Policy*, 72, 61–80.

—— (1989), *Reflections on the Cuban Missile Crisis*, Washington, DC, The Brookings Institution, rev. edn.

—— (1990a), *Deterrence and the Revolution in Soviet Military Doctrine*, Washington, DC, The Brookings Institution.

—— (1990b), 'Evaluating and using historical hearsay', *Diplomatic History*, **14**:2, 223–9.

—— (1991), 'Berlin 1961: the record corrected', *Foreign Policy*, 84, 142–56.

Garver, John (1980), 'The Chinese foreign policy in 1970: the tilt towards the Soviet Union', *The China Quarterly*, 82, 214–49.

Geertz, Clifford (1973), *The Interpretation of Cultures*, London, Fontana.

—— (1983), *Local Knowledge*, London, Fontana.

Gelber, Harry (1973), *Nuclear Weapons and Chinese Policy*, Adelphi paper 99, London, International Institute for Strategic Studies.

Gelman, Harry (1982), *The Soviet Far East Buildup and Soviet Risk-Taking Against China*, R-2943-AF, Santa Monica, CA, RAND Corporation.

George, Alexander L. (1979), 'Case studies and theory development: the method of structured, focused comparison' in Paul Gordon Lauren (ed.), *Diplomacy, New Approaches in History, Theory and Policy*, New York, NY, Free Press, 43–68.

—— (ed.) (1991a), *Avoiding War. Problems of Crisis Management*, Boulder, CO, Westview.

—— (1991b), 'The Cuban missile crisis' in Alexander L. George (ed.), *Avoiding War. Problems of Crisis Management*, Boulder, CO, Westview, 223–68.

—— (1993), *Bridging the Gap. Theory and Practice in Foreign Policy*, Washington, DC, United States Institute of Peace Press.

—— (1994), 'Coercive diplomacy: definition and characteristics' in Alexander L. George and William E. Simons (eds.), *The Limits of Coercive Diplomacy*, Boulder, CO, Westview, 2nd edn., 7–11.

——, David K. Hall and William E. Simons (1971), *The Limits of Coercive Diplomacy: Laos, Cuba, Vietnam*, New York, NY, Little, Brown.

—— and William E. Simons (eds.) (1994), *The Limits of Coercive Diplomacy*, Boulder, CO, Westview, 2nd edn.

—— and Richard Smoke (1974), *Deterrence in American Foreign Policy: Theory and Practice*, New York, NY, Columbia University Press.

Gibbins, John R. (ed.) (1989), *Contemporary Political Culture: Politics in a Postmodern Age*, London, Sage.

Glaser, Charles L. (1992), 'Political consequences of military strategy. Expanding and refining the spiral and deterrence models', *World Politics*, 44:4, 497–538.

Golan, Galia (1990), 'The Soviet Union and the Suez crisis' in Selwyn Ilan Troen and Moshe Shemesh (eds.), *The Suez-Sinai Crisis 1956. Retrospective and Reappraisal*, London, Frank Cass, 274–86.

Gooch, John (1980), 'Clio and Mars: the use and abuse of history', *Journal of Strategic Studies*, 3:3, 21–36.

Gordon, Leonard H. (1985), 'United States opposition to use of force in the Taiwan Strait, 1954–1962', *The Journal of American History*, 72:3, 637–60.

Gottfried, Kurt and Bruce G. Blair (eds.) (1988), *Crisis Stability and Nuclear War*, Oxford, Oxford University Press.

Gray, Colin S. (1979), 'Nuclear strategy and the case for a theory of victory', *International Security*, **4**:1, 54–87.

—— (1982a), *Strategic Studies. A Critical Assessment*, London, Aldwych Press.

—— (1982b), *Strategic Studies and Public Policy: The American Experience*, Philadelphia, PA, Foreign Policy Research Institute.

—— (1984), 'Comparative strategic culture', *Parameters*, **14**:4, 26–33.

—— (1986), *Nuclear Strategy and National Style*, Lanham, MD, Hamilton.

—— (1993), 'Through a missile tube darkly: "new thinking" about nuclear strategy', *Political Studies*, **61**:4, 661–71.

—— and Keith B. Payne (1980), 'Victory is possible', *Foreign Policy*, 39, 14–28.

Green, Philip (1966), *Deadly Logic: The Theory of Nuclear Deterrence*, Columbus, OH, Columbia University Press.

Grieco, Joseph M. (1993), 'The relative gains problem for international cooperation', *American Political Science Review*, **87**:3, 729–43.

Gurtov, Melvin and Byong-Moo Hwang (1980), *China Under Threat*, Baltimore, MD, Johns Hopkins University Press.

Halperin, Morton H. (1987), *Nuclear Fallacy: Dispelling the Myth of Nuclear Strategy*, Cambridge, MA, Ballinger.

Hampson, Fen Osler (1984–85), 'The divided decision-maker. American domestic politics and the Cuban crises', *International Security*, **9**:3, 130–65.

Hao Yufan and Zhai Zhihai (1990), 'China's decision to enter the Korean War: history revisited', *China Quarterly*, 121, 94–115.

Hart, Douglas M. (1984), 'Soviet approaches to crisis management: the military dimension', *Survival*, **26**:5, 214–23.

Hastings, Max and Simon Jenkins (1983), *The Battle for the Falklands*, London, Michael Joseph.

Hayes, Peter (1991), *Pacific Powderkeg. American Nuclear Dilemmas in Korea*, Lexington, MA, Lexington Books, D. C. Heath.

He Di (1990), 'The evolution of the People's Republic of China's policy toward the offshore islands' in Warren I. Cohen and Akira Iriye (eds.), *The Great Powers in East Asia: 1953–1960*, New York, NY, Columbia University Press, 222–45.

Heidelmeyer, Wolfgang and Guenther Hindrichs (eds.) (1963), *Documents on Berlin 1943–1963*, Munich, R. Oldenbourg Verlag.

Heikal, Mohamed (1976), *The Road to Ramadan*, London, Fontana-Collins.

—— (1978), *Sphinx and Commissar. The Rise and Fall of Soviet Influence in the Arab World*, London, Collins.

—— (1992), *Illusions of Triumph. An Arab View of the Gulf War*, London, Fontana.

Herek, Gregory M., Irving L. Janis and Paul Huth (1987), 'Decision making during international crises. Is quality of process related to outcome?', *Journal of Conflict Resolution*, **31**:2, 203–26.

Herken, Gregg (1985), 'The not-quite-absolute weapon: deterrence and the legacy of Bernard Brodie', paper prepared for a conference on 'The Calculus of Terror: Nuclear Strategy and its Discontents', Bellagio, Italy, 9–13 December 1985.

—— (1987), *Counsels of War*, New York, NY, Oxford University Press, expanded edn.

Herman, Edward S. and Noam Chomsky (1988), *Manufacturing Consent: The Political Economy of the Mass Media*, New York, NY, Pantheon.

Hermann, Charles F. (1969), 'International crisis as a situational variable' in James N. Rosenau (ed.), *International Politics and Foreign Policy: A Reader in Research and Theory*, New York, NY, Free Press, rev. edn., 402–21.

Herring, Eric (1991), 'The decline of nuclear diplomacy' in Ken Booth (ed.), *New Thinking about Strategy and International Security*, London, HarperCollins, 90–109.

Herrmann, Richard (1994), 'Coercive diplomacy and the crisis over Kuwait, 1990–91' in Alexander L. George and William E. Simons (eds.), *The Limits of Coercive Diplomacy*, Boulder, CO, Westview, 2nd edn., 229–64.

Hersh, Seymour (1983), *The Price of Power: Henry Kissinger in the Nixon White House*, New York, NY, Summit.

—— (1991), *The Samson Option. America, Israel and the Bomb*, London, Faber & Faber.

Hill, Christopher and P. Beshoff (1994), *Two Worlds of International Relations*, London, Routledge.

Hoffmann, Fritz L. and Olga Mingo Hoffmann (1984), *Sovereignty in Dispute. The Falklands/Malvinas, 1493–1982*, Boulder, CO, Westview Press.

Hollis, Martin and Steve Smith (1990), *Explaining and Understanding International Relations*, Oxford, Clarendon Press.

Holloway, David (1983), *The Soviet Union and the Arms Race*, London, Yale University Press.

—— (1994), *Stalin and the Bomb. The Soviet Union and Atomic Energy, 1939–1956*, London, Yale University Press.

Honeywell, Martin and Jenny Pearce (1982), *Falklands/Malvinas: Whose Crisis?* London, Latin American Bureau.

Hopf, Ted (1991), 'Polarity, the offense-defense balance, and war', *American Political Science Review*, **85**:2, 475–93.

Hopkins, J. C. (1982), *The Development of the Strategic Air Command, 1946–1981. A Chronological History*, Omaha, NB, Office of the Historian, Headquarters, Strategic Air Command.

Hopple, Gerald W. (1984), 'Intelligence and warning: implications and lessons of the Falkland Islands war', *World Politics*, **36**:4, 339–61.

Horelick, Arnold L. and Myron Rush (1966), *Strategic Power and Soviet Foreign Policy*, Chicago, IL, University of Chicago Press.

Howard, Michael (1981), 'On fighting a nuclear war', *International Security*, 5:4, 3–17.

—— (1983), 'Reassurance and deterrence: Western defence in the 1980s' in Michael Howard, *The Causes of War: and Other Essays*, London, Counterpoint, 218–36.

Hsieh, Alice Langley (1962), *Communist China's Strategy in the Nuclear Age*, Englewood Cliffs, NJ, Prentice-Hall.

Huebner, Jon W. (1987), 'The abortive liberation of Taiwan', *The China Quarterly*, 110, 256–75.

Hunt, Michael, David Shambaugh, Warren Cohen and Akira Iriye (1988), *Mutual Images in US-China Relations*, occasional paper 32, Asia Program, The Wilson Center, Smithsonian Institution Building, Washington, DC.

Huntington, Samuel P. (1993), 'Why international primacy matters', *International Security*, **17**:4, 68–83.

Huth, Paul (1988a), 'Extended deterrence and the outbreak of war', *American Political Science Review*, **82**:2, 422–43.

—— (1988b), *Extended Deterrence and the Prevention of War*, New Haven, CT, Yale University Press.

—— and Bruce Russett (1984), 'What makes deterrence work? Cases from 1900 to 1980', *World Politics*, **36**:4, 496–526.

—— (1988), 'Deterrence failure and crisis escalation', *International Studies Quarterly*, **32**:1, 29–45.

—— (1990), 'Testing deterrence theory. Rigor makes a difference', *World Politics*, **42**:4, 466–501.

—— (1993), 'General deterrence between enduring rivals: testing three competing models', *American Political Science Review*, **87**:1, 61–73.

—— (forthcoming), Appendix, in Kenneth A. Oye (ed.), *Specifying and Testing Theories of Deterrence*, Ann Arbor, MI, University of Michigan Press.

Hybel, Alex Roberto (1993), *Power Over Rationality. The Bush Administration and the Gulf Crisis*, Albany, NY, State University of New York Press.

Inglehart, Ronald (1988), 'The renaissance of political culture', *American Political Science Review*, **82**:4, 1203–30.

al Jabar, Faleh' Abd (1991), 'Roots of an adventure. The invasion of Kuwait: Iraqi political dynamics' in Victoria Brittain (ed.), *The Gulf Between Us. The Gulf War and Beyond*, London, Virago, 27–42.

Jacobsen, Carl G. (ed.) (1990), *Strategic Power: USA/USSR*, London, Macmillan.

Janis, Irving L. (1972), *Victims of Groupthink: A Psychological Study of Foreign Policy Decisions and Fiascos*, Boston, MA, Houghton-Mifflin, 2nd edn.

—— and Leon Mann (1977), *Decision Making: A Psychological Analysis of Conflict, Choice and Commitment*, New York, NY, The Free Press.

Jervis, Robert (1970), *The Logic of Images in International Relations*, New York, NY, Columbia University Press.

—— (1976), *Perception and Misperception in International Politics*, Princeton, NJ, Princeton University Press.

—— (1978), 'Cooperation under the security dilemma', *World Politics*, **30**:2, 167–214.

—— (1979), 'Deterrence theory revisited', *World Politics*, **31**:2, 289–324.

—— (1979–80), 'Why nuclear superiority doesn't matter', *Political Science Quarterly*, **94**:4, 617–33.

—— (1982–83), 'Deterrence and perception', *International Security*, **7**:1, 3–30.

—— (1983) 'Security regimes' in Stephen D. Krasner (ed.), *International Regimes*, Ithaca, NY, Cornell University Press, 173–94.

—— (1984), *The Illogic of American Nuclear Strategy*, Ithaca, NY, Cornell University Press.

—— (1985), 'Introduction: Approaches and Assumptions' in Robert Jervis, Richard Ned Lebow and Janice Gross Stein, *Psychology and Deterrence*, Baltimore, MD, Johns Hopkins University Press, 1–12.

—— (1988), 'The political effects of nuclear weapons: A comment', *International Security*, **13**:2, 80–90.

—— (1989a), 'Rational deterrence: theory and evidence', *World Politics*, **41**:2, 183–207.

—— (1989b), *The Meaning of the Nuclear Revolution: Statecraft and the Prospect of Armageddon*, Ithaca, NY, Cornell University Press.

—— (1991), 'Domino beliefs and strategic behavior' in Robert Jervis and Jack Snyder (eds.), *Dominoes and Bandwagons. Strategic Beliefs and Great Power Competition in the Eurasian Rimland*, Oxford, Oxford University Press, 20–50.

—— (1993), 'International primacy: is the game worth the candle?', *International Security*, **17**:4, 52–67.

——, Richard Ned Lebow and Janice Gross Stein (1985), *Psychology and Deterrence*, Baltimore, MD, Johns Hopkins University Press. With contributions by Patrick M. Morgan and Jack L. Snyder.

—— and Jack L. Snyder (eds.) (1991), *Dominoes and Bandwagons. Strategic Beliefs and Great Power Competition in the Eurasian Rimland*, Oxford, Oxford University Press.

Johnson, Robert H. (1983), 'Periods of peril. The window of vulnerability and other myths', *Foreign Affairs*, **16**:4, 950–70.

Johnston, Alastair I. (forthcoming), *Cultural Realism: Strategic Culture and Grand Strategy in Ming China*, Princeton, NJ, Princeton University Press.

Jukes, Geoffrey (1975), 'The military approach to deterrence and defence' in Michael MccGwire, Ken Booth and John McDonnell (eds.), *Soviet Naval Policy. Objectives and Constraints*, New York, NY, Praeger, 479–85.

Kahan, Jerome K. and Anne K. Long (1972), 'The Cuban missile crisis: a study of its strategic context', *Political Science Quarterly*, **87**:4, 564–90.

Kahn, Herman (1960), *On Thermonuclear War*, Princeton, NJ, Princeton University Press.

—— (1962), *Thinking About the Unthinkable*, New York, NY, Avon Books.

—— (1965), *On Escalation: Metaphors and Scenarios*, London, Pall Mall.

Kahneman, Daniel, Paul Slovic and Amos Tversky (eds.) (1982), *Judgment Under Uncertainty: Heuristics and Biases*, Cambridge, Cambridge University Press.

—— and Amos Tversky (1979), 'Prospect theory: an analysis of decision under risk', *Econometrica,* **47**:2, 263–91.

Kalicki, J. H. (1975), *The Pattern of Sino-American Crises: Political-Military Interaction in the 1950s*, Cambridge, Cambridge University Press.

Kaplan, Fred (1984), *The Wizards of Armageddon*, New York, NY, Touchstone.

Kaplan, Stephen S. (1981), *Diplomacy of Power. Soviet Armed Forces as a Political Instrument*, Washington, DC, The Brookings Institution.

Karp, Regina Cowen (1991), *Security With Nuclear Weapons? Different Perspectives on National Security*, Oxford, Oxford University Press for the Stockholm International Peace Research Institute.

Karsh, Efraim and Inari Rautsi (1991a), 'Why Saddam Hussein invaded Kuwait', *Survival*, **33**:1, 18–30.

—— (1991b), *Saddam Hussein: A Political Biography*, London, Macmillan.

Kaufman, Robert G. (1992), 'To balance or to bandwagon? Alignment decisions in 1930s Europe', *Security Studies*, **1**:3, 417–47.

Kavanaugh, Denis (1972), *Political Culture*, London, Macmillan.

Keefer, Edward (1986), 'President Dwight D. Eisenhower and the end of the Korean War', *Diplomatic History*, **10**, 267–89.

Keeny, Jr., Spurgeon M. and Wolfgang K. H. Panofsky (1981–82), 'MAD vs. NUTS: can doctrine or weaponry remedy the mutual hostage relationship of the superpowers?', *Foreign Affairs*, **60**:2, 287–304.

Keesing's [*Keesing's Contemporary Archives*, retitled *Keesing's Record of World Events*], Harlow, Longman.

Kennan, George F. (1982), *The Nuclear Delusion. Soviet-American Relations in the Atomic Age*, New York, NY, Pantheon, expanded, updated edn.

Kennedy-Khrushchev correspondence (1992), 'Back from the brink: the correspondence between President John F. Kennedy and Chairman Nikita S. Khrushchev on the Cuban missile crisis of Autumn 1962', *Problems of Communism*, **41**, 28–120, special edn.

Kennedy, Robert F. (1971), *Thirteen Days. A Memoir of the Cuban Missile Crisis*, New York, NY, W. W. Norton.

Keohane, Robert O. and Joseph S. Nye (Jr.) (1989), *Power and Interdependence. World Politics in Transition*, Boston, MA, Little, Brown, 2nd edn.

Khong, Yuen Foong (1992), *Analogies at War: Korea, Munich, Dien Bien Phu and the Vietnam Decisions of 1965*, Princeton, NJ, Princeton University Press.

Khrushchev, Nikita S. (1971), *Khrushchev Remembers*, London, Book Club Associates. Introduction, commentary and notes by Edward Crankshaw, trans. and ed. Strobe Talbott.

—— (1974), *Khrushchev Remembers. The Last Testament*, Boston, MA, Little, Brown. Introduction by Edward Crankshaw and Jerrold Shecter, trans. and ed. Strobe Talbott.

—— (1990), *Khrushchev Remembers. The Glasnost Tapes*, Boston, MA,

Little, Brown, trans. and ed. Jerrold L. Schecter, with Vyacheslav V. Luchkov.

Khrushchev, Sergei (1990), *Khrushchev on Khrushchev: An Inside Account of the Man and His Era*, Boston, MA, Little, Brown, trans. and ed. William Taubman.

Kinder, Donald R. and Janet A. Weiss (1978), 'In lieu of rationality. Psychological perspectives on foreign policy decision making', *Journal of Conflict Resolution*, **22**:4, 707–35.

King, Gary, Robert O. Keohane and Sidney Verba (1994), *Designing Social Inquiry: Scientific Inference in Qualitative Research*, Princeton, NJ, Princeton University Press.

Kissinger, Henry A. (1957), *A World Restored: Castlereagh, Metternich, and the Problem of Peace, 1812–22*, Boston, MA, Houghton Mifflin.

—— (1979), *The White House Years*, London, Weidenfeld & Nicolson, Michael Joseph.

—— (1982), *Years of Upheaval*, London, Weidenfeld & Nicolson, Michael Joseph.

Klein, Bradley S. (1988), 'Hegemony and strategic culture: American power projection and alliance defence politics', *Review of International Studies*, **14**:2, 133–48.

Klein, Yitzak (1991), 'A theory of strategic culture', *Comparative Strategy*, **10**:1, 3–24.

Klotz, Audie (1992), 'Reconstituting interests: interpretive analysis of norms in international relations', unpublished MS.

Knelman, F. H. (1985), *Reagan, God and the Bomb*, Buffalo, NY, Prometheus.

Knorr, Klaus and Patrick Morgan (eds.) (1983), *Strategic-Military Surprise*, New Brunswick, NJ, Transaction.

Kramer, Mark (1990), 'Remembering the Cuban missile crisis: should we swallow oral history?', *International Security*, **15**:1, 212–16.

Kratochwil, Friedrich (1982), 'On the notion of "interest" in international relations', *World Politics*, **36**:1, 1–30.

—— (1989), *Rules, Norms and Decisions: On the Conditions of Practical and Legal Reasoning in International Relations and Domestic Affairs*, Cambridge, Cambridge University Press.

Krus, David J. and Yoko Ishigaki (1992), 'Kamikaze pilots: the Japanese versus the American perspective', *Psychological Reports*, **70**:2, 599–602.

Kruzel, Joseph P. (1977), 'Military alerts and diplomatic signals' in Ellen P. Stern (ed.), *The Limits of Military Intervention*, Beverly Hills, CA, Sage, 83–99.

Kugler, Jacek (1984), 'Terror without deterrence: reassessing the role of nuclear weapons', *Journal of Conflict Resolution*, **28**:3, 470–506.

Kull, Steven (1988), *Minds at War. Nuclear Reality and the Inner Conflict of Defense Policymakers*, New York, NY, Basic.

Kunz, Diane B. (1989), 'The importance of having money: the economic diplomacy of the Suez crisis' in W. Roger Louis and Roger Owen (eds.), *Suez 1956. The Crisis and its Consequences*, Oxford, Clarendon, 215–32.

Kux, Stephan (1986), *A Synoptical Analysis of Key Terms in the Strategic Doctrines of the Nuclear Powers PR of China, France, Great Britain, Soviet Union and the United States*, PhD dissertation, University of Zurich.

Kyle, Keith (1991), *Suez*, New York, NY, Weidenfeld & Nicolson.

Labs, Eric (1992), 'Do weak states bandwagon?', *Security Studies*, **1**:3.

Laitin, David D. and Aaron Wildavsky (1988), 'Correspondence: political culture and political preferences', *American Political Science Review*, **82**:2, 589–96.

Lambeth, Benjamin (1982–83), 'Uncertainties for the Soviet war planner', *International Security*, 7:3, 139–66.

Laqueur, Walter (1979), *A Continent Astray. Europe 1970–1978*, Oxford, Oxford University Press.

La Rocque, Gene R. and Eugene J. Carroll, Jr. (1991), 'Victory in the desert: superior technology or brute force?' in Victoria Brittain (ed.), *The Gulf Between Us. The Gulf War and Beyond*, London, Virago, 43–60.

Larson, David L. (ed.) (1986), *The 'Cuban Crisis' of 1962. Selected Documents, Chronology and Bibliography*, Lanham, MD, University Press of America, 2nd edn.

Larson, Deborah Welch (1991), 'Bandwagon images in American foreign policy: myth or reality?' in Robert Jervis and Jack Snyder (eds.), *Dominoes and Bandwagons. Strategic Beliefs and Great Power Competition in the Eurasian Rimland*, Oxford, Oxford University Press, 85–111.

Lebow, Richard Ned (1981), *Between Peace and War: The Nature of International Crisis*, Baltimore, MD, Johns Hopkins University Press.

—— (1983), 'The Cuban missile crisis: reading the lessons correctly', *Political Science Quarterly*, **98**:3, 431–58.

—— (1984), 'Windows of opportunity: do states jump through them?', *International Security*, **9**:1, 147–86.

—— (1985a), 'Miscalculation in the South Atlantic: the origins of the Falklands War' in Robert Jervis, Richard Ned Lebow and Janice Gross

Stein, *Psychology and Deterrence*, Baltimore, MD, Johns Hopkins University Press, 89–124. With contributions by Patrick M. Morgan and Jack L. Snyder.

—— (1985b), 'The deterrence deadlock: is there a way out?' in Robert Jervis, Richard Ned Lebow and Janice Gross Stein, *Psychology and Deterrence*, Baltimore, MD, Johns Hopkins University Press, 180–202. With contributions by Patrick M. Morgan and Jack L. Snyder.

—— (1985c), 'Conclusions' in Robert Jervis, Richard Ned Lebow and Janice Gross Stein, *Psychology and Deterrence*, Baltimore, MD, Johns Hopkins University Press, 203–232. With contributions by Patrick M. Morgan and Jack L. Snyder.

—— (1985d), 'Deterrence reconsidered: the challenge of recent research', *Survival*, **27**:1, 20–9.

—— (1987a), *Nuclear Crisis Management: a Dangerous Illusion*, Ithaca, NY, Cornell University Press.

—— (1987b), 'Conventional and nuclear deterrence: are the lessons transferable?', *Journal of Social Issues*, **43**:4, 171–91.

—— (1987c), 'Deterrence failure revisited', *International Security*, **12**:1, 197–213.

—— (1988), 'Was Khrushchev bluffing in Cuba?' *Bulletin of the Atomic Scientists*, **44**:3, 38–42.

—— (1989), 'Deterrence: a political and psychological critique' in Paul Stern, Robert Axelrod, Robert Jervis and Roy Radner (eds.), *Perspectives on Deterrence*, New York, NY, Oxford University Press, 25–51.

—— and Janice Gross Stein (1987a), 'Beyond deterrence', *Journal of Social Issues*, **43**:4, 5–71.

—— (1987b), 'Beyond deterrence: building better theory', *Journal of Social Issues*, **43**:4, 155–69.

—— (1989), 'Rational deterrence theory: I think, therefore I deter', *World Politics*, **41**:2, 208–24.

—— (1990a), 'Deterrence: the elusive dependent variable', *World Politics*, **42**:3, 336–69.

—— (1990b), *When Does Deterrence Succeed and How Do We Know?* Ottawa, Canadian Institute for International Peace and Security.

—— (1994), *We All Lost the Cold War*, Princeton, NJ, Princeton University Press.

—— (forthcoming), 'Review of the data collection on extended deterrence by Paul Huth and Bruce Russett' in Kenneth A. Oye (ed.), *Specifying and Testing Theories of Deterrence*, Ann Arbor, MI, University of Michigan Press.

Lee, Steven P. (1993), *Morality, Prudence and Nuclear Weapons*, Cambridge, Cambridge University Press.

Leebaert, Derek (ed.) (1981), *Soviet Military Thinking*, London, Allen & Unwin.

Legvold, Robert (1979), 'The concept of power in Soviet history' in *Prospects for Soviet Power in the 1980s*, Adelphi paper 151, part 1, London, International Institute for Strategic Studies.

Leitenberg, Milton (1980), 'Appendix 3: threats of the use of nuclear weapons since World War II: an introductory note' in Asbjorn Eide and Marek Thee (eds.), *Problems of Contemporary Militarism*, London, Croom Helm, 388–95.

Leng, Russell J. (1983), 'When will they ever learn: coercive bargaining in recurrent crises', *Journal of Conflict Resolution*, **27**:3, 379–419.

Levy, Jack S. (1984), 'The offensive/defensive balance of military technology: a theoretical and historical analysis', *International Studies Quarterly*, **28**:2, 219–38.

—— (1987), 'Declining power and the preventive motivation for war, *World Politics*', **40**:1, 82–107.

—— (1988), 'Review article: when do deterrent threats work?', *British Journal of Political Science*, **18**:4, 485–512.

—— (1989), 'Quantitative studies of deterrence success and failure' in Paul Stern, Robert Axelrod, Robert Jervis and Roy Radner (eds.), *Perspectives on Deterrence*, New York, NY, Oxford University Press, 98–133.

—— and Michael M. Barnett (1991), 'Domestic sources of alliances and alignments: the case of Egypt, 1962–1973', *International Organization*, **45**:3, 369–95.

—— (1992), 'Alliance formation, domestic political economy, and Third World security', *The Jerusalem Journal of International Relations*, **14**:4, 19–40.

Lewis, John W. and Xue Litai (1988), *China Builds the Bomb*, Stanford, CA, Stanford University Press.

Lieberman, Elli (1992), 'Testing deterrence theory: success and failure in the enduring adversarial relationship between Egypt and Israel, 1948–1979', prepared for the Annual Meeting of the American Political Science Association, Chicago, IL.

Lifton, Robert Jay and Richard Falk (1982), *Indefensible Weapons. The Political and Psychological Cases Against Nuclearism*, New York, NY, Basic Books.

—— and Erik Markusen (1990), *The Genocidal Mentality: Nazi Holocaust and Nuclear Threat*, New York, NY, Basic Books.

Lin, Chong-Pin (1988), *China's Nuclear Weapons Strategy: Tradition Within Evolution*, Lexington, MA, Lexington Books.

Liu, Leo Yueh-Yun (1972), *China as a Nuclear Power in World Politics*, London, Macmillan.

Lord, Carnes (1985), 'American Strategic Culture', *Comparative Strategy*, 5:3, 269–93.

Luttwak, Edward N. (1974), *The Political Uses of Sea Power*, Baltimore, MD, Johns Hopkins University Press.

Macdonald, Douglas J. (1991), 'The Truman Administration and global responsibilities: the birth of the falling domino principle' in Robert Jervis and Jack Snyder (eds.), *Dominoes and Bandwagons. Strategic Beliefs and Great Power Competition in the Eurasian Rimland*, Oxford, Oxford University Press, 112–44.

Maclear, Michael (1982), *Vietnam. The Ten Thousand Day War*, London, Thames, Methuen.

Madeley, John (1985), *Diego Garcia: A Contrast to the Falklands*, London, Minority Rights Group, Report No. 54.

Mandelbaum, Michael (1981), *The Nuclear Revolution*, Cambridge, MA, Cambridge University Press.

Mao's telegrams (1992), 'Mao's dispatch of Chinese troops to Korea: forty-six telegrams July–October 1950', *Chinese Historians*, 5:1, 63–86, trans. and annotated by Li Xiaobing, Wang Xi and Chen Jian.

Maoz, Zeev (1983), 'Resolve, capabilities, and the outcomes of international disputes, 1816–1976', *Journal of Conflict Resolution*, **27**:2, 195–228.

—— (1989), *Paradoxes of War: On the Art of National Self-Entrapment*, Boston, MA, Unwin Hyman.

—— (1990), 'Framing the national interest. The manipulation of foreign policy decisions in group settings', *World Politics*, **43**:1, 77–110.

Marder, Arthur J., Mark Jacobsen and John Horsfield (1990), *Old Friends, New Enemies. The Royal Navy and the Imperial Japanese Navy.* **2** *The Pacific War, 1942–1945*, Oxford, Clarendon Press.

Mason, R. A. (1991), 'The air war in the Gulf', *Survival*, **33**:3, 211–29.

Matson, Robert W. (1983), 'Finlandization, an ahistorical analogy', *Research Studies*, **51**:1, 1–11.

Matthews, Ken (1993), *The Gulf Conflict and International Relations*, London, Routledge.

Maude, George (1981), 'The further shores of Finlandization', *Cooperation and Conflict*, **16**, 3–16.

May, John (1989), *The Greenpeace Book of the Nuclear Age. The Hidden History, the Human Cost*, London, Victor Gollancz.

May, Michael M., George F. Bing and John D. Steinbruner (1988), 'Strategic arsenals after START: the implications of deep cuts', *International Security*, **13**:1, 90–133.

Maxwell, Neville (1973), 'The Chinese account of the 1969 fighting at Chenpao', *The China Quarterly*, 56, 730–39.

Maxwell, Stephen (1968), *Rationality in Deterrence*, Adelphi paper 50, London, International Institute for Strategic Studies.

McCall, Malcolm and Oliver Ramsbotham (eds.) (1990), *Just Deterrence*, London, Brassey's.

McCalla, Robert B. (1992), *Uncertain Perceptions: US Cold War Crisis Decision-Making*, Ann Arbor, MI, University of Michigan Press.

MccGwire, Michael (1980), 'Soviet military doctrine: contingency planning and the reality of world war', *Survival*, **22**:3, 103–13.

—— (1984), 'The dilemmas and delusions of deterrence' in Gwyn Prins (ed.), *The Choice: Nuclear Weapons Versus Security*, London, Chatto & Windus, Hogarth, 75–97.

—— (1985–86), 'Deterrence: the problem – not the solution', *International Affairs*, **62**:1, 55–70.

—— (1987), *Military Objectives in Soviet Foreign Policy*, Washington, DC, The Brookings Institution.

—— (1991), *Perestroika and Soviet National Security*, Washington, DC, The Brookings Institution.

McConnell, James M. (1979), 'The "rules of the game": a theory on the practice of superpower naval diplomacy', in Bradford Dismukes and James M. McConnell (eds.), *Soviet Naval Diplomacy*, New York, NY, Pergamon, 240–80.

McNamara, Robert S. (1983), 'The military role of nuclear weapons: perceptions and misperceptions', *Foreign Affairs*, **62**:1, 59–80.

—— (1987), *Blundering into Disaster. Surviving the First Century of the Nuclear Age*, New York, NY, Pantheon, updated with a new foreword.

Miller, Judith and Laurie Mylroie (1990), *Saddam Hussein and the Crisis in the Gulf*, New York, NY, Times Books.

Morgan, Patrick M. (1983), *Deterrence. A Conceptual Analysis*, London, Sage, 2nd edn.

—— (1985), 'Saving face for the sake of deterrence' in Robert Jervis, Richard Ned Lebow and Janice Gross Stein, *Psychology and Deterrence*, Baltimore, MD, Johns Hopkins University Press, 125–52. With contributions by Patrick M. Morgan and Jack L. Snyder.

—— (1987), *Theories and Approaches to International Politics: What Are We to Think?* New Brunswick, NJ, Transaction, 4th edn.

—— (1991), *Assessing the Republic of China's Deterrence Situation*, SCPS paper 4, Kaohsiun, Taiwan, Republic of China, Sun Yat-Sen Center for Policy Studies, National Sun Yat-Sen University.

Morgenthau, Hans J. (1948), *Politics Among Nations: The Struggle for Power and Peace*, New York, NY, Alfred A. Knopf.

—— (1976), 'The fallacy of thinking conventionally about nuclear weapons' in David Carlton and Carlo Schaerf (eds.), *Arms Control and Technological Innovation*, New York, NY, Wiley and Sons, 255–64.

Moro, Rubén O. (1989), *The History of the South Atlantic Conflict. The War for the Malvinas*, New York, NY, Praeger, trans. Michael Valeur.

Mueller, John (1988), 'The essential irrelevance of nuclear weapons', *International Security*, **13**:2, 55–79.

—— (1989), *Retreat from Doomsday: The Obsolescence of Major War*, New York, NY, Basic Books.

—— (1994), *Policy and Opinion in the Gulf War*, Chicago, IL, University of Chicago Press.

Nash, Philip (1991), 'Nuisance of decision: Jupiter missiles and the Cuban missile crisis', *Journal of Strategic Studies*, **14**:1, 1–26.

Neustadt, Richard E., and Graham T. Allison (1971), 'Afterword' in Robert F. Kennedy, *Thirteen Days: A Memoir of the Cuban Missile Crisis*, New York, NY, Norton, 109–50.

—— and Ernest R. May (1986), *Thinking in Time. The Use of History for Decision Making*, New York, NY, Free Press.

Nitobé, Inazo (1905), *Bushido: The Soul of Japan. An Exposition of Japanese Thought*, London, G.P. Putnam's and Sons, The Knickerbocker Press.

Nixon, Richard M. (1978), *RN: The Memoirs of Richard Nixon*, London, Arrow.

Nolan, Janne E. (1989), *Guardians of the Arsenal: The Politics of Nuclear Strategy*, New York, NY, Basic Books.

Nye Jr., Joseph S. (1987), 'Nuclear learning and US-Soviet security regimes', *International Organization*, **41**:3, 371–402.

Orme, John (1987), 'Deterrence failures: a second look', *International Security*, **11**:4, 96–124.

Ovendale, Ritchie (1985), *The Origins of the Arab-Israeli Wars*, London, Longman.

Owen, Roger (1991), 'Epilogue. Making sense of an earthquake: the Middle East after the Gulf War' in Victoria Brittain (ed.), *The Gulf Between Us. The Gulf War and Beyond*, London, Virago, 159–78.

Panikkar, K. M. (1955), *In Two Chinas: Memoirs of a Diplomat*, London, Allen & Unwin.

Paterson, Thomas G. and William J. Brophy (1986), 'October missiles and November elections: the Cuban missile crisis and American politics', *The Journal of American History*, **73**:1, 87–119.

Paul, T. V. (1994), *Asymmetric Conflicts: War Initiation by Weaker Powers*, Cambridge, Cambridge University Press.

Payne, James L. (1970), *The American Threat: The Fear of War as an Instrument of Foreign Policy*, Chicago, IL, Markham.

Peng Dehuai (1984), *Memoirs of a Chinese Marshal – The Autobiographical Notes of Peng Dehuai (1898–1974)*, Beijing, Foreign Languages Press.

Petersen, Ib Damgaard and Paul Smoker (1993), 'The security paradox and the fear trap' in Håkan Wiberg, Ib Damgaard Petersen and Paul Smoker (eds.), *Inadvertent Nuclear War. The Implications of the Changing Global Order*, Oxford, Pergamon Press, 171–201.

Petersen, Walter J. (1986), 'Deterrence and compellence: a critical assessment of conventional wisdom', *International Studies Quarterly*, **30**:3, 269–94.

Pillsbury, Michael (1975), *SALT on the Dragon: Chinese Views of the Soviet-American Strategic Balance*, RAND P-5457, Santa Monica, CA, RAND Corporation.

Pipes, Richard (1977), 'Why the Soviet Union thinks it can fight and win a nuclear war', *Commentary*, **64**:1, 21–34.

—— (1982), 'Soviet strategic doctrine: another view', *Strategic Review*, **10**:4, 52–8.

Pollack, Jonathan D. (1984), *China and the Global Strategic Balance*, RAND P-6952, Santa Monica, CA, RAND Corporation.

Pope, Ronald R. (ed.) (1982), *Soviet Views on the Cuban Missile Crisis: Myth and Reality in Foreign Policy Analysis*, Washington, DC, University Press.

Post, Jerrold M. (1991), 'Saddam Hussein of Iraq: a political psychology profile', *Political Psychology*, **12**:2.

Prados, John (1986), *The Soviet Estimate: US Intelligence Analysis and Soviet Strategic Forces*, Princeton, NJ, Princeton University Press.

Price, Richard A (1993), 'Genealogy of the Chemical Weapons Taboo', paper prepared for the Annual Meeting of the American Political Science Association, Washington, DC.

—— (1994), 'Interpretation and disciplinary orthodoxy in international relations', *Review of International Studies*, **20**:2, 201–04.

Pringle, Peter and William Arkin (1983), *SIOP. Nuclear War From the Inside*, London, Sphere.

Quandt, William B. (1977a), 'Soviet policy in the October Middle East War – I', *International Affairs*, 53:3, 377–89.

—— (1977b), 'Soviet policy in the October Middle East War – II', *International Affairs*, 53:3, 587–603.

Quattrone, George A. and Amos Tversky (1988), 'Contrasting rational and psychological analyses of political choice', *American Political Science Review*, **82**:3, 719–36.

Quester, George H. (1977), *Offense and Defense in the International System*, New York, NY, John Wiley.

Ravenal, Earl C. (1982), 'Counterforce and alliance: the ultimate connection', *International Security*, **6**:4, 26–43.

—— (1991), 'The logic of nuclear strategy: the US orientation to counterforce' in David Carlton and Carlo Schaerf (eds.), *The Arms Race in an Era of Negotiations*, London, Macmillan, 3–48.

Record, Jeffrey (1993), *Hollow Victory. A Contrary View of the Gulf War*, Washington, DC, Brassey's.

Reiss, Mitchell (1988), *Without the Bomb. The Politics of Nuclear Non-proliferation*, New York, NY, Columbia University Press.

Renshon, Stanley A. (ed.) (1993), *The Political Psychology of the Gulf War. Leaders, Publics, and the Process of Conflict*, Pittsburgh, PA, University of Pittsburgh Press.

Post, Jerrold M. (1991), 'Saddam Hussein of Iraq: a political psychology profile', *Political Psychology*, 12: 2,

Rescher, Nicholas (1988), *Rationality. A Philosophical Inquiry into the Nature and the Rationale of Reason*, Oxford, Clarendon Press.

Rhodes, Edward (1989), *Power and MADness. The Logic of Nuclear Coercion*, New York, NY, Columbia University Press.

Richardson, James L. (1994), *Crisis Diplomacy. The Great Powers Since the Mid-Nineteenth Century*, Cambridge, Cambridge University Press.

Ridgeway, James (ed.) (1991), *The March to War*, New York, NY, Four Walls Eight Windows.

Ridgway, Matthew B. (1967), *The Korean War*, New York, NY, Doubleday.

Robinson, Paul (1981), 'The Sino-Soviet border conflict' in Stephen S. Kaplan, *Diplomacy of Power. Soviet Armed Forces as a Political Instrument*, Washington, DC, The Brookings Institution, 265–313.

Rosenberg, David Alan (1982), 'US nuclear stockpile, 1945 to 1950', *Bulletin of the Atomic Scientists*, **38**:5, 25–30.

—— (1983), 'The origins of overkill: nuclear weapons and American strategy, 1945–1960', *International Security*, 7:4, 3–71.

—— (1987), 'US nuclear strategy: theory vs practice', *Bulletin of the Atomic Scientists*, **43**:2, 20–6.

Rothschild, Joseph (1987), 'Culture and war' in Stephanie G. Neuman and Robert E. Harkavy (eds.), *The Lessons of Recent Wars in the Third World*, vol. II: *Comparative Dimensions*, Lexington, MA, D.C. Heath, 53–72.

Rushkoff, Bennett C. (1981), 'Eisenhower, Dulles and the Quemoy-Matsu crisis, 1954–55', *Political Science Quarterly*, **96**:3, 465–80.

Russett, Bruce (1963), 'The calculus of deterrence', *Journal of Conflict Resolution*, 7:1, 97–106.

—— (1967), 'Pearl Harbor: deterrence theory and decision theory', *Journal of Peace Research*, **4**:2, 89–105.

—— (1969), 'The young science of international politics', *World Politics*, **22**:1, 87–94.

—— ([1970] 1974), 'International behavior research: case studies and cumulation' in Bruce Russett, *Power and Community in World Politics*, San Francisco, CA, W. H. Freeman, 13–30.

Sagan, Scott D. (1983), 'Review of Robert Dallek, *The American Style of Foreign Policy: Cultural Politics and Foreign Affairs*', *Survival*, 25, 191.

—— (1985), 'Nuclear alerts and crisis management', *International Security*, **9**:4, 99–139.

—— (1989), *Moving Targets. Nuclear Strategy and National Security*, Princeton, NJ, Princeton University Press.

—— (1993), *The Limits of Safety. Organizations, Accidents, and Nuclear Weapons*, Princeton, NJ, Princeton University Press.

Salinger, Pierre, with Eric Laurent (1991), *Secret Dossier. The Hidden Agenda Behind the Gulf War*, London, Penguin.

Schecter, Jerrold L. and Peter S. Deriabin (1992), *The Spy Who Saved The World*, New York, NY, Charles Scribner's Sons.

Scheer, Robert (1983), *With Enough Shovels: Reagan, Bush and Nuclear War*, New York, NY, Vintage Books, updated edn.

Schell, Jonathan (1982), *The Fate of the Earth*, London, Picador.

—— (1984), *The Abolition*, London, Picador.

Schelling, Thomas C. ([1960] 1980), *The Strategy of Conflict*, Cambridge, MA, Harvard University Press, 2nd edn.

—— (1966), *Arms and Influence*, New Haven, NJ, Yale University Press.

Schick, Jack (1971), *The Berlin Crisis: 1958–1962*, Philadelphia, PA, University of Pennsylvania Press.

Schirokauer, Conrad (1986), 'Rationality in Chinese philosophy: an exploration' in Martin Tamny and K. D. Irani (eds.), *Rationality in Thought and Action*, New York, NY, Greenwood Press, 217–27.

Schlesinger, Jr., Arthur M. (1965), *A Thousand Days: John F. Kennedy in the White House*, Cambridge, MA, Houghton Mifflin.

—— (1992), 'Onward and upward from the missile crisis', *Problems of Communism*, **41**, 5–7, special edn.

Schubert, Klaus (1991), 'France' in Regina Cowen Karp (ed.), *Security With Nuclear Weapons? Different Perspectives on National Security*, Oxford, Oxford University Press for Stockholm International Peace Research Institute, 162–88.

Schwartz, David C. (1967), 'Decision theories and crisis behavior: an empirical study of nuclear deterrence in international political crises', *Orbis*, **11**:2, 459–90.

Schweller, Randall L. (1994), 'Bandwagoning for profit: bringing the revisionist state back in', *International Security*, **19**:1, 72–107.

Scott, Len (1991), 'Close to the brink? Britain and the Cuban missile crisis', *Contemporary Record*, **5**:3, 507–18.

Segal, Gerald (1983–84), 'Strategy and ethnic chic', *International Affairs*, **60**:1, 15–30.

—— (1985a), 'Defence culture and Sino-Soviet relations', *Journal of Strategic Studies*, **8**:2, 180–98.

—— (1985b), *Defending China*, Oxford, Oxford University Press.

—— (1991), 'China' in Regina Cowen Karp (ed.), *Security With Nuclear Weapons? Different Perspectives on National Security*, Oxford, Oxford University Press for Stockholm International Peace Research Institute, 189–205.

Sergeev, V. M., V. P. Akimov, V. B. Lukov and P. B. Parshin (1987), 'Interdependence in a crisis situation: simulating the Caribbean crisis', MS.

Shenfield, Stephen (1987), *The Nuclear Predicament: Explorations in Soviet Ideology*, Chatham House paper 37, London, Routledge & Kegan Paul for the Royal Institute of International Affairs.

—— (1989), *Minimum Nuclear Deterrence: The Debate Among Soviet Civilian Analysts*, Center for Foreign Policy Development working paper, Providence, RI, Center for Foreign Policy Development.

—— (1990), 'Crisis management: the Soviet approach' in Carl G. Jacobsen (ed.), *Strategic Power: USA/USSR*, London, Macmillan, 198–205.

Shevchenko, Arkady N. (1985), *Breaking With Moscow*, New York, Ballantine.

Shih, Chih-Yu (1990), *The Spirit of Chinese Foreign Policy: A Psycho-cultural View*, London, Macmillan.

Shlaim, Avi (1983), *The United States and the Berlin Blockade, 1948–1949. A Study in Crisis Decision-Making*, Berkeley, CA, University of California Press.

—— (1983–84), 'Britain, the Berlin blockade and the Cold War', *International Affairs*, 60:1, 1–14.

Simon, Herbert A. ([1972] 1982), 'Theories of bounded rationality' in Herbert A. Simon (ed.), *Models of Bounded Rationality* 2 *Behavioral Economics and Business Organization*, Cambridge, MA, MIT Press, 408–23.

—— ([1976] 1982), 'From substantive to procedural rationality' in Herbert A. Simon (ed.), *Models of Bounded Rationality* 2 *Behavioral Economics and Business Organization*, Cambridge, MA, MIT Press, 424–43.

Simpson, John (1991), *From the House of War*, London, Arrow.

Singleton, F. B. (1978), 'Finland between East and West', *The World Today*, 34:8, 321–32.

Slusser, Robert M. (1973), *The Berlin Crisis of 1961: Soviet-American Relations and the Struggle for Power in the Kremlin*, Baltimore, MD, Johns Hopkins University Press.

—— (1978), 'The Berlin crises of 1958–59 and 1961' in Barry M. Blechman and Stephen Kaplan, *Force Without War: U.S. Armed Forces as a Political Instrument*, Washington, DC, The Brookings Institution, 343–439.

Smith, Jean Edward (1963), *The Defense of Berlin*, Baltimore, MD, Johns Hopkins University Press.

—— (1992), *George Bush's War*, New York, NY, Henry Holt and Company.

Smoke, Richard and Andrei Kortunov (eds.) (1991), *Mutual Security: A New Approach to Soviet-American Relations*, London, Macmillan.

Snidal, Duncan (1991), 'International cooperation among relative gains maximizers', *International Studies Quarterly*, 35, 387–402.

Snyder, Glenn H. and Paul Diesing (1977), *Conflict Among Nations: Decision Making and System Structure in International Crises*, Princeton, NJ, Princeton University Press.

Snyder, Jack L. (1977), *The Soviet Strategic Culture: Implications for Limited Nuclear Options*, RAND R-2154, Santa Monica, CA, RAND Corporation.

—— (1978), 'Rationality at the brink: the role of cognitive processes in failures of deterrence', *World Politics*, 30:3, 345–65.

—— (1984), *The Ideology of the Offensive. Military Decision Making and the Disasters of 1914,* Ithaca, NY, Cornell University Press.

—— (1984–85), 'Richness, rigor and relevance in the study of Soviet foreign policy', *International Security*, 9:3, 89–108.

—— (1987–88), 'The Gorbachev revolution: a waning of Soviet expansionism?', *International Security*, **12**:3, 93–131.

—— (1988), 'Science and Sovietology: bridging the methods gap in Soviet foreign policy studies', *World Politics*, **40**:2, 169–93.

—— (1990), 'The concept of strategic culture: *caveat emptor*' in Carl G. Jacobsen (ed.), *Strategic Power: USA/USSR*, London, Macmillan, 3–9.

—— (1991a), 'Introduction' in Robert Jervis and Jack Snyder (eds.), *Dominoes and Bandwagons. Strategic Beliefs and Great Power Competition in the Eurasian Rimland*, Oxford, Oxford University Press, 3–19.

—— (1991b), 'Conclusion', in Robert Jervis and Jack Snyder (eds.), *Dominoes and Bandwagons. Strategic Beliefs and Great Power Competition in the Eurasian Rimland*, Oxford, Oxford University Press, 276–90.

—— (1991c), *Myths of Empire: Domestic Politics and International Ambition*, Ithaca, NY, Cornell University Press.

Stein, Janice Gross (1985a), 'Calculation, miscalculation and conventional deterrence I: the view from Cairo', in Robert Jervis, Richard Ned Lebow and Janice Gross Stein, *Psychology and Deterrence*, Baltimore, MD, Johns Hopkins University Press, 34–59. With contributions by Patrick M. Morgan and Jack L. Snyder.

—— (1985b), 'Calculation, miscalculation and conventional deterrence II: the view from Jerusalem', in Robert Jervis, Richard Ned Lebow and Janice Gross Stein, *Psychology and Deterrence*, Baltimore, MD, Johns Hopkins University Press, 60–88. With contributions by Patrick M. Morgan and Jack L. Snyder.

—— (1988), 'Building politics into psychology: the misperception of threat', *Political Psychology*, **9**:2, 245–71.

—— (1991a), 'Deterrence and reassurance', in Philip E. Tetlock, Jo L. Husbands, Robert Jervis, Paul C. Stern and Charles Tilly (eds.), *Behavior, Society and Nuclear War*, **2**, New York, NY, Oxford University Press, 8–72.

—— (1991b), 'Reassurance in international conflict management', *Political Science Quarterly*, 106, 431–51.

—— (1992), 'Deterrence and compellence in the Gulf, 1990–91: a failed or impossible task?', *International Security*, **17**:2, 147–79.

—— (1993), 'International cooperation and loss avoidance: framing the problem' in Janice Gross Stein and Louis W. Pauly (eds.), *Choosing to Co-operate. How States Avoid Loss*, Baltimore, MD, Johns Hopkins University Press, 2–34.

—— and Louis W. Pauly (eds.) (1993), *Choosing to Co-operate. How States Avoid Loss*, Baltimore, MD, Johns Hopkins University Press.

Steinbruner, John (1974), *The Cybernetic Theory of Decision*, Princeton, NJ, Princeton University Press.

—— (1976), 'Beyond rational deterrence: the struggle for new conceptions', *World Politics*, **28**:2, 223–45.

—— (1979), 'An assessment of nuclear crises' in Franklyn Griffiths and John C. Polyani (eds.), *The Dangers of Nuclear War*, Toronto, University of Toronto Press, 34–49.

Stephenson, Michael and John Weal (1985), *Nuclear Dictionary*, Harlow, Longman.

Stern, Paul, Robert Axelrod, Robert Jervis and Roy Radner (1989), 'Conclusions' in Stern, Paul, Robert Axelrod, Robert Jervis and Roy Radner (eds.) (1989), *Perspectives on Deterrence*, New York, NY, Oxford University Press, 294–321.

Strode, Rebecca V. (1981–82), 'Soviet strategic style', *Comparative Strategy*, **3**:4, 319–39.

Sunday Times Insight Team (1982), *The Falklands War*, London, André Deutsch.

Sun Tzu ([*c*.400 BC] 1988) *The Art of War*, Shaftesbury, Shambala, trans. Thomas Cleary.

Tanham, Geoffrey (1992), 'Indian strategic culture', *Washington Quarterly*, **15**:1, 129–42.

Taubman, William (1982), *Stalin's American Policy. From Entente to Detente to Cold War*, New York, NY, W. W. Norton.

—— (1992), 'The correspondence: Khrushchev's motives and his views of Kennedy', *Problems of Communism*, **41**, 14–18, special edn.

Taylor, Maxwell D. (1979), *Swords and Plowshares*, New York, NY, W. W. Norton.

Taylor, Philip M. (1992), *War and the Media. Propaganda and Persuasion in the Gulf War*, Manchester, Manchester University Press.

Taylor, Jr., William J. and James Blackwell (1991), 'The ground war in the Gulf', *Survival*, **33**:3, 230–45.

Thatcher, Margaret (1993), *The Downing Street Years*, London, HarperCollins.

Trachtenberg, Marc (1985), 'The influence of nuclear weapons in the Cuban missile crisis', *International Security*, **10**:1, 137–63.

—— (1988a), *The Development of American Strategic Thought: Writings on Strategy, 1961–1969, and Retrospectives*, New York, NY, Garland, 6 vols.

—— (1988b), 'A "wasting asset": American strategy and the shifting nuclear balance, 1949–1954', *International Security*, **13**:3, 5–49.

—— (1991), 'The Berlin crisis' in Marc Trachtenberg, *History and Strategy*, Princeton, NJ, Princeton University Press, 169–234.

Train, John (1991), 'The Gulf War and the future of NATO', *Armed Forces Journal International*, July, 24.

Trofimenko, Henry (1980), *Changing Attitudes Towards Deterrence*, ACIS working paper 25, University of California, Center for International and Strategic Affairs.

—— (1986), *The US Military Doctrine*, Moscow, Progress.

Tsou, Tang (1963), *America's Failure in China, 1941–1950*, Chicago, IL, University of Chicago Press.

Tucker, Robert W. and David C. Hendrickson (1992), *The Imperial Temptation: The New World Order and America's Purpose*, New York, NY, Council on Foreign Relations Press.

Tusa, Ann and John Tusa (1988), *The Berlin Blockade*, London, Hodder & Stoughton.

Tversky, Amos and Daniel Kahneman (1981), 'The framing of decisions and the psychology of choice', *Science*, 211, 453–8.

—— (1986), 'Rational choice and the framing of decisions', *The Journal of Business*, **59**:2, 251–78.

Ulam, Adam M. (1974), *Expansion and Coexistence: Soviet Foreign Policy 1917–73*, New York, NY, Holt, Rinehart & Winston, 2nd edn.

Vertzberger, Yaacov Y. I. (1990), *The World in Their Minds: Information Processing, Cognition and Perception in Foreign Policy Decisionmaking*, Stanford, CA, Stanford University Press.

Wagner, Harrison R. (1988), 'Reputation and the credibility of military threats: rational choice vs. psychology', paper prepared for the Annual Meeting of the American Political Science Association, Washington, DC.

Walker, Martin (1994), *The Cold War: And the Making of the Modern World*, London, Vintage.

Walt, Stephen M. (1985), 'Alliance formation and the balance of world power', *International Security*, **9**:4, 3–43.

—— (1987), *The Origins of Alliances*, Ithaca, NY, Cornell University Press.

—— (1988), 'Testing theories of alliance formation: the case of Southwest Asia', *International Organization*, **43**:2, 275–316.

—— (1989), 'The case for finite containment: analyzing US grand strategy', *International Security*, **14**:1, 5–49.

—— (1991), 'Alliance formation in Southwest Asia: balancing and bandwagoning in Cold War competition' in Robert Jervis and Jack Snyder (eds.), *Dominoes and Bandwagons. Strategic Beliefs and Great Power Competition in the Eurasian Rimland*, Oxford, Oxford University Press, 51–84.

—— (1992), 'Alliances, threats and US grand strategy: a reply to Kaufman and Labs', *Security Studies*, **1**:3, 448–82.

Waltz, Kenneth N. (1979), *Theory of International Politics*, Reading, MA, Addison-Wesley.

—— (1981), *The Spread of Nuclear Weapons: More May be Better*, Adelphi paper 171, London, International Institute for Strategic Studies.

—— (1990), 'Nuclear myths and political realities', *American Political Science Review*, **84**:3, 738–45.

Watson, Bruce, Bruce George, Peter Tsouras and B. L. Cyr (1991), *Military Lessons of the Gulf War*, London, Greenhill Books.

Weber, Steven (1990), 'Realism, détente, and nuclear weapons', *International Organisation*, **44**:1, 55–82.

Weinberg, Alvin M. (1985), 'The sanctification of Hiroshima', *Bulletin of the Atomic Scientist*, **41**:11, 34.

Weiszäcker, Carl Friedrich von (1980), 'Can a Third World War be prevented?', *International Security*, **5**:1, 198–205.

Welch, David A. (ed.) (1988), *Proceedings of the Cambridge Conference on the Cuban Missile Crisis, 11–12 October 1987*, Cambridge, MA, Center for Science and International Affairs, Harvard University.

—— (ed.) (1989), *Proceedings of the Hawk's Cay Conference on the Cuban Missile Crisis, 5–8 March 1987*, Cambridge, MA, Center for Science and International Affairs, Harvard University, Working Paper 89–1.

—— (1993a), 'The politics and psychology of restraint: Israeli decision-making in the Gulf War' in Janice Gross Stein and Louis W. Pauly (eds.) (1993), *Choosing to Co-operate. How States Avoid Loss*, Baltimore, MD, Johns Hopkins University Press, 128–69.

—— (1993b), *Justice and the Genesis of War*, Cambridge, Cambridge University Press.

—— and James G. Blight (1987–88), 'An introduction to the ExComm transcripts', *International Security*, **12**:3, 5–29.

Wendt, Alexander (1992), 'Anarchy is what states make of it: the social construction of power politics', *International Organization*, **46**:2, 391–405.

Weston, Burns H. (ed.) (1991), *Alternative Security. Living Without Nuclear Deterrence*, Boulder, CO, Westview Press.

White, Mark (1992), 'Belligerent beginnings: John F. Kennedy on the opening day of the Cuban missile crisis', *Journal of Strategic Studies*, **15**:1, 30–49.

Whiting, Allen S. (1960), *China Crosses the Yalu*, New York, NY, Macmillan.

—— (1975), *The Chinese Calculus of Deterrence. India and Indochina*, Ann Arbor, MI, University of Michigan Press.

—— (1991), 'The US-China War in Korea' in Alexander L. George (ed.), *Avoiding War. Problems of Crisis Management*, Boulder, CO, Westview Press, 103–25.

Wiberg, Håkan (1993), 'Accidental nuclear war: the problematique' in Håkan Wiberg, Ib Damgaard Petersen and Paul Smoker (eds.), *Inadvertent Nuclear War. The Implications of the Changing Global Order*, Oxford, Pergamon Press, 3–30.

Wich, Richard (1980), *Sino-Soviet Crisis Politics. A Study of Political Change and Communication*, Cambridge, MA, Harvard University Press.

Wildavsky, Aaron (1985), 'Change in political culture', *Politics*, 20.

—— (1987), 'Choosing preferences by constructing institutions: a cultural theory of preference formation', *American Political Science Review*, **81**:1, 3–21.

Wilkenfeld, Jonathan, Michael Brecher and Sheila Moser (1988), *Crises in the Twentieth Century:* vol. 2, *Handbook of Foreign Policy Crises*, Oxford, Pergamon Press.

Williams, Phil (1983), 'Miscalculation, crisis management and the Falklands conflict', *The World Today*, **39**:4, 144–9.

Wohlforth, William Curti (1993), *The Elusive Balance. Power and Perceptions During the Cold War*, Ithaca, NY, Cornell University Press.

Wohlstetter, Albert (1959), 'The delicate balance of terror', *Foreign Affairs*, **37**:2, 211–34.

Wolfers, Arnold (1962), *Discord and Collaboration: Essays on International Politics*, Baltimore, MD, Johns Hopkins University Press.

Woodward, Bob (1991), *The Commanders*, London, Simon & Schuster.

Wright, George (1985), 'Organizational, group, and individual decision making in cross-cultural perspective' in George Wright (ed.), *Behavioral Decision Making*, New York, NY, Plenum Press, 149–65.

Yakovlev, Alexander (1985), *On the Edge of an Abyss: From Truman to Reagan. The Doctrines and Realities of the Nuclear Age*, Moscow, Progress.

Young, Oran (1969), 'Professor Russett: industrious tailor to a naked emperor', *World Politics*, **21**:3, 586–611.

Yu, Bin (1993), 'The study of Chinese foreign policy: problems and prospect', *World Politics*, **46**:2, 235–61.

Zhang, Shu Guang (1993), *Deterrence and Strategic Culture – Chinese-American Confrontations, 1949–1958*, Ithaca, NY, Cornell University Press.

Zubok, Vladislav M. (1992), 'The missile crisis and the problem of Soviet learning', *Problems of Communism*, **41**, 19–23, special edn.

INDEX

Index

Index